P9-DUQ-501

WITHDRAWN

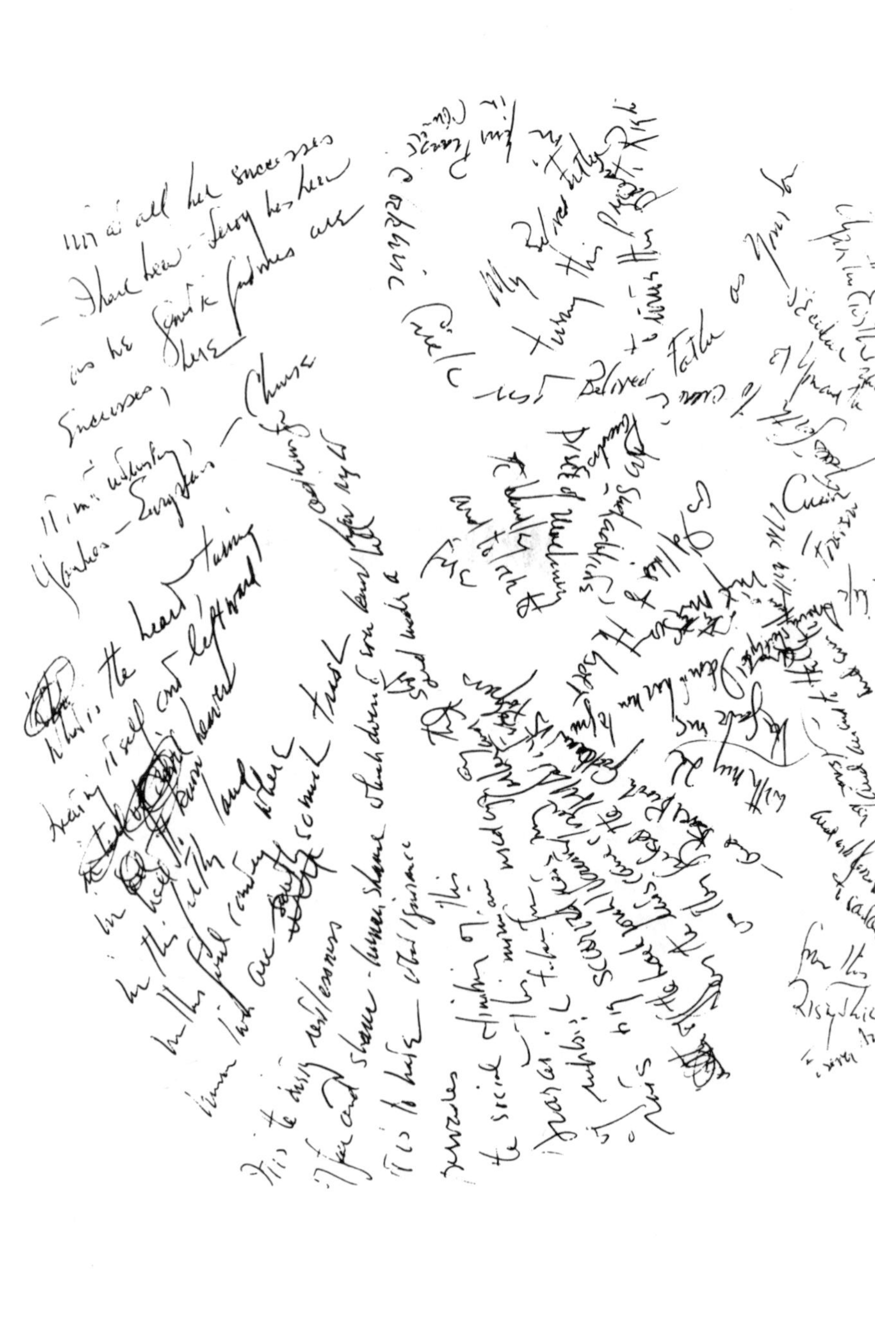

AMERICAN POETRY SINCE 1950

INNOVATORS AND OUTSIDERS

AN ANTHOLOGY

EDITED BY ELIOT WEINBERGER

MARSILIO PUBLISHERS
New York

Acknowledgments for permission to reproduce
previously published material
appear on pages 431 through 433, which are
an extension of this copyright page.

853 Broadway, New York, NY 10003

frontispiece:
manuscript page from *The Maximus Poems*
by Charles Olson: "The Land as Haithubu."
reprinted by permission of the
University of Connecticut Library, Storrs.

distributed in the U.S.A. by
Consortium Book Sales & Distribution
1045 Westgate Drive, Saint Paul, MN 55114-1065

hardcover ISBN 0-941419-91-6
paperback ISBN 0-941419-92-4

LOC 92-62373

printed in the United States of America
Second Printing
book design by Charles Nix

CONTENTS

A Note on the Selection

For decades American poetry has been divided into two camps, not quite Republicans and Democrats, but more like the ruling and opposition parties in some particularly messy parliamentary system, full of defections, unaligned members, splinter parties, internecine disputes and ideas stolen across the aisle.

On the one side is a ruling party that insists there is no ruling party, and thus no opposition; that there are only good or bad poets, publishers, literary magazines; that the others are simply those who failed to make the grade. Yet it is a party that clearly exists in the minds of those outside it, who have derided it with adjectives like *conventional, establishment, official, academic,* and have pitched their own poetics as alternatives to the prevailing humdrum. On the other side is an opposition still intensely aware of its outsider status, yet now increasingly dissatisfied with the banners under which it once rallied: *avant-garde, experimental, non-academic, radical.*

The distinction between the two parties has always been blurred at the edges and, over the decades, the issues of debate have changed: "free" verse vs. traditional prosody, colloquial speech vs. literary language, America vs. England, direct presentation vs. elaborate metaphor, "closed" vs. "open" forms. (And even more confusing: the ruling party tends to adopt, years later, the opposition platform.) But there is no doubt that inequities, most visible during the lifetimes of the poets, have indeed existed. Today, in the current population explosion of poets, they are greater than ever.

The channels of recognition, however slight for poets in the United States, have always been controlled by the ruling party. Consider the writers in this book: Few among them have ever won a major prize. (Even William Carlos Williams only received a Pulitzer posthumously.) Few are published or reviewed in the national magazines or newspapers; few appear under the imprint of a large press. Most of the "standard" anthologies of contemporary American poetry omit many of these poets, and no anthology includes all of them.

Of the poets now deceased, more than half died with most of their work unpublished or out of print. Yet, within a few years after their deaths, nearly all of them were recognized as having been among the central poets of their time. Most are now decked with critical apparatus from the academy—book-length studies, biographies, annotated texts, collections of letters, bibliographies—and some of them have become the models for the new generations of establishment poets to imitate. (Meanwhile, those laureled in life seem to have vanished from their graves: read the lists of the prize-winners of decades past.) For the poets of the opposition, it seems, the first condition of immortality is death.

In a society where all poets are outsiders, most of the poets here are, or have been, outside the outside. All of them are innovators, those who make it new, amidst the more visible legions of renovators, those who make it like new. Nearly all have devised idiosyncratic forms of prosody or musical composition, and have introduced worlds of historical, mythological, political, scientific, biological and geographical matter into their poems. The ruling party has always maintained a policy of exclusion: only certain forms, certain subjects and ways of dealing with them have been deemed permissible at any given moment. For the opposition, poetry is a place where one can, one should, talk about everything, and where the diversity of content determines the variety of forms.

The book opens with the last works of the great Modernists (William Carlos Williams, Ezra Pound and H.D.) and follows through four poetic generations of writers who generally considered themselves, at least in part, to be their heirs. Only poems first published in book form since 1950—the date of the magazine appearance of Charles Olson's "The Kingfishers," the first major work by a new writer in the postwar American poetry renaissance—are included. The most recent poems here were written or published just last year. For "American" I have adopted the narrow scope of work written in English by citizens of the United States; for "poetry," that which its own author considers to be poetry.

Only thirty-five poets have been included, to give them sufficient space to be heard in at least one aspect of their work. (Anthologies with many more poets, represented by a few short poems, serve mainly to reinforce friendships with the editor.) No poets born after World War II are included, thanks to that ruling demon, space, and because many of the precursors to the present younger generations—the contexts in which the latest developments are occurring—remain so little known.

The demographic complexity of the United States is reflected in the work itself, rather than in the police-blotter profiles of the individual poets. The book opens on the Mexican-American border, and is concerned throughout, as the poetry has been, with the migration of cultural stuff from every part of the world. (American—it couldn't be otherwise—is unquestionably the most internationalist of the world's poetries.) Those who count heads according to gender and race should first consider how many poets genuinely qualify within these chronological limits. (This situation has now changed radically: a subsequent selection of the innovators from the post–World War II generations would probably contain a majority of women, with a greater number of non-white poets, male and female.)

When only thirty-five poets have been chosen from among many hundreds, each reader will inevitably find conspicuous absences, absences which in turn form another anthology to be dreamed or published. There are as many anthologies of American poetry as there are its readers; none is, or should be, a papal decree of sanctity or excommunication. (Only fundamentalists and academic critics believe in definitive editions.) Nevertheless, this present selection will, I think, have a coherence for those who are familiar with, or just entering, the territory. It is the delineation of a "group" only in the largest sense that most of the poets here, it may be imagined, generally respect or would have respected one another. American poetry has rarely had the organized movements common to the rest of the world. It has been written mainly in isolation—from the cultural life of the nation as well as from other poets—and distant reciprocal admiration may well be as cohesive as it ever gets.

The selection, like poetry itself, begins with "the dance" and ends with "language." Individual poems have been chosen not as discrete examples of the author's "best," but rather for the way in which they interact with the other poems: the intention is a hubbub of conversations, not a series of monologues. And the book, as a whole, attempts to serve four functions: as a place to find certain amazing poems; as an introduction to the work of this historical moment; as an alternative to the existing anthologies; and above all, as a signpost pointing to the books of the individual poets.

—E.W.

A NOTE ON THE TEXT

The date in brackets at the end of each poem is intended as a rough approximation of its chronological context: usually first book publication, sometimes first magazine appearance. The emphasis is on the moment when the poem was first read, rather than when it was written. However, in the cases where there is a long period of time between composition and publication, two dates, separated by a slash bar, are given. Where more than one poem is taken from the same book, the last poem in the group contains the date of publication. The few editorial deletions are indicated by an ellipsis in square brackets [...].

AMERICAN POETRY SINCE 1950

Innovators and Outsiders

William Carlos Williams

THE DESERT MUSIC

—the dance begins: to end about a form
propped motionless—on the bridge
between Juárez and El Paso—unrecognizable
in the semi-dark

Wait!

The others waited while you inspected it,
on the very walk itself .

Is it alive?

—neither a head,
legs nor arms!

It isn't a sack of rags someone
has abandoned here . torpid against
the flange of the supporting girder . ?

an inhuman shapelessness,
knees hugged tight up into the belly

Egg-shaped!

What a place to sleep!
on the International Boundary. Where else,
interjurisdictional, not to be disturbed?

How shall we get said what must be said?

Only the poem.

Only the counted poem, to an exact measure:
to imitate, not to copy nature, not
to copy nature

NOT, prostrate, to copy nature
                                        but a dance! to dance
two and two with him—
                              sequestered there asleep,
                                        right end up!

        A music
supersedes his composure, hallooing to us
across a great distance . .

                                        wakens the dance
who blows upon his benumbed fingers!

                                        Only the poem
only the made poem, to get said what must
be said, not to copy nature, sticks
in our throats .

The law? The law gives us nothing
but a corpse, wrapped in a dirty mantle.
The law is based on murder and confinement,
long delayed,
but this, following the insensate music,
is based on the dance:

                              an agony of self-realization
bound into a whole
by that which surrounds us .

                                    I cannot escape

I cannot vomit it up

Only the poem!

Only the made poem, the verb calls it
                                        into being.

                              —it looks too small for a man.
A woman.   Or a very shriveled old man.
Maybe dead.   They probably inspect the place
and will cart it away later   .

                              Heave it into the river.
A good thing.

Leaving California to return east, the fertile desert,
                              (were it to get water)
surrounded us, a music of survival, subdued, distant, half
                              heard; we were engulfed
by it as in the early evening, seeing the wind lift
                              and drive the sand, we
passed Yuma. All night long, heading for El Paso to
                              meet our friend,
we slept fitfully.   Thinking of Paris, I waked to the tick
                              of the rails.   The
jagged desert   .

                                        —to tell
      what subsequently I saw and what heard

                                   —to place myself (in
my nature) beside nature

                                   —to imitate
nature (for to copy nature would be a
      shameful thing)

                              I lay myself down:

The Old Market's a good place to begin:
Let's cut through here—
                                        tequila's only

a nickel a slug in these side streets.
Keep out though. Oh, it's all right at
this time of day but I saw H. terribly
beaten up in one of those joints. He
asked for it. I thought he was going to
be killed. I do
my drinking on the main drag .

That's the bull ring
Oh, said Floss, after she got used to the
change of light .
What color! Isn't it
wonderful!

—paper flowers (*para los santos*)
baked red-clay utensils, daubed
with blue, silverware,
dried peppers, onions, print goods, children's
clothing . the place deserted all but
for a few Indians squatted in the
booths, unnoticing (don't you think it)
as though they slept there .

There's a second tier. Do you
want to go up?

What makes Texans so tall?
We saw a woman this morning in a mink cape
six feet if she was an inch. What a woman!

Probably a Broadway figure.

—tell you what else we saw: about a million
sparrows screaming their heads off
in the trees of that small park where
the buses stop, sanctuary,
I suppose,
from the wind driving the sand in that way
about the city .

Texas rain they call it

—and those two alligators in the fountain .

There were four

I saw only two

They were looking
right at you all the time .

Penny please! Give me penny please, mister.

Don't give them anything.

. instinctively
one has already drawn one's naked
wrist away from those obscene fingers
as in the mind a vague apprehension speaks
and the music rouses .

Let's get in here.
a music! cut off as
the bar door closes behind us.

We've got
another half hour.

—returned to the street,
the pressure moves from booth to booth along
the curb. Opposite, no less insistent
the better stores are wide open. Come in
and look around. You don't have to buy: hats,
riding boots, blankets .

Look at the way,
slung from her neck with a shawl, that young
Indian woman carries her baby!

—a stream of Spanish,
as she brushes by, intense, wide-
eyed in eager talk with her boy husband

—three half-grown girls, one of them eating a
pomegranate. Laughing.

and the serious tourist,
man and wife, middle-aged, middle-western,
their arms loaded with loot, whispering
together—still looking for bargains .

and the aniline
red and green candy at the little booth
tended by the old Indian woman.
Do you suppose anyone actually
buys—and eats the stuff?

My feet are beginning to ache me.

We still got a few minutes.
Let's try here. They had the mayor
up last month for taking $3000 a week from
the whorehouses of the city. Not much left
for the girls. There's a show on.

Only a few tables
occupied. A conventional orchestra—this
place livens up later—playing the usual local
jing-a-jing—a boy and girl team, she
confidential with someone
off stage. Laughing: just finishing the act.

So we drink until the next turn—a strip tease.

Do you mean it? Wow! Look at her.

You'd have to be
pretty drunk to get any kick out of that.
She's no Mexican. Some worn-out trouper from
the States. Look at those breasts .

There is a fascination
seeing her shake
the beaded sequins from
a string about her hips

She gyrates but it's
not what you think,
one does not laugh
to watch her belly.

One is moved but not
at the dull show.   The
guitarist yawns.   She
cannot even sing. She

has about her painted
hardihood a screen
of pretty doves which
flutter their wings.

Her cold eyes perfunc-
torily moan but do not
smile.   Yet they bill
and coo by grace of
a certain candor.   She

is heavy on her feet.
That's good.   She
bends forward leaning
on the table of the
balding man sitting
upright, alone, so that
everything hangs for-
ward.
        What the hell
are you grinning
to yourself about?   Not
at *her?*
        The music!
I like her.   She fits

the music   .

Why don't these Indians get over this nauseating prattle
about their souls and their loves and sing us something
else for a change?

This place is rank
with it. She
at least knows she's
part of another tune,
knows her customers,
has the same
opinion of them as I
have. That gives her
one up . one up
following the lying
music .

There is another music. The bright-colored candy
of her nakedness lifts her unexpectedly
to partake of its tune .

Andromeda of those rocks,
the virgin of her mind . those unearthly
greens and reds

in her mockery of virtue
she becomes unaccountably virtuous .
though she in no
way pretends it .

Let's get out of this.

In the street it hit
me in the face as we started to walk again. Or
am I merely playing the poet? Do I merely invent
it out of whole cloth? I thought .

What in the form of an old whore in
a cheap Mexican joint in Juárez, her bare
can waggling crazily can be
so refreshing to me, raise to my ear
so sweet a tune, built of such slime?

Here we are. They'll be along any minute.
The bar is at the right of the entrance,
a few tables opposite which you have to pass
to get to the dining room, beyond.

A foursome, two oversize Americans, no
longer young, got up as cowboys,
hats and all, are drunk and carrying on
with their gals, drunk also,

especially one inciting her man, the
biggest, *Yip ee*! to dance in
the narrow space, oblivious to everything
—she is insatiable and he is trying

stumblingly to keep up with her.
Give it the gun, pardner! *Yip ee*! We
pushed by them to our table, seven
of us. Seated about the room

were quiet family groups, some with
children, eating. Rather a better
class than you notice
on the streets. So here we are. You

can see through into the kitchen
where one of the cooks, his shirt sleeves
rolled up, an apron over
the well-pressed pants of a street

suit, black hair neatly parted,
a tall
good-looking man, is working
absorbed, before a chopping block

Old Fashioneds all around?

So this is William
Carlos Williams, the poet .

Floss and I had half consumed
our quartered hearts of lettuce before
we noticed the others hadn't touched theirs .
You seem quite normal. Can you tell me? Why
does one want to write a poem?

Because it's there to be written.

Oh. A matter of inspiration then?

Of necessity.

Oh. But what sets it off?

I am that he whose brains
are scattered
aimlessly

—and so,
the hour done, the quail eaten, we were on
our way back to El Paso.

Good night. Good
night and thank you . No. Thank you. We're
going to walk .

—and so, on the naked wrist, we feel again
those insistent fingers .

Penny please, mister.
Penny please. Give me penny.

Here! now go away.

—but the music, the music has reawakened
as we leave the busier parts of the street
and come again to the bridge in the semi-dark,
pay our fee and begin again to cross .
seeing the lights along the mountain back of El
Paso and pause to watch the boys calling out

to us to throw more coins to them standing
in the shallow water . so that's
where the incentive lay, with the annoyance
of those surprising fingers.

So you're a poet?
a good thing to be got rid of—half drunk,
a free dinner under your belt, even though you
get typhoid—and to have met people you
can at least talk to .

relief from that changeless, endless
inescapable and insistent music . .

What else, Latins, do you yourselves
seek but relief!
with the expressionless ding dong you dish up
to us of your souls and your loves, which
we swallow. Spaniards! (though these are mostly
Indians who chase the white bastards
through the streets on their Independence Day
and try to kill them) .

What's that?

Oh, come on.

But what's THAT?

the music! the
music! as when Casals struck
and held a deep cello tone
and I am speechless .

There it sat
in the projecting angle of the bridge flange
as I stood aghast and looked at it—
in the half-light: shapeless or rather returned
to its original shape, armless, legless,
headless, packed like the pit of a fruit into

that obscure corner—or
a fish to swim against the stream—or
a child in the womb prepared to imitate life,
warding its life against
a birth of awful promise.   The music
guards it, a mucus, a film that surrounds it,
a benumbing ink that stains the
sea of our minds—to hold us off—shed
of a shape close as it can get to no shape,
a music! a protecting music   .

I *am* a poet! I
am.   I am.   I am a poet, I reaffirmed, ashamed

Now the music volleys through as in
a lonely moment I hear it.   Now it is all
about me.   The dance!   The verb detaches itself
seeking to become articulate   .

And I could not help thinking
of the wonders of the brain that
hears that music and of our
skill sometimes to record it.

[1954]

Ezra Pound

from *The Confucian Odes*:

SIX POEMS
(translated from the Chinese)

"Hid! Hid!" the fish-hawk saith,
by isle in Ho the fish-hawk saith:
"Dark and clear,
Dark and clear,
So shall be the prince's fere."

Clear as the stream her modesty;
As neath dark boughs her secrecy,
reed against reed
tall on slight
as the stream moves left and right,
dark and clear,
dark and clear.
To seek and not find
as a dream in his mind,
think how her robe should be,
distantly, to toss and turn,
to toss and turn.

High reed caught in *ts'ai* grass
so deep her secrecy;
lute sound in lute sound is caught,
touching, passing, left and right.
Bang the gong of her delight.

* * *

Locusts a-wing, multiply.
Thick be thy
                    posterity.

Locusts a-wing with heavy sound;
strong as great rope may thy line
                                        abound.

Wing'd locust, that seem to cease,
in great companies hibernate,
So may thy line last and be great
                              in hidden ease.

* * *

Lies a dead deer on younder plain
whom white grass covers,
A melancholy maid in spring
                                    is luck
                                    for
                                    lovers.

Where the scrub elm skirts the wood,
be it not in white mat bound,
as a jewel flawless found,
                         dead as doe is maidenhood.

Hark!
Unhand my girdle-knot,
                         stay, stay, stay
                         or the dog
                         may
                         bark.

* * *

Pine boat a-shift
on drift of tide,
for flame in the ear, sleep riven,
driven; rift of the heart in dark

no wine will clear,
nor have I will to playe.

Mind that 's no mirror to gulp down all 's seen,
brothers I have, on whom I dare not lean,
angered to hear a fact, ready to scold.

My heart no turning-stone, mat to be rolled,
right being right, not whim nor matter of count,
true as a tree on mount.

Mob's hate, chance evils many, gone through,
aimed barbs not few;
at bite of the jest in heart
start up as to beat my breast.

O'ersoaring sun, moon malleable
alternately
lifting a-sky to wane;
sorrow about the heart like an unwashed shirt, I
clutch here at words,
having no force to fly.

* * *

Green robe, green robe, lined with yellow,
Who shall come to the end of sorrow?

Green silk coat and yellow skirt,
How forget all my heart-hurt?

Green the silk is, you who dyed it;
Antient measure, now divide it?

Nor fine nor coarse cloth keep the wind
from the melancholy mind;
Only antient wisdom is
solace to man's miseries.

* * *

Heaven conserve thy course in quietness,
Solid thy unity, thy weal endless
that all the crops increase and nothing lack
in any common house.

Heaven susteyne thy course in quietness
that thou be just in all, and reap
so, as it were at ease, that every day
seem festival.

Heaven susteyne thy course in quietness
To abound and rise as mountain hill and range
constant as rivers flow that all augment
steady th' increase in ever cyclic change.

Pure by the victuals of thy sacrifice
throughout the year as autumns move to springs,
above the fane to hear "ten thousand years"
spoke by the manes of foregone dukes and kings.

Spirits of air assign felicity:
thy folk be honest, in food and drink delight;
dark-haired the hundred tribes concord
in act born of thy true insight.

As moon constant in phase; as sun to rise;
as the south-hills nor crumble nor decline;
as pine and cypress evergreen the year
be thy continuing line.

[1954]

CANTO XC

Animus humanus amor non est,
sed ab ipso amor procedit, et
ideo seipso non diligit, sed amore
qui seipso procedit.

"From the colour the nature
& by the nature the sign!"
Beatific spirits welding together
as in one ash-tree in Ygdrasail.
Baucis, Philemon.
Castalia is the name of that fount in the hill's fold,
the sea below,
narrow beach.
Templum aedificans, not yet marble,
"Amphion!"

And from the San Ku 三

to the room in Poitiers where one can stand
casting no shadow,
That is Sagetrieb,
that is tradition.
Builders had kept the proportion,
did Jacques de Molay
know these proportions?
and was Erigena ours?
Moon's barge over milk-blue water
Kuthera δεινά
Kuthera sempiterna
Ubi amor, ibi oculus.
Vae qui cogitatis inutile.
quam in nobis similitudine divinae
reperetur imago.
"Mother Earth in thy lap"
said Randolph
ἠγάπησεν πολύ

liberavit masnatos.
Castalia like the moonlight
                    and the waves rise and fall,
Evita, beer-halls, semina motuum,
                    to parched grass, now is rain
not arrogant from habit,
    but furious from perception,
                                        Sibylla,
from under the rubble heap
                                        m'elevasti
from the dulled edge beyond pain,
                                        m'elevasti
out of Erebus, the deep-lying
    from the wind under the earth,
                                        m'elevasti
from the dulled air and the dust,
                                        m'elevasti
by the great flight,
                        m'elevasti,
                                        Isis Kuanon
        from the cusp of the moon,
                                        m'elevasti
the viper stirs in the dust,
                                        the blue serpent
glides from the rock pool
    And they take lights now down to the water
the lamps float from the rowers
    the sea's claw drawing them outward.
"De fondo" said Juan Ramón,
        like a mermaid, upward,
but the light perpendicular, upward
and to Castalia,
                    water jets from the rock
and in the flat pool as Arethusa's
                    a hush in papyri.
Grove hath its altar
        under elms, in that temple, in silence
a lone nymph by the pool.
        Wei and Han rushing together

two rivers together
bright fish and flotsam
torn bough in the flood
and the waters clear with the flowing
Out of heaviness where no mind moves at all
"birds for the mind" said Richardus,
"beasts as to body, for know-how"
Gaio! Gaio!
To Zeus with the six seraphs before him
The architect from the painter,
the stone under elm
Taking form now,
the rilievi,
the curled stone at the marge
Faunus, sirenes,
the stone taking form in the air
ac ferae,
cervi,
the great cats approaching.
Pardus, leopardi, Bagheera
drawn hither from woodland,
woodland ἐπὶ χθονί
the trees rise
and there is a wide sward between them
οἱ χθόνιοι myrrh and olibanum on the altar stone
giving perfume,
and where was nothing
now is furry assemblage
and in the boughs now are voices
grey wing, black wing, black wing shot with crimson
and the umbrella pines
as in Palatine,
as in pineta. χελιδών, χελιδών
For the procession of Corpus
come now banners
comes flute tone
οἱ χθόνιοι
to new forest,
thick smoke, purple, rising

bright flame now on the altar
        the crystal funnel of air
out of Erebus, the delivered,
        Tyro, Alcmene, free now, ascending,
e i cavalieri,
        ascending,
no shades more,
        lights among them, enkindled,
and the dark shade of courage
                'Ηλέκτρα
        bowed still with the wrongs of Aegisthus.
Trees die & the dream remains
        Not love but that love flows from it
        ex animo
        & cannot ergo delight in itself
        but only in the love flowing from it.
    UBI AMOR IBI OCULUS EST.

[1955]

from CANTO CXV

The scientists are in terror
        and the European mind stops
Wyndham Lewis chose blindness
        rather than have his mind stop.
Night under wind mid garofani,
        the petals are almost still
Mozart, Linnaeus, Sulmona,
When one's friends hate each other
        how can there be peace in the world?
Their asperities diverted me in my green time.
A blown husk that is finished
        but the light sings eternal
a pale flare over marshes
        where the salt hay whispers to tide's change

Editor's note: "*from* Canto CXV" is the original title. The complete Canto has never been published.

Time, space,
        neither life nor death is the answer.
And of man seeking good,
          doing evil.
In meiner Heimat
                where the dead walked
                        and the living were made of cardboard.

CANTO CXVI

Came Neptunus
            his mind leaping
                        like dolphins,
These concepts the human mind has attained.
To make Cosmos—
To achieve the possible—
Muss., wrecked for an error,
But the record
          the palimpsest—
a little light
            in great darkness—
cuniculi—
An old "crank" dead in Virginia.
Unprepared young burdened with records,
The vision of the Madonna
            above the cigar butts
                  and over the portal.
"Have made a mass of laws"
                        (mucchio di leggi)
Litterae nihil sanantes
                        Justinian's,
a tangle of works unfinished.

I have brought the great ball of crystal;
                who can lift it?
Can you enter the great acorn of light?
          But the beauty is not the madness
Tho' my errors and wrecks lie about me.
And I am not a demigod,

I cannot make it cohere.
If love be not in the house there is nothing.
The voice of famine unheard.
How came beauty against this blackness,
Twice beauty under the elms—
To be saved by squirrels and bluejays?
"plus j'aime le chien"
Ariadne.
Disney against the metaphysicals,
and Laforgue more than they thought in him,
Spire thanked me in proposito
And I have learned more from Jules
(Jules Laforgue) since then
deeps in him,
and Linnaeus.
chi crescerà i nostri—
but about that terzo
third heaven,
that Venere,
again is all "paradiso"
a nice quiet paradise
over the shambles,
and some climbing
before the take-off,
to "see again,"
the verb is "see," not "walk on"
i.e. it coheres all right
even if my notes do not cohere.
Many errors,
a little rightness,
to excuse his hell
and my paradiso.
And as to why they go wrong,
thinking of rightness
And as to who will copy this palimpsest?
al poco giorno
ed al gran cerchio d'ombra
But to affirm the gold thread in the pattern
(Torcello)

al Vicolo d'oro
(Tigullio).
To confess wrong without losing rightness:
Charity I have had sometimes,
I cannot make it flow thru.
A little light, like a rushlight
to lead back to splendour.

[1968]

H.D.

from *Hermetic Definition*:

RED ROSE AND A BEGGAR

[1]

Why did you come
to trouble my decline?
I am old (I was old till you came);

the reddest rose unfolds,
(which is ridiculous
in this time, this place,

unseemly, impossible,
even slightly scandalous),
the reddest rose unfolds;

(nobody can stop that,
no immanent threat from the air,
not even the weather,

blighting our summer fruit),
the reddest rose unfolds,
(they've got to take that into account).

[2]

Take me anywhere, anywhere;
I walk into you,
Doge — Venice —

you are my whole estate;
I would hide in your mind
as a child hides in an attic,

what would I find there?
religion or majic — both? neither?
one or the other? together, matched,

mated, exactly the same,
equal in power, together yet separate,
your eyes' amber.

[3]

Isis, Iris,
fleur-de-lis,
Bar-Isis is son of Isis,

(bar ou ber ou ben, signifiant fils).
so Bar-Isis is Par-Isis?
Paris, anyway;

because you do not drink our wine,
nor salt our salt,
I would enter your senses

through burnt resin and pine-cones
smouldering in a flat dish;
were you a cave-hermit?

why do they punish us?
come out, come out of the darkness;
will I be burnt to cinders in this heat?

[4]

They say the hieratic and heraldic iris
is the lotus, martigan-lily,
magenta, purple — do I blaspheme?

cowering under the rain,

I think of the hot sand,
and call and call again

Bar-Isis, Paris;
I call Paris, Paris,
not to the Greek

nor to the courtly suitor of Verona
"where we lay our scene,"
though Verona is not far,

now I walk into you,
Doge — Venice —
you are my whole estate.

[5]

Venice — Venus?
this must be my stance,
my station: though you brushed aside

my verse,
I can't get away from it,
I've tried to;

true, it was "fascinating...
if you can stand its preciousness,"
you wrote of what I wrote;

why must I write?
you would not care for this,
but She draws the veil aside,

unbinds my eyes,
commands,
write, write or die.

[6]

This is my new prayer;
I pray to you?
Paris, Bar-Isis? to Osiris?

or to Isis-self, Egyptian flower,
Notre Dame — do you ever go there?
the stones hold secrets;

they tell us vibration was brought over
by ancient alchemists;
Our Lady keeps tryst,

she commands with her sceptre, *(Astrologie*
is the first door?)
and the Child champions us;

bid me not despair,
Child of the ancient hierarchy...
and you to-day.

[7]

Saint Anne is the last door, (Magie,
Cybele, they once called her,
the grand-mother),

and where are we now?
certainly there is the rush, the fervour,
the trampling of lush grass,

the bare feet entanglement,
the roar of the last desperate charge,
the non-escape, the enchantment,

the tremor, the earthquake,
nothing, nothing, nothing more,
nothing further; the pine-cone

we left smouldering in the flat dish,
is flaming, is fire,
no before, no after — escape?

who can escape life, fever,
the darkness of the abyss?
lost, lost, lost,

the last desperate non-escape,
the reddest rose,
the unalterable law. . .

[8]

is it you?
is it some thundering pack
of steers, bulls? is it one?

is it many?
voices from the past, from the future,
so far, no further,

now total abasement;
were you ever here?
were you ever in this room?

how did I endure your presence,
and afterwards, just once,
in a strange place, with others there,

silly talk, mine,
and you wouldn't drink our wine,
("then fruit-juice?" "yes"),

and you wouldn't touch our salt —
almonds — pecans — what happened?
you were so late,

why didn't you come sooner?
why did you come at all?
why did you come

to trouble my decline,
I am old,
(I was old till you came.)

[9]

The middle door is Judgement, *(Alchimie)*,
judge this, judge me implacable;
there is yet time to crawl back

to security? no — there is no time left:
almonds, pecans without salt,
scatter them near some sand-coast

for a wind-break, beyond is the wax flower,
the thyme, honeymyrtle and the coral heath,
these are new to me, different,

as you are new to me, different,
but of an old, old sphere;
these are some small wild dogroses, I think,

but all this is nothing
when the desert wind bears the white
gumblossom eucalypts' fragrance;

no, no, this is too much,
we can not escape to a new continent;
the middle door is judgement,

I am judged — prisoner?
the reddest rose unfolds,
can I endure this?

[10]

Because you can not drink our wine
nor eat our salt,
(I asked "do you like salt?"

you said, "yes,") I keep remembering
my glass of red wine; one glass every day
becomes an orgy,

greed devours me,
wine is the sacrament,
salt has not lost its savour;

savour? saviour?
this is a new intensity,
but you are far away,

not so far — Paris;
hidden on or under a transept cross-bar,
the *Notre Dame* dedication is enigmatic,

each of the 18 Latin words has a double sense,
they tell us; I find *Secondo*, the 7th word,
means *Seconde, aide, et favorise*

l'action de la Nature...
and this was inscribed in 1257;
I think we will go far,

going nowhere; Cybele
(*Cybèle*, they write it),
is set over the last door.

[11]

It is heart,
this no-salt, they say,
you might go at any moment,

but that might be said of any of us,
so I must stand apart, keep away;
an intimate of my youth,

a poet wrote,
so slow is the rose to open,
so I contemplate these words

and the Latin dedication,
and would decipher my own fate;
I know the poet that I speak of

wouldn't hesitate,
perhaps humility is more becoming
in a woman;

la rose est la fleur du creuset,
and the *creuset* is the crucible
that I called a flat dish when I wrote [3],

I would enter your senses
through burnt resin
and pine-cones.

[12]

... but I must finish what I have begun
the tall god standing
where the race is run;

did the pine-cones in the flat dish
light an Olympic torch?
my fever, fervour was for one not born

when I wrote this;
the Red-Roses-for-Bronze
roses were for an abstraction;

now with like fervour, with fever,
I offer them to a reality;
the ecstasy comes through you

but goes on;
the torch was lit from another before you,
and another and another before that...

[13]

We leave the old bronze doors, 1257,
for another bronze, 1960,
I am thinking of the young athlete

with the spear, the poised javelin
as I saw him in the picture,
"U.S. Decathlon star ,"

there is living bronze there,
the vibration of sun, desperate endeavour,
ambition, achievement, simplicity,

sheer strength reaching sublimity,
goodness that we might emulate,
(I might, at any rate),

"I like people,
I want to do all I can to help them,
in whatever little way I can,"

we can not compete
but perhaps we meet somewhere;
I with my seven-string lyre,

seem helpless, effete,
but where there is Olympia, Delphi is not far,
sublimation, recognition,

the very aspect of the Decathlon
slays desperation, as long ago (to-day)
Helios slays the Python.

[14]

So my *Red Roses for Bronze* (1930)
bring me to-day, a prophecy,
so these lyrics that would only embarrass you,

perhaps reach further into the future;
if it took 30 years for my *Red Roses for Bronze*
to find the exact image,

perhaps in 30 years,
life's whole complexity will be annulled,
when this *reddest rose unfolds*;

I won't be here,
probably you won't either;
in the meantime, there is beauty and valour

in these contests and passionate excitement as well,
and who was I to shrug and pass them by?
perhaps it was my "preciousness,"

as you called it,
but that was long ago,
last April,

and last May
when you came so late, in a strange place,
with others there.

[15]

The poet of *so slow is the rose to open*
writes, "what have I done with my life?"
what have I done with mine?

I stand again on the threshold,
on my left are the angels Astaroth, Lilith,
on my right, Raphael, Michael;

Astar — a star — Lili — a flower —
Raphael, Michael — why are you there?
would you guide me with dignity

into a known port?
would you champion my endeavour?
Astaroth, you can not be malign

with so beautiful a name,
have you brought me here?
Lilith, why do they call you a devil

with Lucifer and Asmodel?
true the *noms démoniaques* are
donnés sous toutes réserves. . .

[16]

Sesame
seed,
string
minute granules
on a white thread
or red,
will they split
on my needle?
do I need a thimble?
sesame
seed
from South Asia,
that is far away,
what comes between?
hemp — seed,
fleur de chanvre,
from India?
that is the *hachish supérieur*
of dream;
is it better to string
poppy-seeds?
they are too small;
they worshipped the Stars
on the top of the towers,
dites tours à parfums:
I need no rosary

of sesame,
only the days' trial,
reality . . .
faint,
faint,
faint,
O scent of roses
in this room.

[17]

O most august
and sacred host,
so do I turn and fade,

a candle in your light,
burnt to the quick;
you know I offered you my best,

hours, minutes, days, years spent
to proffer a small grain
of worship, incense,

my last breath (I thought)
to assemble in my song,
lines competent to praise,

of shame no taint, no *noms démoniaques*
invoked, no fallen angel
called by name;

now I am forced to hold my lines in doubt,
give me the answer,
let me know your grace,

whose is the Judgement?
there is One
indifferent to the realm of time and space,

Azrael; ironic and subtle in his smile,
near and familiar in his face,
(are his eyes amber?)

"is this your throw with Death?
right, left?
win, lose?

you court the end?
you call this life?
your rose so red

is bondage, stamp and seal,
you asked, 'I am judged prisoner?'
you spoke of Asmodel,

your rose so red
withers in any case,
renouncement? *feu d'enfer?*

now choose,
right, left,
win, lose."

[18]

Azrael said,
"you spoke of Asmodel,"
as if in reproval,

and I am temporarily astray;
I can't find Asmodel
in dictionary or reference book,

certainly not in the Saints' calendar;
Azrael is the Mohammedan angel of Death,
but we know that;

should we delete Asmodel
and find another?
who is he, anyway?

angels may become devils,
devils may become angels,
he'd better stay;

I must keep my identity,
walk unfalteringly toward a Lover,
the *hachish supérieur* of dream.

[1960/1972]

Charles Reznikoff

from *Holocaust*:

MASSACRES

1

The first day the Germans came into the city
where the young woman lived
they took Jewish men and ordered them to gather the dirt on the streets
with their hands.
Then the Jews had to undress
and behind each Jew was a German soldier with a fixed bayonet
who ordered him to run;
if the Jew stopped,
he would be stabbed in the back with the bayonet.
Almost all the Jews came home bleeding—
among them her father.
Later, after the German garrison had left the market place,
large trucks were suddenly there,
and about a dozen soldiers jumped off each truck—
in green uniforms with steel helmets:
these were S.S. men.
They went from house to house
and took Jewish men—young and old—
and brought them to the market place;
here the Jews had to hold their hands on the back of their necks.
About thirty Jews were taken that day;

Author's note: All that follows is based on a United States government publication, *Trials of the Criminals before the Nuerenberg Military Tribunal* and the records of the Eichmann trial in Jerusalem.

among them the young woman's father.
They were then put on one of the trucks and carried off.
The young woman ran after the truck
until she reached a woods in the neighborhood.
There she found all the Jews who had been taken—
dead.

They had been shot
and were stretched out on the ground
in a pattern:
Jews and Poles
in groups of five
but Jews and Poles in separate groups.
She kissed her father:
he was ice-cold
although it was only an hour after he had been taken.

2

Her father had a shop for selling leather
and was one of the notables in a Polish Jewish community
when the Germans entered.
They put their horses into the synagogue and turned it into a stable.
On a Saturday afternoon, peasants from neighboring villages
came to tell the Jews of the town
that the Gemans were killing Jews: they should run away and hide.
But the rabbi and other elders of the town
thought running away useless;
besides, they thought the Germans might take a few of the young men
    to work for them
but that no one would be killed.

The next day, before sunrise, a Jew from a neighboring village
ran into the town shouting:
"Jews, run for your lives!
The Germans are out to kill us,"
and the townspeople saw the Germans coming in.
The young woman's grandfather said, "Run and hide, children, but I
    will stay:

they will do no harm to me."
Those who could hid in a neighboring forest.
During the day they heard shooting—
single shots and cries;
but towards evening they thought the Germans would be leaving the town
and, sure enough, peasants from the neighborhood met them
and said: "You can go back now.
The Germans killed everybody left behind."

When the Jews came back,
they found that the Germans had rounded up about one hundred and
fifty Jews,
including the rabbi and other notables.
They told the rabbi to take his prayer shawl along—
the other Jews had been gathered in the center of the town—
and he was told to put on his prayer shawl
and sing and dance. He would not
and was beaten up. And so were the other Jews.
Then they were driven to the cemetery.
Here a shallow grave had been dug for them.
They were told to lie down in fours
and were shot. But her father remained behind in the town—alive:
he had said he was cutting the leather in his shop for shoes
and was registered as a shoemaker.

Later, the Germans went into the town to take whatever they could find;
the place was swarming with Germans—four or five to every Jew.
Many were put upon a large truck;
those who could not climb on themselves
were thrown on; and those for whom there was no room on the truck
were ordered to run after it.
All the Jews were counted and the Germans searched for every missing
person on their list.
The young woman was among those who ran,
her little daughter in her arms.
There were those, too, who had two or three children
and held them in their arms as they ran after the truck.
Those who fell were shot—right where they fell.

When the young woman reached the truck,
all who had been on it were down and undressed and lined up;
the rest of her family among them.
There was a small hill there and at the foot of the hill a dugout.
The Jews were ordered to stand on top of the hill
and four S.S. men shot them—killed each separately.
When she reached the top of the hill and looked down
she saw three or four rows of the dead already on the ground.
Some of the young people tried to run
but were caught at once
and shot right there.
Children were taking leave of their parents;
but her little daughter said to her,
"Mother, why are we waiting? Let us run!"

Her father did not want to take off all of his clothes
and stood in his underwear.
His children begged him to take it off
but he would not and was beaten.
Then the Germans tore off his underwear
and he was shot.
They shot her mother, too,
and her father's mother—
she was eighty years old
and held two children in her arms;
and they shot her father's sister;
she also had babies in her arms
and was shot on the spot.
Her younger sister went up to one of the Germans—
with another girl, one of her sister's friends—
and they asked to be spared,
standing there naked before him.
The German looked into their eyes
and shot them both—her sister and the young friend;
they fell
embracing each other.

The German who had shot her younger sister
turned to her
and asked, "Whom shall I shoot first?"

She was holding her daughter in her arms and did not answer.
She felt him take the child from her;
the child cried out and was shot.
Then he aimed at her: took hold of her hair
and turned her head around.
She remained standing and heard a shot
but kept on standing. He turned her head around again
and shot her;
and she fell into the dugout
among the bodies.

Suddenly she felt that she was choking;
bodies had fallen all over her.
She tried to find air to breathe
and began climbing towards the top of the dugout,
and felt people pulling at her
and biting at her legs.
At last she came to the top.
Bodies were lying everywhere
but not all of them dead:
dying, but not dead;
and children were crying, "Mamma! Papa!"
She tried to stand up but could not.

The Germans were gone.
She was naked,
covered with blood and dirty with the excrement of those in the dugout,
and found that she had been shot in the back of the head.
Blood was spurting from the dugout
in many places;
and she heard the cries and screams of those in it still alive.
She began to search among the dead for her little girl
and kept calling her name;
trying to join the dead,
and crying out to her dead mother and father,
"Why didn't they kill me, too?"

She was there all night.
Suddenly she saw Germans on horseback
and sat down in a field

and heard them order all the corpses heaped together;
and the bodies—many who had been shot but were still alive—
were heaped together with shovels.
Children were running about.
The Germans caught the children
and shot them, too;
but did not come near her. And left again
and with them the peasants from around the place—
who had to help—
and the machine-guns and trucks were taken away.

She remained in the field, stretched out.
Shepherds began driving their flocks into the field;
and threw stones at her,
thinking her dead or mad.
Afterwards, a passing farmer saw her,
fed her
and helped her join Jews in the forest nearby.

3

Jewish women were lined up by German troops in charge of the territory,
told to undress,
and they stood in their undergarments.
An officer, looking at the row of women,
stopped to look at a young woman—
tall, with long braided hair, and wonderful eyes.
He kept looking at her, then smiled and said,
"Take a step forward."
Dazed—as they all were—she did not move
and he said again: "Take a step forward!
Don't you want to live?"
She took that step
and then he said: "What a pity
to bury such beauty in the earth.
Go!
But don't look backwards.
There is the street to the boulevard.
Follow that."
She hesitated

and then began to walk as told.
The other women looked at her—
some no doubt with envy—
as she walked slowly, step by step.
And the officer took out his revolver
and shot her in the back.

4

The soldier doing the shooting was sitting at the narrow end of the pit,
his feet dangling into it;
smoking a cigarette,
the machine-gun on his knees.

As each truck came, those who had been on it—
Jewish men, women, and children of all ages—
had to undress
and put their clothing at fixed places,
sorted in great piles—
shoes, outer clothing, and underwear.

The S.S. man at the pit,
shouted to his comrade
and he counted off twenty, now completely naked,
and told them to go down the steps cut in the clay wall of the pit:
here they were to climb over the heads of the dead
to where the soldier pointed.
As they went towards the pit,
a slender young woman with black hair,
passing a German civilian who was watching,
pointed to herself and said,
"I am twenty-three."
An old woman with white hair
was holding a child about a year old
in her arms,
singing to it and tickling it,
and the child was cooing with delight;
and a father was holding the hand of his little son—
—the child about to burst into tears—
speaking to the child softly,

stroking his head
and pointing to the sky.

Bodies were soon heaped in the large pit,
lying on top of each other,
heads still to be seen and blood running over their shoulders;
but some were still moving,
lifting arms and turning heads.

5

They gathered some twenty *Hasidic* Jews from their homes,
in the robes these wear,
wearing their prayer shawls, too,
and holding prayer books in their hands.
They were led up a hill.
Here they were told to chant their prayers
and raise their hands for help to God
and, as they did so,
the officers poured kerosene under them
and set it on fire.

[1975]

Langston Hughes

from MONTAGE OF A DREAM DEFERRED

DREAM BOOGIE

Good morning, daddy!
Ain't you heard
The boogie-woogie rumble
Of a dream deferred?

Listen closely:
You'll hear their feet
Beating out and beating out a—

You think
It's a happy beat?

Listen to it closely:
Ain't you heard
something underneath
like a—

What did I say?

Sure,
I'm happy!
Take it away!

Hey, pop!
Re-bop!
Mop!

Y-e-a-h!

SISTER

That little Negro's married and got a kid.
Why does he keep on foolin' around Marie?
Marie's my sister—not married to me—
But why does he keep on foolin' around Marie?
Why don't she get a boy-friend
I can understand—some decent man?

Did it ever occur to you, son,
the reason Marie runs around with trash
is she wants some cash?

Don't decent folks have dough?

Unfortunately usually no!

Well, anyway, it don't have to be a married man.

Did it ever occur to you, boy,
that a woman does the best she can?

Comment on Stoop

So does a man.

PREFERENCE

I likes a woman
six or eight or ten years older'n myself.
I don't fool with these young girls.
Young girl'll say,
Daddy, I want so-and-so.
I needs this, that, and the other.
But a old woman'll say,
Honey, what does YOU *need?*
I just drawed my money tonight
and it's all your'n.
That's why I likes a older woman
who can appreciate me:
When she conversations you
it ain't forever, *Gimme!*

NECESSITY

Work?
I don't have to work.
I don't have to do nothing
but eat, drink, stay black, and die.
This little old furnished room's
so small I can't whip a cat
without getting fur in my mouth
and my landlady's so old
her features is all run together
and God knows she sure can overcharge—
Which is why I reckon I *does*
have to work after all.

QUESTION

Said the lady, *Can you do*
what my other man can't do—
That is
love me, daddy—
and feed me, too?

Figurine

De-dop!

EASY BOOGIE

Down in the bass
That steady beat
Walking walking walking
Like marching feet.

Down in the bass
That easy roll,
Rolling like I like it
In my soul.

Riffs, smears, breaks.

Hey, Lawdy, Mama!
Do you hear what I said?
Easy like I rock it
In my bed!

TELL ME

Why should it be *my* loneliness,
Why should it be *my* song,
Why should it be *my* dream
deferred
overlong?

NEON SIGNS

WONDER BAR
.
. .
.
WISHING WELL
.
. .
.
MONTEREY
.
. .
.
MINTON'S
(ancient altar of Thelonious)
.
. .
.
MANDALAY
Spots where the booted
and unbooted play
.
. .
.

SMALL'S

.

. .

.

CASBAH

.

. .

.

SHALIMAR

.

. .

.

Mirror-go-round
where a broken glass
in the early bright
smears re-bop
sound

.

. .

.

DEAD IN THERE

Sometimes
A night funeral
Going by
Carries home
A cool bop daddy.

Hearse and flowers
Guarantee
He'll never hype
Another paddy.

It's hard to believe,
But dead in there,
He'll never lay a
Hype nowhere!

He's my ace-boy,
Gone away.
Wake up and live!
He used to say.

Squares
Who couldn't dig him,
Plant him now—
Out where it makes
No diff' no how.

SITUATION

When I rolled three 7's
in a row
I was scared to walk out
with the dough.

TOMORROW

Tomorrow may be
a thousand years off:

TWO DIMES AND A NICKLE ONLY

says this particular
cigarette machine.

Others take a quarter straight.

Some dawns
wait.

GAUGE

Hemp…
A stick…
A roach…
Straw…

BAR

That whiskey will cook the egg.
Say not so!
Maybe the egg
will cook the whiskey.
You ought to know!

BE-BOP BOYS

Imploring Mecca
to achieve
six discs
with Decca.

BOOGIE: 1 A.M.

Good evening, daddy!
I know you've heard
The boogie-woogie rumble
Of a dream deferred
Trilling the treble
And twining the bass
Into midnight ruffles
Of cat-gut lace.

SO LONG

So long
is in the song
and it's in the way you're gone
but it's like a foreign language
in my mind
and maybe was I blind
I could not see
and would not know
you're gone so long
so long.

DEFERRED

This year, maybe, do you think I can graduate?
I'm already two years late.
Dropped out six months when I was seven,
a year when I was eleven,
then got put back when we come North.
To get through high at twenty's kind of late—
But maybe this year I can graduate.

Maybe now I can have that white enamel stove
I dreamed about when we first fell in love
eighteen years ago.
But you know,
rooming and everything
then kids,
cold-water flat and all that.
But now my daughter's married
And my boy's most grown—
quit school to work—
and where we're moving
there ain't no stove—
Maybe I can buy that white enamel stove!

Me, I always did want to study French.
It don't make sense—
I'll never go to France,
but night schools teach French.
Now at last I've got a job
where I get off at five,
in time to wash and dress,
so, si'l-vous plait, I'll study French!

Someday,
I'm gonna buy two new suits
at once!

All I want is
one more bottle of gin.

All I want is to see
my furniture paid for.
All I want is a wife who will
work with me and not against me. Say,
baby, could you see your way clear?

Heaven, heaven, is my home!
This world I'll leave behind
When I set my feet in glory
I'll have a throne for mine!

I want to pass the civil service.

I want a television set.

You know, as old as I am,
I ain't never
owned a decent radio yet?

I'd like to take up Bach.

> *Montage*
> *of a dream*
> *deferred.*

Buddy, have you heard?

PASSING

On sunny summer Sunday afternoons in Harlem
when the air is one interminable ball game
and grandma cannot get her gospel hymns
from the Saints of God in Christ
on account of the Dodgers on the radio,
on sunny Sunday afternoons
when the kids look all new
and far too clean to stay that way,
and Harlem has its
washed-and-ironed-and-cleaned-best out,

the ones who've crossed the line
to live downtown
miss you,
Harlem of the bitter dream,
since their dream has
come true.

NIGHTMARE BOOGIE

I had a dream
and I could see
a million faces
black as me!
A nightmare dream:
Quicker than light
All them faces
Turned dead white!
Boogie-woogie,
Rolling bass,
Whirling treble
of cat-gut lace.

NEIGHBOR

Down home
he sets on a stoop
and watches the sun go by.
In Harlem
when his work is done
he sets in a bar with a beer.
He looks taller than he is
and younger than he ain't.
He looks darker than he is, too.
And he's smarter than he looks,

He ain't smart.
That cat's a fool.

Naw, he ain't neither.
He's a good man,
except that he talks too much.
In fact, he's a great cat.
But when he drinks,
he drinks fast.

Sometimes
he don't drink.

True,
he just
lets his glass
set there.

CHORD

Shadow faces
In the shadow night
Before the early dawn
Bops bright.

FACT

There's been an eagle on a nickel,
An eagle on a quarter, too.
But there ain't no eagle
On a dime.

HOPE

He rose up on his dying bed
and asked for fish.
His wife looked it up in her dream book
and played it.

DREAM BOOGIE: VARIATION

Tinkling treble,
Rolling bass,
High noon teeth
In a midnight face,
Great long fingers
On great big hands,
Screaming pedals
Where his twelve-shoe lands,
Looks like his eyes
Are teasing pain,
A few minutes late
For the Freedom Train.

HARLEM

What happens to a dream deferred?

Does it dry up
like a raisin in the sun?
Or fester like a sore—
And then run?
Does it stink like rotten meat?
Or crust and sugar over—
like a syrupy sweet?

Maybe it just sags
like a heavy load.

Or does it explode?

GOOD MORNING

Good morning, daddy!
I was born here, he said,
watched Harlem grow
until colored folks spread
from river to river

across the middle of Manhattan
out of Penn Station
dark tenth of a nation,
planes from Puerto Rico,
and holds of boats, chico,
up from Cuba Haiti Jamaica,
in buses marked New York
from Georgia Florida Louisiana
to Harlem Brooklyn the Bronx
but most of all to Harlem
dusky sash across Manhattan
I've seen them come dark
    wondering
    wide-eyed
    dreaming
out of Penn Station—
but the trains are late.
The gates open—
Yet there're bars
at each gate.

    What happens
    to a dream deferred?

Daddy, ain't you heard?

SAME IN BLUES

I said to my baby,
Baby, take it slow.
I can't, she said, I can't!
I got to go!

    There's a certain
    amount of traveling
    in a dream deferred.

Lulu said to Leonard,
I want a diamond ring.
Leonard said to Lulu,
You won't get a goddamn thing!

A certain
amount of nothing
in a dream deferred.

Daddy, daddy, daddy,
All I want is you.
You can have me, baby—
but my lovin' days is through.

A certain
amount of impotence
in a dream deferred.

Three parties
On my party line—
But that third party,
Lord, ain't mine!

There's liable
to be confusion
in a dream deferred.

From river to river,
Uptown and down,
There's liable to be confusion
when a dream gets kicked around.

COMMENT ON CURB

You talk like
they don't kick
dreams around
downtown.

I expect they do—
But I'm talking about
Harlem to you!

[1951]

Lorine Niedecker

Who was Mary Shelley?
What was her name
before she married?

She eloped with this Shelley
she rode a donkey
till the donkey had to be carried.

Mary was Frankenstein's creator
his yellow eye
before her husband was to drown

Created the monster nights
after Byron, Shelley
talked the candle down.

Who was Mary Shelley?
She read Greek, Italian
She bore a child

Who died
and yet another child
who died

[1950's/1969]

PAEAN TO PLACE

And the place was water

Fish
  fowl
    flood
  Water lily mud
My life

in the leaves and on water
My mother and I
        born
in swale and swamp and sworn
to water

My father
thru marsh fog
    sculled down
        from high ground
saw her face

at the organ
bore the weight of lake water
    and the cold—
he seined for carp to be sold
that their daughter

might go high
on land
    to learn
Saw his wife turn
deaf

and away
She
    who knew boats
        and ropes
no longer played

She helped him string out nets
for tarring
        And she could shoot
                He was cool
to the man

who stole his minnows
by night and next day offered
        to sell them back
                He brought in a sack
of dandelion greens

if no flood
No oranges—none at hand
        No marsh marigolds
                where the water rose
He kept us afloat

I mourn her not hearing canvasbacks
their blast-off rise
        from the water
                Not hearing sora
rail's sweet

spoon-tapped waterglass-
descending scale-
        tear-drop-tittle
                Did she giggle
as a girl?

His skiff skimmed
the coiled celery now gone
        from these streams
                due to carp
He knew duckweed

fall-migrates
toward Mud Lake bottom

Knew what lay
under leaf decay
and on pickerelweeds

before summer hum
To be counted on:
new leaves
new dead
leaves

He could not
—like water bugs—
stride surface tension
He netted
loneliness

As to his bright new car
my mother—her house
next his—averred:
A hummingbird
can't haul

Anchored here
in the rise and sink
of life—
middle years' nights
he sat

beside his shoes
rocking his chair
Roped not 'looped
in the loop
of her hair'

I grew in green
slide and slant
of shore and shade
Child-time—wade
thru weeds

Maples to swing from
Pewee-glissando
        sublime
                slime-
song
        . . .
Grew riding the river
Books
        at home-pier
                Shelley could steer
as he read

I was the solitary plover
a pencil
        for a wing-bone
From the secret notes
I must tilt

upon the pressure
execute and adjust
        In us sea-air rhythm
'We live by the urgent wave
of the verse'

Seven-year molt
for the solitary bird
        and so young
Seven years the one
dress

for town once a week
One for home
        faded blue-striped
as she piped
her cry

Dancing grounds
my people had none
        woodcocks had—
        backland-
air around

Solemnities
such as what flower
        to take
        to grandfather's grave
unless

water lilies—
he who'd bowed his head
        to grass as he mowed
        Iris now grows
on fill

for the two
and for him
        where they lie
        How much less am I
in the dark than they?

Effort lay in us
before religions
        at pond bottom
                All things move toward
the light

except those
that freely work down
        to oceans' black depths
                In us an impulse tests
the unknown

River rising—flood
Now melt and leave home
    Return—broom wet
        naturally wet
Under

soak-heavy rug
water bugs hatched—
    no snake in the house
        Where were they?—
she

who knew how to clean up
after floods
    he who bailed boats, houses
        Water endows us
with buckled floors

You with sea water running
in your veins sit down in water
    Expect the long-stemmed blue
        speedwell to renew
itself

O my floating life
Do not save love
    for things
        Throw *things*
to the flood

ruined
by the flood
    Leave the new unbought—
        all one in the end—
water

I possessed
the high word:
    The boy my friend
        played his violin
in the great hall

On this stream
my moonnight memory
washed of hardships
maneuvers barges
thru the mouth

of the river
They fished in beauty
It was not always so
In Fishes
red Mars

rising
rides the sloughs and sluices
of my mind
with the persons
on the edge

[1970]

DARWIN

I

His holy
slowly
mulled over
matter

not all 'delirium
of delight'
as were the forests
of Brazil

'Species are not
(it is like confessing
a murder)
immutable'

He was often becalmed
in this Port Desire by illness
or rested from species
at billiard table

As to Man
'I believe Man...
in the same predicament
with other animals'

II

Cordilleras to climb—Andean
peaks 'tossed about
like the crust
of a broken pie'

Icy wind
Higher, harder
Chileans advised eat onions
for shortness of breath

Heavy on him:
Andes miners carried up
great loads—not allowed
to stop for breath

Fossil bones near Santa Fé
Spider-bite-scauld
Fever
Tended by an old woman

'Dear Susan...
I am ravenous
for the sound
of the pianoforte'

III

FitzRoy blinked—
        sea-shells on mountain tops!
                The laws of change
    rode the seas

without the good captain
        who could not concede
                land could rise from the sea
    until—before his eyes

earthquake—
        Talcahuana Bay drained out
                all-water wall
    up from the ocean

—six seconds—
        demolished the town
                The will of God?
    Let us pray

And now the Galapagos Islands—
        hideous black lava
                The shore so hot
    it burned their feet

through their boots
        Reptile life
                Melville here later
    said the chief sound was a hiss

A thousand turtle monsters
        drive together to the water
                Blood-bright crabs hunt ticks
    on lizards' backs

Flightless cormorants
        Cold-sea creatures—
                penguins, seals
    here in tropical waters

Hell for FitzRoy
but for Darwin Paradise Puzzle
with the jig-saw gists
beginning to fit

IV

Years...balancing
probabilities
I am ill, he said
and books are slow work

Studied pigeons
barnacles, earthworms
Extracted seeds
from bird dung

Brought home Drosera—
saw insects trapped
by its tentacles—the fact
that a plant should secrete

an acid acutely akin
to the digestive fluid
of an animal! Years
till he published

He wrote Lyell: Don't forget
to send me the carcass
of your half-bred African cat
should it die

V

I remember, he said
those tropical nights at sea—
we sat and talked
on the booms

Tierra del Fuego's
shining glaciers translucent
blue clear down
(almost) to the indigo sea

(By the way Carlyle
thought it most ridiculous
anyone should care
whether a glacier

moved a little quicker
or a little slower
or moved at all)
Darwin

sailed out
of Good Success Bay
to carcass-
conclusions—

the universe
not built by brute force
but designed by laws
The details left

to the working of chance
'Let each man hope
and believe
what he can'

[1976]

Louis Zukofsky

"*A*" – 11

for Celia and Paul

River that must turn full after I stop dying
Song, my song, raise grief to music
Light as my loves' thought, the few sick
So sick of wrangling: thus weeping,
Sounds of light, stay in her keeping
And my son's face—this much for honor.

Freed by their praises who make honor dearer
Whose losses show them rich and you no poorer
Take care, song, that what stars' imprint you mirror
Grazes their tears; draw speech from their nature or
Love in you—faced to your outer stars—purer
Gold than tongues make without feeling
Art new, hurt old: revealing
The slackened bow as the stinging
Animal dies, thread gold stringing
The fingerboard pressed in my honor.

Honor, song, sang the blest is delight knowing
We overcome ills by love. Hurt, song, nourish
Eyes, think most of whom you hurt. For the flowing
River 's poison where what rod blossoms. Flourish
By love's sweet lights and sing *in them I flourish.*
No, song, not any one power
May recall or forget, our
Love to see your love flows into
Us. If Venus lights, your words spin, to
Live our desires lead us to honor.

Graced, your heart in nothing less than in death, go—
I, dust—raise the great hem of the extended
World that nothing can leave; having had breath go
Face my son, say: 'If your father offended
You with mute wisdom, my words have not ended
His second paradise where
His love was in her eyes where
They turn, quick for you two—sick
Or gone cannot make music
You set less than all. Honor

His voice in me, the river's turn that finds the
Grace in you, four notes first too full for talk, leaf
Lighting stem, stems bound to the branch that binds the
Tree, and then as from the same root we talk, leaf
After leaf of your mind's music, page, walk leaf
Over leaf of his thought, sounding
His happiness: song sounding
The grace that comes from knowing
Things, her love our own showing
Her love in all her honor.'

[1950/1966]

from "*A*"-15

An
   hinny
by
   stallion
out of
  she-ass

He neigh ha lie low h'who y'he gall mood
So roar cruel hire
Lo to achieve an eye leer rot off
Mass th'lo low o loam echo
How deal me many coeval yammer
Naked on face of white rock—sea.

Then I said: Liveforever my nest
Is arable   hymn
Shore she   root to water
Dew anew to branch.

Wind: Yahweh at Iyyob
Mien His roar 'Why yammer
Measly make short hates oh
By milling bleat doubt?
Eye sore gnaw key heaver haul its core
Weigh as I lug where hide any?
If you—had you towed beside the roots?
How goad Him—you'd do it by now—
My sum My made day a key to daw?
O Me not there allheal—a cave.

All mouth deny hot bough?
O Me you're raw—Heaven pinned Dawn stars
Brine I heard choir and weigh by care—
Why your ear would call by now Elohim:
Where was soak—bid lot tie in hum—
How would you have known to hum
How would you all oats rose snow lay
Asśay how'd a rock light rollick ore
Had the rush in you curb, ah bay,
Bay the shophar yammer *heigh horse*'

Wind: Yahweh at Iyyob 'Why yammer,'
Wind: Iyyob at Yahweh, 'Why yammer
How cold the mouth achieved echo.'
Wind: Yahweh at Iyyob 'Why yammer
Ha neigh now behēmoth and share I see see your make
Giddy pair—stones—whose rages go
Weigh raw all gay where how spill lay who'
Wind: Iyyob
'Rain without sun hated? *hurt no one*
In two we shadow, how hide any.'

[1964]

from "*A*" – 18

An unearthing
my valentine
if I say it now will
it always be said.
I always know
it is I who have died
yet in that state

sorrow for you
by yourself.
Thinking of you
without me
without years
of hours
that time is.
Selfish of
me to wish you
to merely
live long

to fulfill
no time
where your
thought for
me has no sense
for with
that thought
it is I have died.
I mean don't cry
in that sense
I cannot now

get around
thinking I am dead
where with you
now I have no place
as I say
it now
and you sense
it always said.

[...]
When they use elbow or arm boards to
cover the whole keyboard fast rather than their
fingers spanning octave to octave they fly to
lunes together and the epicene stentorian drops
bass lower than his stones we're to watch see.
The young o young-eyed pitiful cannot bear that
gnawing pain sorrow sorrow and 'the music saves
it' I may not ever translate it precisely
carried having enough its hoving over. THRONGS OF
VIETNAMESE PILGRIMS VISIT POND OF MIRACULOUS FISH
'The pond is in Quang Nam about 30
miles west of Danang where hate between Buddhists
(about 80 per cent of the population) and
Roman Catholics equals "*strong*." The miracle happened about
two months ago in the middle of the crisis
the Buddhists accusing the Government of discriminating against
them. Word spread. A giant fish apparently a
carp swimming in a pond the incarnate Buddha.
The fish was so big and could be
seen so easily it was attracting the attention
of the villagers. From all over the province
Vietnamese came to the pond to be its
fish. At this point the district chief a
newly shrived Catholic told American aide that the
"pilgrimage" was an act of opposition. American decided
to clean out *his* pond. With new troops
from Col. Le Quang Tung's special forces both
marched to that pond to *get* that fish.
Troops fired their automatic weapons into *their* pond.
They placed ten mines in said pond and
set them off. They blew up and killed
everything in that pond except the fish. He
came on swimming. They started feeding it bread
so to tempt him up to the surface.
They followed bread with hand grenades pitched into
the water twice. Twice terrific explosions twice the
fish officially "continued" to swim. *Ich hub dir*
in bud (Kentuckian for *jump in the lay-ake*
brother tongue too.) Other continents enroach' as

we can see by the belly-fanny dancing
of the tights over the buttocks of "our"
women the slim erectile trousers of "their" men.
Not that we digged original sin reading Gibbon's
"an useful scavenger" of a defender of persecution
who used saints for his history in support of
his arguments. Rather noted a statesman hump TV-
free face between a pumpkin and a shark.
For a roman à clef all resemblance to living or
dead obviously intended if these find their identities
in them. For the young starting out: better
ordure than order's arrogance of 'ideas' and 'ideals.'
We warm us may ah Lesbia what cue
may maim us the theatre marquees too big
to read, a friend writes 'the song preserves
recurring saves us' the song preserves a store's
preserves packed rancid: death wars' commonplace no hurt
wars not Old Glory's archaic even for MacArthur
'How many killings per Diem Phu on Nhu'
housewife alarmed veteran unpacking from the supermarket 'I
told him not to put the encyclopedia with
the vegetables, PENTHOUSE FLOOR send the elevator down.'

[...]

He has become as
talkative as Bottom a weaver and says for
me all that follows: 'we laugh at that elixir
that promises to prolong life to a thousand
years and with equal justice may be derided?
Who shall imagine that his dictionary can enbalm his
language, that it is in his power to
change sublunary nature. Sounds are too volatile for
legal restraints. To enchain syllables and to lash
the wind are equally undertakings of pride unwilling
to measure its desires by its strength. That
signs might be permanent..like the things?
To explain requires the use of terms less
abstruse than that which is to be explained
and such terms cannot always be found. Words
hourly shifting, names have often many ideas, few

ideas many names. But every art is obscure
to those that have not learned (?) it. The
exuberance of words, to admit no testimony of
living authors, but when my heart in the
tenderness of friendship solicited admission for a favorite
name—to *per*sue perfection was like the first
inhabitants of Arcadia to *chace* the sun, which
when they had reached the hill where he
seemed to rest, was still beheld at some
distance from them: that I set limits to
my work which would in time be ended
tho not completed, that he whose design includes
whatever language can express must often speak of
what he does not understand: writes hurried by
eagerness to the end—that the *English Dictionary*
was written with little assistance of the learned,
and without any patronage of the great; not
in the soft obscurities of retirement, or under
the shelter of academic*k* bowers, but amidst inconvenience
and distraction, in sickness and in sorrow—success and
miscarriage..empty sounds..having little to fear
from censure or from praise.'

[...]

Weeping: the food he eats.
The spirits would not return to rest under
the huts burnt to the ground their lifegiving
handful of rice smoke when the rice paddies
fired. The marine with the cigarette lighter did
not know nor the air cavalry bombing indiscriminately
cultured now like the innocent child shamed by
the pain his birth caused perverse burned hating all
males who impregnate. Here an old woman weeps
as in the Melanesian tale the old woman's
spirit crouched under the bedstead not known scalded
after the Harvest Tide when the dead return
for their Day then all but the longing spirit
return all the dead to return remembered only
in the next Harvest Tide the Year's Time
scalded unknown by the day's broth her daughter

spilled from a coconut cup weeps heard known
to 'I thought you were here only for
the one Day' weeps 'I shall go now'
known now cutting a coconut in half as
alive keeping the half with three eyes giving
her daughter the other 'I am giving you
the half that is blind tho you look you
will not see me I am taking the
half with the eyes and I shall see
you when I come back with the others.'
Trobrianders: born of these spirits *Baloma bogè isaika*
the baloma gave it of the father's way
with the child's into the womb they'll say
or know nothing: when the *Baloma* the dead
soul is old his teeth fall out his
skin's loose and wrinkled he goes to the
beach and bathes in salt water throws off
his skin like snake becomes child again a
waiwaia in *utero* (belly: cavity of earth) or
just born: baloma woman's there with a basket
or plaits coconut leaf to carry *waiwaia* to
Kiriwina village places it into the womb of
(that's later) its mother so she is *nasusuma*
pregnant: or the *waiwaia* go into the sea
hide in *popèwo* floating scum in washed on
stones *dukupi* or come along on large tree-
trunk *kaibilabala* or attach to dead leaves *libulibu*:
when wind and high tide blow plenty of
this stuff towards the shore girls are afraid
to bathe in the sea: while bathing may
feel a thing touch or hurt: sometimes cry
A fish has bitten me: th' *waiwaia* being inserted:
or in a dream *baloma* inserts the *waiwaia.*
As to your "cause" *U'ula* a mere share:
dripping water a finger may also—not man:
also the fatherless always *the baloma gave it*
tho the girl with *waiwaia* no father's "no good"
gala taitala Cikopo'i where is no father no
man to take it in his arms.

[1966]

from CATULLUS LXIV

laeva colum molli lana retinebat amictum,
dextera tum leviter deducens fila supinis
formabat digitis, tum prono in pollice torquens
libratum tereti versabat turbine fusum,
atque ita decerpens aequabat semper opus dens,
laneaque aridulis haerebant morsa labellis,
quae prius in levi fuerant extantia filo:
ante pedes autem candentis mollia lanae
vellera virgati custodibant calathisci.
haec tum clarisona pellentes vellera voce
talia divino fuderunt carmine fata,
carmine, perfidiae quod post nulla arguet aetas.

O decus eximium magnis virtutibus augens,
Emathiae tutamen opis, clarissime nato,
accipe, quod laeta tibi pandunt luce sorores,
veridicum oraclum. sed vos, quae fata sequuntur,
currite ducentes subtegmina, currite, fusi.

adveniet titi iam portans optata maritis
Hesperus, adveniet fausto cum sidere coniunx,
quae tibi flexanimo mentem perfundat amore
languidulosque paret tecum coniungere somnos,
levia substernens robusto bracchia collo.
currite ducentes subtegmina, currite, fusi.

nulla domus tales umquam contexit amores,
nullus amor tali coniunxit foedere amantes,
qualis adest Thetidi, qualis concordia Peleo.
currite ducentes subtegmina, currite, fusi.

nascetur vobis expers terroris Achilles,
hostibus haud tergo, sed forti pectore notus,
qui persaepe vago victor certamine cursus
flammea praevertet celeris vestigia cervae.
currite ducentes subtegmina, currite, fusi.

from CATULLUS LXIV
(translated from the Latin by Louis & Celia Zukofsky)

Left hand holding distaff and wool retained on it (ah mixture)
dexter hand will levitate take down these threads (feels *up* in these
formed about digitals) thumb pronate 'down' policy torque wanes
liberate the spindle whorl 's about round in now fusing,
and what thread they cure pain 's about smoothed bitten off with their teeth,
wool ends as of arid locks of hair abound morsels on bit lips,
what previously would furl on the thread extant if a lull:
at their feet always near candescent more light than wool white
rolls of fleece well guarded custom bound small willow baskets.
Hike t'whom clarisonous pelting the rolls of fleece, voiced then
the tale ah divinely poured from the harmony Fate their
harmony, perfidy could in no late time argue its heart.

Honor his excellence, magnanimity, virtues your gains,
Emathia, to your men powers, clear 's the fame of your son,
ah keep the good light of today span we looked into—Sisters'
wayridden true oracle. Said once, why Fate has to sing under,
hurry the skeins and the spinning and ah hurry what few see.

Advent and yet to be, come portent and hope to th' married here
Hesperus, advent and yet wish to come, star in their conscience,
how 't will be flows on in her meant him pour forth love and more love
languidly who's closer by it take him into your young slumbers,
lave ah sustaining arms his robust neck your column.
Hurry the skeins and the spinning and ah hurry what few see.

No loves' home has told us weaving on one text of lovers
no loves have more to tell conjoin seek further rayed mandates
while all that is is Thetis, all is concord with her Peleus.
Hurry the skeins and the spinning and ah hurry what few see.

Now seed your own blood's fearless of terrors Achilles,
host of foes, how to go? set forth is breast torn no truce,
quick pass by peer why *go* victor certain win his coursers
flaming outferret th' deer gale ere his vestige will care why.
Hurry the skeins and the spinning and ah hurry what few see.

non illi quisquam bello se conferet heros,
cum Phyrgii Teucro manabunt sanguine rivi,
Troicaque obsidens longinquo moenia bello
periuri Pelopis vastabit tertius heres.
currite ducentes subtegmina, currite, fusi.

illius egregias virtutes claraque facta
saepe fatebuntur gnatorum in funere matres,
cum incultum cano solvent a vertice crinem
putridaque infirmis variabunt pectora palmis.
currite ducentes subtegmina, currite, fusi.

namque velut densas praecerpens cultor aristas
sole sub ardenti flaventia demetit arva,
Troiugenum infesto prosternet corpora ferro.
currite ducentes subtegmina, currite, fusi.

testis erit magnis virtutibus unda Scamandri,
quae passim rapido diffunditor Hellesponto,
cuius iter caesis angustans corporum acervis
alta tepefaciet permixta flumina caede.
currite ducentes subtegmina, currite, fusi.
. . . .

denique testis erit morti quoque reddita praeda,
cum teres excelso coacervatum aggere bustum
excipiet niveos percussae virginis artus.
currite ducentes subtegmina, currite, fusi.

nam simul ac fessis dederit fors copiam Achivis
urbis Dardaniae Neptunia solvere vincla,
alta Polyxenia madefient caede sepulcra,
quae, velut ancipiti succumbens victima ferro,
proiciet truncum submisso poplite corpus.
currite ducentes subtegmina, currite, fusi.

quare agite optatos animi coniungite amores.
accipiat coniunx felici foedere divam,
dedatur cupido iamdudum nupta marito.
currite ducentes subtegmina, currite, fusi.

None who'll quest war'll bellow he compares with this hero,
come Phrygian Teucrian man in one sanguine river,
Troy crashing walls sift down longing call turmoil and bellow
perjurer Pelops lay waste to it—the third of his heirs.
    Hurry the skeins and the spinning and ah hurry what few see.

He will with his excellent virtues such clarified acts as
cipher Fate bring to their dead sons funereal mothers,
come uncoiling long hair sobbing ah averted crowned gray
putrid at heart infirm as they rave and beat old breasts with their palms.
    Hurry the skeins and the spinning and ah hurry what few see.

Now come will it dense as ripe crops of corn th' farmer harvests
sunlight so ardent of yellow flame demitted arable:
Troy's young mown down with foe's steel prostrate and corpses in furrow.
    Hurry the skeins and the spinning and ah hurry what few see.

Test his air earth mog knees virtue to be 's under Scamander,
what passing rapid o diffused into Hellespont o
who is in the crush sees anguished slain corpses in great heaps
altered to deep tepefied purr mixture of blood and cold tide.
    Hurry the skeins and the spinning and ah hurry what few see.

................................[lacuna MSS]................................

Then ache cue test his air earth mortal booty ready to pride ah
coom earth's ash excels so cumbustible heap round barrow burns now
she is given as new white snow pierced corpse by him virgin odd truce.
    Hurry the skeins and the spinning and ah hurry what few see.

Name simulacra fagged deed dared Fortune's *come on* Achaeans
your bid 's Dardania her Neptune's own dissolving link wall,
(all told!) Polyxenia made of we win blood for sepulcher,
aie will it and cut two-edged succumb head victim of error,
broken headless trunk submits so poppled knee corpse pus.
    Hurry the skeins and the spinning and ah hurry what few see.

Quarry ah go to your hoped host animate conjunction of lovers.
Ah keep that goddess, man, felicity faith of her, dear one,
do deed her, Cupid, to him do do nuptial marry them.
    Hurry the skeins and the spinning and ah hurry what few see.

non illam nutrix orienti luce revisens
hesterno collum poterit circumdare filo,
anxia nec mater discordis maestra puellae
secubitu caros mittet sperare nepotes.
currite ducentes subtegmina, currite, fusi.

Talia praefantes quondam felicia Pelei
carmina divino cecinerunt pectore Parcae.
praesentes namque ante domos invisere castas
heroum et sese mortali ostendere coetu
caelicolae nondum spreta pietate solebant.
saepe pater divum templo in fulgente revisens
annua cum festis venissent sacra diebus,
conspexit terra centum procumbere tauros.
saepe vagus Liber Parnasi vertice summo
Thyadas effusis euantis crinibus egit,
cum Delphi tota certatim ex urbe ruentes
acciperent laeti divum fumantibus aris.
saepe in letifero belli certamine Mavors
aut rapidi Tritonis era aut Rhamnusia virgo
armatas hominumst praesens hortata catervas.
sed postquam tellus scelerest imbuta nefando,
iustitiamque omnes cupida de mente fugarunt,
perfudere manus fraterno sanguine fratres,
destitit extinctos natus lugere parentes,
optavit genitor primaevi funera nati,
liber ut innuptae poteretur flore novercae,
ignaro mater substernens se impia nato
impia non veritast divos scelerare parentes:
omnia fanda nefanda malo permixta furore
iustificam nobis mentem avertere deorum.
quare nec tales dignantur visere coetus,
nec se contingi patiuntur lumine claro.

Nor will her nurse tricks of the rising sun looking in sense
yesterday, collar for her neck now too small for her love,
nor anxious nag mother, discord's mist on a puling girl
sigh the bride lies alone despair ever of the little ones.
    Hurry the skeins and the spinning and ah hurry what few see.

    Tally all prophecies one time felicity hailed Peleus
harmony divinely chanted from the breasts of the Parcae.
Presences Gods came once to visit the homes of the pious,
heroes might yet see mortal and gods stand there together—
godly call high no man would spurn piety his holy bond.
Saw Father of the Gods temple refulgent revisit His
annual Kalends feast venerated sacrifices he'd
come to see on earth count them by hundred prone taurine.
Saw Bacchus as Liber, Parnassus' vertigo summon
Thyades effuse his *hey on* tease crinite heads *ay get*,
'come Delphic townsfolk hurl toward him exuberance routings,
ah keep Your Own Light here Dear God fume mount! busy altars.'
Siding in lethal war o beleaguered town 'Ah mien of Mavors!
out rapid heed Triton's own daughter! out Rhamnusian virgin!'
armored as men whom god's presence exhorted to courage.
Said past come tell us sclerous crime imbued earth, men founder,
justice has gone and always cupidity and mind figure ground,
perfidy on their hands brothers now strangle their brothers,
destitute extinct those sons who looked after their parents,
mourned them, but today's father primps at junior's funeral
libertine impatience bother to deflower his new mother,
innocent martyr son steered to impious incest,
impious no fear or taste divines scald wrath of her parent gods:
all law once founded unfounded malice a mixture of furor
justifying no blest mind may await gods' ray where or home.
Where there are no tales dignifying Their Ways They cut us,
nor seek contingent patient touch to illumine clear air.

[1969]

Kenneth Rexroth

THE SIGNATURE OF ALL THINGS

My head and shoulders, and my book
In the cool shade, and my body
Stretched bathing in the sun, I lie
Reading beside the waterfall—
Boehme's "Signature of all Things."
Through the deep July day the leaves
Of the laurel, all the colors
Of gold, spin down through the moving
Deep laurel shade all day. They float
On the mirrored sky and forest
For a while, and then, still slowly
Spinning, sink through the crystal deep
Of the pool to its leaf gold floor.
The saint saw the world as streaming
In the electrolysis of love.
I put him by and gaze through shade
Folded into shade of slender
Laurel trunks and leaves filled with sun.
The wren broods in her moss domed nest.
A newt struggles with a white moth
Drowning in the pool. The hawks scream,
Playing together on the ceiling
Of heaven. The long hours go by.
I think of those who have loved me,
Of all the mountains I have climbed,
Of all the seas I have swum in.
The evil of the world sinks.
My own sin and trouble fall away

Like Christian's bundle, and I watch
My forty summers fall like falling
Leaves and falling water held
Eternally in summer air.

Deer are stamping in the glades,
Under the full July moon.
There is a smell of dry grass
In the air, and more faintly,
The scent of a far off skunk.
As I stand at the wood's edge,
Watching the darkness, listening
To the stillness, a small owl
Comes to the branch above me,
On wings more still than my breath.
When I turn my light on him,
His eyes glow like drops of iron,
And he perks his head at me,
Like a curious kitten.
The meadow is bright as snow.
My dog prowls the grass, a dark
Blur in the blur of brightness.
I walk to the oak grove where
The Indian village was once.
There, in blotched and cobwebbed light
And dark, dim in the blue haze,
Are twenty Holstein heifers,
Black and white, all lying down,
Quietly together, under
The huge trees rooted in the graves.

When I dragged the rotten log
From the bottom of the pool,
It seemed heavy as stone.
I let it lie in the sun
For a month; and then chopped it
Into sections, and split them

For kindling, and spread them out
To dry some more. Late that night,
After reading for hours,
While moths rattled at the lamp—
The saints and the philosophers
On the destiny of man—
I went out on my cabin porch,
And looked up through the black forest
At the swaying islands of stars.
Suddenly I saw at my feet,
Spread on the floor of night, ingots
Of quivering phosphorescence,
And all about were scattered chips
Of pale cold light that was alive.

LYELL'S HYPOTHESIS AGAIN

An Attempt to Explain the Former
Changes of the Earth's Surface by
Causes Now in Operation
Subtitle of Lyell: Principles of Geology

The mountain road ends here,
Broken away in the chasm where
The bridge washed out years ago.
The first scarlet larkspur glitters
In the first patch of April
Morning sunlight. The engorged creek
Roars and rustles like a military
Ball. Here by the waterfall,
Insuperable life, flushed
With the equinox, sentient
And sentimental, falls away
To the sea and death. The tissue
Of sympathy and agony
That binds the flesh in its Nessus' shirt;
The clotted cobweb of unself
And self; sheds itself and flecks
The sun's bed with darts of blossom
Like flagellant blood above
The water bursting in the vibrant

Air. This ego, bound by personal
Tragedy and the vast
Impersonal vindictiveness
Of the ruined and ruining world,
Pauses in this immortality,
As passionate, as apathetic,
As the lava flow that burned here once;
And stopped here; and said, 'This far
And no further.' And spoke thereafter
In the simple diction of stone.

Naked in the warm April air,
We lie under the redwoods,
In the sunny lee of a cliff.
As you kneel above me I see
Tiny red marks on your flanks
Like bites, where the redwood cones
Have pressed into your flesh.
You can find just the same marks
In the lignite in the cliff
Over our heads. *Sequoia*
Langsdorfii before the ice,
And *sempervirens* afterwards,
There is little difference,
Except for all those years.

Here in the sweet, moribund
Fetor of spring flowers, washed,
Flotsam and jetsam together,
Cool and naked together,
Under this tree for a moment,
We have escaped the bitterness
Of love, and love lost, and love
Betrayed. And what might have been,
And what might be, fall equally
Away with what is, and leave
Only these ideograms
Printed on the immortal
Hydrocarbons of flesh and stone.

ANDREE REXROTH

MT. TAMALPAIS

The years have gone. It is spring
Again. Mars and Saturn will
Soon come on, low in the West,
In the dusk. Now the evening
Sunlight makes hazy girders
Over Steep Ravine above
The waterfalls. The winter
Birds from Oregon, robins
And varied thrushes, feast on
Ripe toyon and madroñe
Berries. The robins sing as
The dense light falls.
Your ashes
Were scattered in this place. Here
I wrote you a farewell poem,
And long ago another,
A poem of peace and love,
Of the lassitude of a long
Spring evening in youth. Now
It is almost ten years since
You came here to stay. Once more,
The pussy willows that come
After the New Year in this
Outlandish land are blooming.
There are deer and raccoon tracks
In the same places. A few
New sand bars and cobble beds
Have been left where erosion
Has gnawed deep into the hills.
The rounds of life are narrow.
War and peace have past like ghosts.
The human race sinks towards
Oblivion. A bittern
Calls from the same rushes where
You heard one on our first year
In the West; and where I heard
One again in the year
Of your death.

KINGS RIVER CANYON

My sorrow is so wide
I cannot see across it;
And so deep I shall never
Reach the bottom of it.
The moon sinks through deep haze,
As though the Kings River Canyon
Were filled with fine, warm, damp gauze.
Saturn gleams through the thick light
Like a gold, wet eye; nearby,
Antares glows faintly,
Without sparkle. Far overhead,
Stone shines darkly in the moonlight —
Lookout Point, where we lay
In another full moon, and first
Peered down into this canyon.
Here we camped, by still autumnal
Pools, all one warm October.
I baked you a bannock birthday cake.
Here you did your best paintings —
Innocent, wondering landscapes.
Very few of them are left
Anywhere. You destroyed them
In the terrible trouble
Of your long sickness. Eighteen years
Have passed since that autumn.
There was no trail here then.
Only a few people knew
How to enter this canyon.
We were all alone, twenty
Miles from anybody;

A young husband and wife,
Closed in and wrapped about
In the quiet autumn,
In the sound of quiet water,
In the turning and falling leaves,
In the wavering of innumerable
Bats from the caves, dipping
Over the odorous pools
Where the great trout drowsed in the evenings.

Eighteen years have been ground
To pieces in the wheels of life.
You are dead. With a thousand
Convicts they have blown a highway
Through Horseshoe Bend. Youth is gone,
That only came once. My hair
Is turning grey and my body
Heavier. I too move on to death.
I think of Henry King's stilted
But desolated *Exequy*,
Of Yuan Chen's great poem,
Unbearably pitiful;
Alone by the Spring river
More alone than I had ever
Imagined I would ever be,
I think of Frieda Lawrence,
Sitting alone in New Mexico,
In the long drought, listening
For the hiss of the milky Isar,
Over the cobbles, in a lost Spring.

[1950]

from THE LOVE POEMS OF MARICHIKO

I

I sit at my desk.
What can I write to you?
Sick with love,
I long to see you in the flesh.
I can write only,
"I love you. I love you. I love you."

Author's note: Marichiko is the pen name of a contemporary young woman who lives near the temple of Marishi-ben in Kyoto. Marishi-ben is an Indian, pre-Aryan, goddess of the dawn who is a bodhisattva in Buddhism and patron of geisha, prostitutes, women in childbirth, and lovers, and, in another aspect, once of samurai. Few temples or shrines to her or even statues exist in Japan, but her presence is indicated by statues, often in avenues like sphinxes, of wild boars, who also draw her chariot. She has three faces: the front of compassion; one side, a sow; the other a woman in ecstasy. She is a popular, though hidden, deity of tantric, Tachigawa Shingon. As the Ray of Light, the Shakti, or Prajna, the Power or Wisdom of Vairocana (the primordial Buddha, Dainichi Nyorai), she is seated on his lap in sexual bliss, Myōjō—the Morning Star.

Love cuts through my heart
And tears my vitals.
Spasms of longing suffocate me
And will not stop.

II

If I thought I could get away
And come to you,
Ten thousand miles would be like one mile.
But we are both in the same city
And I dare not see you,
And a mile is longer than a million miles.

III

Oh the anguish of these secret meetings
In the depth of night,
I wait with the shoji open.
You come late, and I see your shadow
Move through the foliage
At the bottom of the garden.
We embrace—hidden from my family.
I weep into my hands.
My sleeves are already damp.
We make love, and suddenly
The fire watch loom up
With clappers and lantern.
How cruel they are
To appear at such a moment.
Upset by their apparition,
I babble nonsense
And can't stop talking
Words with no connection.

IV

You ask me what I thought about
Before we were lovers.
The answer is easy.
Before I met you
I didn't have anything to think about.

VI

Just us.
In our little house
Far from everybody,
Far from the world,
Only the sound of water over stone.
And then I say to you,
"Listen. Hear the wind in the trees."

IX

You wake me,
Part my thighs, and kiss me.
I give you the dew
Of the first morning of the world.

X

Frost covers the reeds of the marsh.
A fine haze blows through them,
Crackling the long leaves.
My full heart throbs with bliss.

XII

Come to me, as you come
Softly to the rose bed of coals
Of my fireplace
Glowing through the night-bound forest.

XIII

Lying in the meadow, open to you
Under the noon sun,
Hazy smoke half hides
My rose petals.

XIV

On the bridges
And along the banks
Of Kamo River, the crowds
Watch the character "Great"

Burst into red fire on the mountain
And at last die out.
Your arm about me,
I burn with passion.
Suddenly I realize—
It is life I am burning with.
These hands burn,
Your arm about me burns,
And look at the others,
All about us in the crowd, thousands,
They are all burning—
Into embers and then into darkness.
I am happy.
Nothing of mine is burning.

XVI

Scorched with love, the cicada
Cries out. Silent as the firefly,
My flesh is consumed with love.

XVII

Let us sleep together here tonight.
Tomorrow, who knows where we will sleep?
Maybe tomorrow we will lie in the fields,
Our heads on the rocks.

XVIII

Fires
Burn in my heart.
No smoke rises.
No one knows.

XIX

I pass the day tense, day-
Dreaming of you. I relax with joy
When in the twilight I hear
The evening bells ring from temple to temple.

XX

Who is there? Me.
Me who? I am me. You are you.
You take my pronoun,
And we are us.

XXIII

I wish I could be
Kannon of eleven heads
To kiss you, Kannon
Of the thousand arms,
To embrace you forever.

XXIV

I scream as you bite
My nipples, and orgasm
Drains my body, as if I
Had been cut in two.

XXV

Your tongue thrums and moves
Into me, and I become
Hollow and blaze with
Whirling light, like the inside
Of a vast expanding pearl.

XXVI

It is the time when
The wild geese return. Between
The setting sun and
The rising moon, a line of
Brant write the character "heart."

XXVII

As I came from the
Hot bath, you took me before
The horizontal mirror
Beside the low bed, while my
Breasts quivered in your hands, my
Buttocks shivered against you.

XXVIII

Spring is early this year.
Laurel, plums, peaches,
Almonds, mimosa,
All bloom at once. Under the
Moon, night smells like your body.

XXXI

Some day in six inches of
Ashes will be all
That's left of our passionate minds,
Of all the world created
By our love, its origin
And passing away.

XXXII

I hold your head tight between
My thighs, and press against your
Mouth, and float away
Forever, in an orchid
Boat on the River of Heaven.

XXXIII

I cannot forget
The perfumed dusk inside the
Tent of my black hair,
As we awoke to make love
After a long night of love.

XXXIV

Every morning, I
Wake alone, dreaming my
Arm is your sweet flesh
Pressing my lips.

XXXV

The uguisu sleeps in the bamboo grove,
One night a man traps her in a bamboo trap,
Now she sleeps in a bamboo cage.

XXXVI

I am sad this morning.
The fog was so dense,
I could not see your shadow
As you passed my shoji.

XL

As the wheel follows the hoof
Of the ox that pulls the cart,
My sorrow follows your footsteps,
As you leave me in the dawn.

XLII

How many lives ago
I first entered the torrent of love,
At last to discover
There is no further shore.
Yet I know I will enter again and again.

XLIII

Two flowers in a letter.
The moon sinks into the far off hills.
Dew drenches the bamboo grass.
I wait.
Crickets sing all night in the pine tree.
At midnight the temple bells ring.
Wild geese cry overhead.
Nothing else.

XLVII

How long, long ago.
By the bridge at Uji,
In our little boat,
We swept through clouds of fireflies.

XLVIII

Now the fireflies of our youth
Are all gone,
Thanks to the efficient insecticides
Of our middle age.

L

In the park a crow awakes
And cries out under the full moon,
And I awake and sob
For the years that are gone.

LI

Did you take me because you loved me?
Did you take me without love?
Or did you just take me
To experiment on my heart?

LII

Once I shone afar like a
Snow-covered mountain.
Now I am lost like
An arrow shot in the dark.
He is gone and I must learn
To live alone and
Sleep alone like a hermit
Buried deep in the jungle.
I shall learn to go
Alone, like the unicorn.

LIII

Without me you can only
Live at random like

A falling pachinko ball.
I am your wisdom.

LVI

This flesh you have loved
Is fragile, unstable by nature
As a boat adrift.
The fires of the cormorant fishers
Flare in the night.
My heart flares with this agony.
Do you understand?
My life is going out.
Do you understand?
My life.
Vanishing like the stakes
That hold the nets against the current
In Uji River, the current and the mist
Are taking me.

LVII

Night without end. Loneliness.
The wind had driven a maple leaf
Against the shoji. I wait, as in the old days,
In our secret place, under the full moon.
The last bell crickets sing.
I found your old love letters,
Full of poems you never published.
Did it matter? They were only for me.

LVIII

Half in a dream
I become aware
That the voices of the crickets
Grow faint with the growing Autumn.
I mourn for this lonely
Year that is passing
And my own being
Grows fainter and fades away.

[1978]

George Oppen

ROUTE

'the void eternally generative'
the *Wen Fu* of Lu Chi

1

Tell the beads of the chromosomes like a rosary,
Love in the genes, if it fails

We will produce no sane man again

I have seen too many young people become adults, young friends
        become old people, all that is not ours,

The sources
And the crude bone

                —we say

Took place

Like the mass of the hills.

'The sun is a molten mass'. Therefore

Fall into oneself—?

Reality, blind eye
Which has taught us to stare—

Your elbow on a car-edge
Incognito as summer,

I wrote. Not you but a girl
At least

Clarity, clarity, surely clarity is the most beautiful thing in the world,
A limited, limiting clarity

I have not and never did have any motive of poetry
But to achieve clarity

2

Troubled that you are not, as they say,
Working—
I think we try rather to understand,
We try also to remain together

There is a force of clarity, it is
Of what is not autonomous in us,
We suffer a certain fear

Things alter, surrounded by a depth
And width

The unreality of our house in moonlight
Is that if the moonlight strikes it
It is truly there tho it is ours

3

Not to reduce the thing to nothing—

I might at the top of my ability stand at a window
and say, look out; out there is the world.

Not the desire for approval nor even for love—O,
that trap! From which escaped, barely—if it fails

We will produce no sane man again

4

Words cannot be wholly transparent. And that is the 'heartlessness'
of words.

Neither friends nor lovers are coeval...

as for a long time we have abandoned those in extremity and we find it
unbearable that we should do so...

The sea anemone dreamed of something, filtering the sea water thru
its body,

Nothing more real than boredom—dreamlessness, the experience of
time, never felt by the new arrival, never at the doors, the
thresholds, it is the native

Native in native time...

The purity of the materials, not theology, but to present the circumstances

5

In Alsace, during the war, we found ourselves on the edge of the Battle of the Bulge. The front was inactive, but we were spread so thin that the situation was eerily precarious. We hardly knew where the next squad was, and it was not in sight—a quiet and deserted hill in front of us. We dug in near a farmhouse. Pierre Adam, tho he was a journeyman mason, lived with his wife and his children in that farmhouse.

During the occupation the Germans had declared Alsace a part of Greater Germany. Therefore they had drafted Alsatian men into the German army. Many men, learning in their own way that they were to be called, dug a hole. The word became a part of the language: *faire une trou.* Some men were in those holes as long as two and three years. It was necessary that someone should know where those holes were; in winter it was impossible for a man to come out of his hole without leaving footprints in the snow. While snow was actually falling, however, a friend could come to the hole with food and other help.

Pierre, whom many people trusted, knew where some two dozen of those holes were.

The Germans became aware that men were going into hiding, and they began to make reprisals. If the man was young and unmarried, they killed his parents. If the man was married, they took his wife into Germany to the army brothels, it was said. They took the children into Germany, and it was not certain whether those children would remember where they came from. Pierre told me this story:

Men would come to Pierre and they would say: I am thinking of making a hole. Pierre would say: yes. They would say then: but if I do they will kill my parents; or: they will take my wife and my children. Then Pierre would say, he told me: *if* you dig a hole, I will help you.

He knew, of course, what he was telling me. You must try to put yourself into those times. If one thought he knew anything, it was that a man should not join the Nazi army. Pierre himself learned, shortly before the Americans arrived, that he was about to be drafted. He and his wife discussed the children. They thought of tattooing the children's names and addresses on their chests so that perhaps they could be found after the war. But they thought that perhaps the tattooing would be cut out of the children… They did not, finally, have to make that decision, as it turned out. But what a conversation between a man and his wife—

There was an escape from that dilemma, as, in a way, there always is. Pierre told me of a man who, receiving the notification that he was to report to the German army, called a celebration and farewell at his home. Nothing was said at that party that was not jovial. They drank and sang. At the proper time, the host got his bicycle and waved goodbye. The house stood at the top of the hill and, still waving and calling farewells, he rode with great energy and as fast as he could down the hill, and, at the bottom, drove into a tree.

It must be hard to do. Probably easier in an automobile. There is, in an automobile, a considerable time during which you cannot change your mind. Riding a bicycle, since in those woods it is impossible that the tree should be a redwood, it must be necessary to continue aiming at the tree right up to the moment of impact. Undoubtedly difficult to do. And, of course, the children had no father. Thereafter.

6

Wars that are just? A simpler question: In the event, will you or will you not want to kill a German. Because, in the event, if you do not want to, you won't.

...and my wife reading letters she knew were two weeks late and did not prove I was not dead while she read. Why did I play all that, what was I doing there?

We are brothers, we are brothers?—these things are composed of a moral substance only if they are untrue. If these things are true they are perfectly simple, perfectly impenetrable, those primary elements which can only be named.

A man will give his life for his friend provided he wants to.

In all probability a man will give his life for his child provided his child is an infant.

...One man could not understand me because I was saying simple things; it seemed to him that nothing was being said. I was saying: there is a mountain, there is a lake

A picture seen from within. The picture is unstable, a moving picture, unlimited drift. Still, the picture exists.

The circumstances:

7

And if at 80

He says what has been commonly said
It is for the sake of old times, a cozy game

He wishes to join again, an unreasonable speech
Out of context

8

Cars on the highway filled with speech,
People talk, they talk to each other;

Imagine a man in the ditch,
The wheels of the overturned wreck
Still spinning—

I don't mean he despairs, I mean if he does not
He sees in the manner of poetry

9

The cars run in a void of utensils
—the powerful tires—beyond
Happiness

Tough rubbery gear of invaders, of the descendents
Of invaders, I begin to be aware of a countryside
And the exposed weeds of a ditch

The context is history
Moving toward the light of the conscious

And beyond, culvert, blind curb, there are also names
For these things, language in the appalling fields

I remember my father as a younger man than I am now,
My mother was a tragic girl
Long ago, the autonomous figures are gone,
The context is the thousands of days

10

Not the symbol but the scene this pavement leads
To roadsides—the finite

Losing its purposes
Is estranged

All this is reportage.

If having come so far we shall have
Song

Let it be small enough.

Virgin
what was there to be thought

comes by the road

11

Tell the life of the mind, the mind creates the finite.

All punishes him. I stumble over these stories—
Progeny, the possibility of progeny, continuity

Or love that tempted him

He is punished by place, by scene, by all that holds
all he has found, this pavement, the silent symbols

Of it, the word it, never more powerful than in this
moment. Well, hardly an epiphany, but there the thing
is all the same

All this is reportage

12

To insist that what is true is good, no matter, no matter,
   a definition—?

That tree
   whose fruit…

The weight of air
Measured by the barometer in the parlor,
Time remains what it was

Oddly, oddly insistent

haunting the people in the automobiles,

shining on the sheetmetal,

open and present, unmarred by indifference,

wheeled traffic, indifference,
the hard edge of concrete continually crumbling

into gravel in the gravel of the shoulders,
Ditches of our own country

Whom shall I speak to

13

Department of Plants and Structures—obsolete, the old name
In this city, of the public works

Tho we meant to entangle ourselves in the roots of the world

An unexpected and forgotten spoor, all but indestructible shards

To owe nothing to fortune, to chance, nor by the power of his heart
or her heart to have made these things sing
But the benevolence of the real

Tho there is no longer shelter in the earth, round helpless belly
Or hope among the pipes and broken works

'Substance itself which is the subject of all our planning'

And by this we are carried into the incalculable

14

There was no other guarantee

Ours aren't the only madmen tho they have burned thousands
of men and women alive, perhaps no madder than most

Strange to be here, strange for them also, insane and criminal,
who hasn't noticed that, strange to be man, we have come
rather far

We are at the beginning of a radical depopulation of the earth

Cataclysm...cataclysm of the plains, jungles, the cities

Something in the soil exposed between two oceans

As Cabeza de Vaca found a continent of spiritual despair
in campsites

His miracles among the Indians heralding cataclysm

Even Cortés greeted as revelation...No I'd not emigrate,
I'd not live in a ship's bar wherever we may be headed

These things at the limits of reason, nothing at the limits
of dream, the dream merely ends, by this we know it is the
real

That we confront

[1968]

from SOME SAN FRANCISCO POEMS

1

Moving over the hills, crossing the irrigation
canals perfect and profuse in the mountains the
streams of women and men walking under the high-
tension wires over the brown hills

in the multiple world of the fly's
multiple eye the songs they go to hear on
this occasion are no one's own

Needle's eye   needle's eye   but in the ravine
again and again on the massive spike the song
clangs

as the tremendous volume of the music takes
over obscured by their long hair they seem
to be mourning

2

A MORALITY PLAY: PREFACE

Lying full length
On the bed in the white room

Turns her eyes to me

Again,

Naked...

Never to forget her naked eyes

Beautiful and brave
Her naked eyes

Turn inward

Feminine light

The unimagined
Feminine light

Feminine ardor

Pierced and touched

Tho all say
Huddled among each other

'Love'

The play begins with the world

A city street
Leads to the bay

Tamalpais in cloud

Mist over farmlands

Local knowledge
In the heavy hills

The great loose waves move landward
Heavysided in the wind

Grass and trees bent
Along the length of coast in the continual wind

The ocean pounds in her mind
Not the harbor leading inward
To the back bay and the slow river
Recalling flimsy Western ranches
The beautiful hills shine outward

Sunrise   the raw fierce fire
Coming up past the sharp edge

And the hoof marks on the mountain

Shines in the white room

Provincial city
Not alien enough

To naked eyes

This city died young

You too will be shown this

You will see the young couples

Leaving again in rags

3

So with artists. How pleasurable
to imagine that, if only they gave
up their art, the children would be
healed,   would live.

Irving Younger in *The Nation*

'AND THEIR WINTER AND NIGHT IN DISGUISE'

The sea and a crescent strip of beach
Show between the service station and a deserted shack

A creek drains thru the beach
Forming a ditch
There is a discarded super-market cart in the ditch
That beach is the edge of a nation

There is something like shouting along the highway
A California shouting
On the long fast highway over the California mountains

Point Pedro
Its distant life

It is impossible the world should be either good or bad
If its colors are beautiful or if they are not beautiful
If parts of it taste good or if no parts of it taste good
It is as remarkable in one case as the other
As against this

We have suffered fear, we know something of fear
And of humiliation mounting to horror

The world above the edge of the foxhole belongs to the flying bullets,
leaden superbeings
For the men grovelling in the foxhole danger, danger in being drawn
to them

These little dumps
The poem is about them

Our hearts are twisted
In dead men's pride

Dead men crowd us
Lean over us

In the emplacements

The skull spins
Empty of subject

The hollow ego

Flinching from the war's huge air

Tho we are delivery boys and bartenders

We will choke on each other

Minds may crack

But not for what is discovered

Unless that everyone knew
And kept silent

Our minds are split
To seek the danger out

From among the miserable soldiers

4

ANNIVERSARY POEM

'the picturesque
common lot' the unwarranted light

Where everyone has been

The very ground of the path
And the litter grow ancient

A shovel's scratched edge
So like any other man's

We are troubled by incredulity
We are troubled by scratched things

Becoming familiar
Becoming extreme

Let grief
Be
So it be ours

Nor hide one's eyes
As tides drop along the beaches in the thin wash of
breakers

And so desert each other

—lest there be nothing

The Indian girl walking across the desert, the
sunfish under the boat

How shall we say how this happened, these stories, our
stories

Scope, mere size, a kind of redemption

Exposed still and jagged on the San Francisco hills

Time and depth before us, paradise of the real, we
know what it is

To find now depth, not time, since we cannot, but depth

To come out safe,   to end well

We have begun to say good bye
To each other
And cannot say it

[1972]

Charles Olson

THE KINGFISHERS

1

What does not change / is the will to change

He woke, fully clothed, in his bed. He
remembered only one thing, the birds, how
when he came in, he had gone around the rooms
and got them back in their cage, the green one first,
she with the bad leg, and then the blue,
the one they had hoped was a male

Otherwise? Yes, Fernand, who had talked lispingly of Albers & Angkor Vat.
He had left the party without a word. How he got up, got into his coat,
I do not know. When I saw him, he was at the door, but it did not matter,
he was already sliding along the wall of the night, losing himself
in some crack of the ruins. That it should have been he who said, "The kingfishers!
who cares
for their feathers
now?"

His last words had been, "The pool is slime." Suddenly everyone,
ceasing their talk, sat in a row around him, watched
they did not so much hear, or pay attention, they
wondered, looked at each other, smirked, but listened,
he repeated and repeated, could not go beyond his thought
"The pool   the kingfishers' feathers were wealth   why
did the export stop?"

It was then he left

2

I thought of the E on the stone, and of what Mao said
la lumiere"
but the kingfisher
de l'aurore"
but the kingfisher flew west
est devant nous!
he got the color of his breast
from the heat of the setting sun!

The features are, the feebleness of the feet (syndactylism of the 3rd & 4th digit)
the bill, serrated, sometimes a pronounced beak, the wings
where the color is, short and round, the tail
inconspicuous.

But not these things were the factors. Not the birds.
The legends are
legends. Dead, hung up indoors, the kingfisher
will not indicate a favoring wind,
or avert the thunderbolt. Nor, by its nesting,
still the waters, with the new year, for seven days.
It is true, it does nest with the opening year, but not on the waters.
It nests at the end of a tunnel bored by itself in a bank. There,
six or eight white and translucent eggs are laid, on fishbones
not on bare clay, on bones thrown up in pellets by the birds.

On these rejectamenta
(as they accumulate they form a cup-shaped structure) the young are born.
And, as they are fed and grow, this nest of excrement and decayed fish becomes
a dripping, fetid mass
Mao concluded:
nous devons
nous lever
et agir!

3

When the attentions change / the jungle
leaps in
          even the stones are split
                                        they rive

Or,
enter
that other conqueror we more naturally recognize
he so resembles ourselves

But the E
cut so rudely on that oldest stone
sounded otherwise,
was differently heard

as, in another time, were treasures used:

(and, later, much later, a fine ear thought
a scarlet coat)

          "of green feathers   feet, beaks and eyes
          of gold

          "animals likewise,
          resembling snails

          "a large wheel, gold, with figures of unknown four-foots,
          and worked with tufts of leaves, weight
          3800 ounces

          "last, two birds, of thread and featherwork, the quills
          gold, the feet
          gold, the two birds perched on two reeds

          gold, the reeds arising from two embroidered mounds,
          one yellow, the other
          white.

"And from each reed hung
seven feathered tassels.

In this instance, the priests
(in dark cotton robes, and dirty,
their dishevelled hair matted with blood, and flowing wildly
over their shoulders)
rush in among the people, calling on them
to protect their gods

And all now is war
where so lately there was peace,
and the sweet brotherhood, the use
of tilled fields.

4

Not one death but many,
not accumulation but change, the feed-back proves, the feed-back is
the law

> Into the same river no man steps twice
> When fire dies air dies
> No one remains, nor is, one

Around an appearance, one common model, we grow up
many. Else how is it,
if we remain the same,
we take pleasure now
in what we did not take pleasure before? love
contrary objects? admire and / or find fault? use
other words, feel other passions, have
nor figure, appearance, disposition, tissue
the same?

> To be in different states without a change
> is not a possibility

We can be precise. The factors are
in the animal and / or the machine the factors are

communication and / or control, both involve
the message. And what is the message? The message is
a discrete or continuous sequence of measurable events distributed in time

is the birth of air, is
the birth of water, is
a state between
the origin and
the end, between
birth and the beginning of
another fetid nest

is change, presents
no more than itself

And the too strong grasping of it,
when it is pressed together and condensed,
loses it

This very thing you are

II

They buried their dead in a sitting posture
serpent   cane   razor   ray of the sun

And she sprinkled water on the head of the child, crying
"Cioa-coatl! Cioa-coatl!"
with her face to the west

Where the bones are found, in each personal heap
with what each enjoyed, there is always
the Mongolian louse

The light is in the east. Yes. And we must rise, act. Yet
in the west, despite the apparent darkness (the whiteness
which covers all), if you look, if you can bear, if you can, long enough

as long as it was necessary for him, my guide
to look into the yellow of the longest-lasting rose

so you must, and, in that whiteness, into that face, with what candor, look

and, considering the dryness of the place
      the long absence of an adequate race

            (of the two who first came, each a conquistador, one healed, the other
            tore the eastern idols down, toppled
            the temple walls, which, says the excuser
            where black from human gore)

hear
hear, where the dry blood talks
      where the old appetite walks

                  la piu saporita et migliore
                  che si possa truovar al mondo

where it hides, look
in the eye how it runs
in the flesh / chalk

            but under these petals
            in the emptiness
            regard the light, contemplate
            the flower

whence it arose

        with what violence benevolence is bought
        what cost in gesture justice brings
        what wrongs domestic rights involve
        what stalks
        this silence

what pudor pejorocracy affronts
how awe, night-rest and neighborhood can rot
what breeds where dirtiness is law
what crawls
below

III

I am no Greek, hath not th'advantage.
And of course, no Roman:
he can take no risk that matters,
the risk of beauty least of all.

But I have my kin, if for no other reason than
(as he said, next of kin) I commit myself, and,
given my freedom, I'd be a cad
if I didn't. Which is most true.

It works out this way, despite the disadvantage.
I offer, in explanation, a quote:
si j'ai du goût, ce n'est guères
que pour la terre et les pierres

Despite the discrepancy (an ocean   courage   age)
this is also true: if I have any taste
it is only because I have interested myself
in what was slain in the sun

        I pose you your question:

shall you uncover honey / where maggots are?

        I hunt among stones

[1950]

"The chain of memory is resurrection..."

The chain of memory is resurrection   I am a vain man
I am interested in the size of the brain-case
of CroMagnon man and that his descendants are Guanches
right now in the Canary Islands, and that my father & mother
lie buried beside each other in the Swedish cemetery

in Worcester, Massachusetts. And my grandmother too.
Even if the Hineses are in St John's cemetery. Those stones
speak to me, my ear is their sea-shell as in Marin County
the big trees as well as the eucalyptus hold sounds
of Asia and Indians the myrtle, comes from Australia

The vector of space is resurrection. We walk on the earth
under which they lie who also matter to us, as well as those
who are distant, from whom we have got separated (as we are
separated from those we have not yet known: the loveliness
of man, that he shoots up men suddenly on the horizon
there is a new person who speaks as Ed Marshall does

and all the back country, the roads I have ridden
without headlights the moon was so bright on the houses
and I was coming from a love in Lawrence, and Georgetown
Rowley Ipswich lay out in the night, not blank at all as
now that Marshall has spoken, all the faces
and the stones
and Concord Avenue
rise into being: the onslaught,
he calls it,
resurrection

The being of man is resurrection, the genetic flow
of each life which has given life, the tenderness
none of us
is without. Let it come back. Let it be
where it is:

"My soul is Chichester and my origin
is a womb whether one likes it or not."

My ugliness,
said Juan Belmonte—to every Spaniard
I was part of himself:

the bull (or whether he's a lion
or a horse or the great snake)
hammers us, mine beat me against
the brick wall until I thought
this is it, and it was only a redheaded boy
diverted him

Direction—a directed magnitude—is
resurrection

All that has been
suddenly is: time

is the face
of recognition, Rhoda Straw; or my son
is a Magyar. The luminousness
of my daughter
to her mother
by a stream:
apocatastasis
how it occurs, that in this instant I seek to speak
as though the species were a weed-seed a grass a barley corn
in the cup of my palm. And I was trying
to hear what it said, I was putting my heart down
to catch the pain
Resurrection
is. It is the avowal. It is the admission. The renewal
is the restoration: the man in the dark with the animal

fat lamp
is my father. Or my grandfather. And the fat lady
who was weak from a heart attack and her granddaughter
I used to see courtin the boy on the motorcycle,
is my mother. Or my grandmother. The Venus
of Willendorf. We move
between two horns, the gate
of horn. And the animal or snake who warns us
propels: we must woo the thing
to get its feet together so that its shoulder blades
are open, so that the aorta

One of the horns
is resurrection, the other horn
is any one of us: a river
is my sword, the Annisquam is my metal
you will have yours (a meadow his was, gone,
boy, in the dance and another
had a tree or there was a third
had a bicycle seat, and the face of all women,
he said,
they sat on. Bless the powers
that be

This is a poem of celebration of the powers that be.
The large theme
is the smallest (the thumbtack
in the way of the inkbottle, the incident
which does not change the course even if the surface
of the day is changed because a hand followed a diaper
into the wringer up to the elbow, the smallest content

is a grit of occasion, the irrelevant
is only known
like the shape of the soul
to the person involved, the absolutes
sit in the palm of the hand which can't close
from the pain. I do not know
what you know at the same time that I do. My vanity
is only the excercise
of my privilege as yours, conceivably,
might be as hers, the peahen, is
also brilliant when she takes it up: Willendorf,
the stone, breathes back
into life. The resurrection
at the farthest point, and

out of the green poison
now the death of spring the jungle
is in the gulley the growth
has gone to the tropics small spring
is over

small spring
   while where my river flows
spring is long. Here where the ice
and the jungle once were identical
spring is small

the blossoms
are already gone green green
the worst green
like paint floods

the sky
is like a bedroom wall
in a motel

the horrors
of season too fast.
Without resurrection
all is too fast. The trees
crawl over everything like facts
like the fascination of irrelevant
events: to hew

o the dirty summer too early
for a man to catch up with

spring is dead! spring the horn
is dead. I Adonis

Lift me, life of being

I lift
the shape of my soul. In the face of spring
gone
into the growth
as the body was burned
on the sticks and went up
as smoke into the pale sky
o father

o mother
put into the ground

(o the beloved ones

they must dance

the thick green
which covers us, the appetite of nature
we stand off, the loss
of loss

In the chain of being
we arise, we make sparse
the virid covering, we lay bare
the dead, the winter ground, the snow
which makes the forsythia first
the first blossom

and in the two weeks of spring:
damn the green growth gone
to green bloom, the resurrection
is sparse   Desire
is spare   The confusion

of physical enjoyment
and desire Desire

is resurrection

The soul
is an onslaught

[1956/1987]

from *The Maximus Poems*, Book III:

POEM 143. THE FESTIVAL ASPECT.

The World
has become divided
from the Universe. Put the three Towns
together

The Individual
has become divided
from the Absolute, it is the times promised
by the poets. They shall drop delta
and lingam, all forms
of symbol
and mystery. As well as all
naturalism. And literalness. The truth

is fingers holding it all up
underneath, the Lotus
is a cusp, and its stalk
holds up it all.
It isn't even a burning point, it is a bow
of fingers shooting
a single arrow. The three Towns
are to be destroyed, as well as
that they are to be made known,
that they are to be known,
that there is no three Towns
now, that without three Towns
there is no Society, there is no
known
Absolute: we shall stand on our heads and hands
truly, kicking
all false form off
the surface
of the still, or active,
water-surface. There is no image
which is a reflection. Or a condition. There is solely
the Lotus

upside down. When the World is one again
with the Universal the Flower
will grow down, the Sun
will be stamped
on the leather
like a growing
Coin, the earth
will be the light, the air and the dust
of the air will be the perfume
of sense, the *gloire*
will have returned
of the body seen
against the window. The flesh
will glow.
            The three Towns
will have become populated
again. In the first Town
somebody will have addressed
themselves
to someone else. There will be no need
of the explicit. In the second Town
the earth
will have replaced
the sun. In the third Town the man
shall have arisen, he shall have concluded
any use of reason, the Dialogue
will have re-begun. The earth
shall have preceded love. The sun
shall have given back its deadly
rays, there shall be no longer any
need to be so careful. The third Town
shall have revealed
itself.

The third Town
is the least known. The third Town
is the one which is the most interesting—and is overpopulated—
behind the Western
sun. It shall only come forth
from underneath. The foot of the Lotus

is not its face, but the roots
of its stalk. The Elephant
moves easily
through any trees. He is Ganesh
with the big Hands. His hands alone
offer all. Through the mountain
through the bole
of any tree through the adamantine
he passes
as though it were nothing. Only the God Himself
of whom he is the frazzled stalk
in each of the coolness, and ease, of his power
is more than water. Water is not equal
                    to the
                    Flower. The three Towns
                    are the fairest
                    which the Flower
                    is. Only when the Flower—only when the uproar
                    has driven the Soul
                    out of me, only then shall the God
                    strike
                    the three Towns. The three Towns
                    shall first
                    be born again. The Flower shall
                    grow down. The mud of the bottom
                    is the floor
                    of the Upside Down. The present
                    is an uproar, the present
                    is the times of the re-birth of
                    the Lotus. Ganesh
                    is walking
                    through anything. There is no obs-
                    tacle. There will be no more
                    anger. There is only one
                    anyway. It is too early
                    for anger. The third Town
                    has only just
                    begun.

[1965/1975]

William Everson

A CANTICLE TO THE WATERBIRDS

Clack your beaks you cormorants and kittiwakes,
North on those rock-croppings finger-jutted into the rough Pacific surge;
You migratory terns and pipers who leave but the temporary clawtrack
written on sandbars there of your presence;
Grebes and pelicans; you comber-picking scoters and you shorelong gulls;
All you keepers of the coastline north of here to the Mendocino beaches;
All you beyond upon the cliff-face thwarting the surf at Hecate Head;
Hovering the under-surge where the cold Columbia grapples at the bar;
North yet to the Sound, whose islands float like a sown flurry of chips upon
the sea;
Break wide your harsh and salt-encrusted beaks unmade for song
And say a praise up to the Lord.

And you freshwater egrets east in the flooded marshlands skirting the sea-level
rivers, white one-legged watchers of shallows;
Broad-headed kingfishers minnow-hunting from willow stems on meandering
valley sloughs;
You too, you herons, blue and supple-throated, stately, taking the air majestical
in the sunflooded San Joaquin,
Grading down on your belted wings from the upper lights of sunset,
Mating over the willow clumps or where the flatwater rice fields shimmer;
You killdeer, high night-criers, far in the moon-suffusion sky;
Bitterns, sand-waders, all shore-walkers, all roost-keepers,
Populates of the 'dobe cliffs of the Sacramento:
Open your water-dartling beaks,
And make a praise up to the Lord.

For you hold the heart of His mighty fastnesses,
And shape the life of His indeterminate realms.
You are everywhere on the lonesome shores of His wide creation.
You keep seclusion where no man may go, giving Him praise;
Nor may a woman come to lift like your cleaving flight her clear
contralto song
To honor the spindrift gifts of His soft abundance.
You sanctify His hermitage rocks where no holy priest may kneel to
adore, nor holy nun assist;
And where His true communion-keepers are not enabled to enter.

And well may you say His praises, birds, for your ways
Are verved with the secret skills of His inclinations,
And your habits plaited and rare with the subdued elaboration of His
intricate craft;
Your days intent with the direct astuteness needful for His outworking,
And your nights alive with the dense repose of His infinite sleep.
You are His secretive charges and you serve His secretive ends,
In His clouded, mist-conditioned stations, in His murk,
Obscure in your matted nestings, immured in His limitless ranges.
He makes you penetrate through dark interstitial joinings of His
thicketed kingdoms,
And keep your concourse in the deeps of His shadowed world.

Your ways are wild but earnest, your manners grave,
Your customs carefully schooled to the note of His serious mien.
You hold the prime condition of His clean creating,
And the swift compliance with which you serve His minor means
Speaks of the constancy with which you hold Him.
For what is your high flight forever going home to your first beginnings,
But such a testament to your devotion?
You hold His outstretched world beneath your wings, and mount
upon His storms,
And keep your sheer wind-lidded sight upon the vast perspectives of
His mazy latitudes.

But mostly it is your way you bear existence wholly within the context
of His utter will and are untroubled.
Day upon day you do not reckon, nor scrutinize tomorrow, nor
multiply the nightfalls with a rash concern,

But rather assume each instant as warrant sufficient of His final seal.
Wholly in Providence you spring, and when you die you look on
    death in clarity unflinched,
Go down, a clutch of feather ragged upon the brush;
Or drop on water where you briefly lived, found food,
And now yourselves made food for His deep current-keeping fish, and
    then are gone:
Is left but the pinion-feather spinning a bit on the uproil
Where lately the dorsal cut clear air.

You leave a silence. And this for you suffices, who are not of the
    ceremonials of man,
And hence are not made sad to now forgo them.
Yours is of another order of being, and wholly it compels.
But may you, birds, utterly seized in God's supremacy,
Austerely living under His austere eye—
Yet may you teach a man a necessary thing to know,
Which has to do of the strict conformity that creaturehood entails,
And constitutes the prime commitment all things share.
For God has given you the imponderable grace to *be* His verification,
Outside the mulled incertitude of our forensic choices;
That you, our lessers in the rich hegemony of Being,
May serve as testament to what a creature is,
And what creation owes.

Curlews, stilts and scissortails, beachcomber gulls,
Wave-haunters, shore-keepers, rockhead-holders, all cape-top vigilantes,
Now give God praise.
Send up the strict articulation of your throats,
And say His name.

[1950]

John Cage

from: DIARY: HOW TO IMPROVE THE WORLD (YOU WILL ONLY MAKE MATTERS WORSE) 1965–1967

VIII. *The daily warmth we*
experience, my father said, is not
transmitted by Sun to Earth but is what
Earth does in response to Sun.
Measurements, he said, measure
measuring means. Bashō: Matsutake ya
shiranu ko no ha no hebaritsuku.
The leaf of some unknown tree sticking
on the mushroom (Blythe). Mushroom does
not know that leaf is sticking on it
(Takemitsu). Project: Discover way to
translate Far Eastern texts so western men
can read orientally.
Communication? Bakarashi! Words
without syntax, each word

Author's note: This text[...]is a mosaic of ideas, statements, words, and stories. It is also a diary. For each day, I determined by chance operations how many parts of the mosaic I would write and how many words there would be in each. The number of words per day was to equal, or, by the last statement written, to exceed one hundred words.[...]I used an IBM Selectric typewriter to print my text. I used twelve different type faces, letting chance operations determine which face would be used for which statement. So, too, the left marginations were determined, the right marginations being the result of not hyphenating words and at the same time keeping the number of characters per line forty-three or less. The present typography follows the original chance-determined plan.

Editor's note: Selections from the 90 entries of the first three years of John Cage's "Diary" were determined by the stations of the Seventh Avenue I.R.T. in New York City, the subway line that was the most convenient to Cage's loft: 8 (standing for Sheridan Square), 14, 18, 23, 28, 34, 42, and so on. (This was also George Oppen's example of a mathematical "discrete series," as an explanation for the title of his first book.)

polymorphic. **He wanted me to agree that**
the piano tuner and the piano maker have
nothing to do with it (the composition).
The younger ones had said: Whoever makes
the stretcher isn't separate from the
painting. (It doesn't stop there
either.)
XIV. Since the
Spirit's omnipresent, there's a difference
in things but no difference in spirit.
McLuhan was able to say "The medium is
the message" because he started from
no concern with content. Or choose
quantity, not quality (we get
quality willy-nilly): i.e. we'd like
to stay alive, the changes that are
taking place are so many and so
interesting. Composition'll have, he
said, less and less to do with what
happens. Things happen more
quickly. One of the signs you'll get
that'll tell you things are going well is
that you and everyone else you know will
be inhabiting lightweight Dymaxion
houses, disengaged from ownership and
from violated Earth spot (read
Fuller).
XVIII. Hearing of past actions
(politics, economics), people soon
won't be able to imagine how such
things could've happened. Fusing
politics with economics prepared
disappearance of both. Still
invisible. Arriving, realizing we
never departed. He mentioned heads
on the ceiling. Seeing them, noticed
him too. Fusion of credit card with
passport. Means of making one's voice
heard: refusal to honor credit card.
End of the month? That too may be

changed: the measurement of time,
what season it is, whether it's
night or day. In any case, no bills,
just added information. **"Take it easy,
but take it."** What'll we do? (Before
lunch.) "Wing it."

**XXIII. LET'S CALL IT THE
COLLECTIVE CONSCIOUSNESS (WE'VE GOT
THE COLLECTIVE UNCONSCIOUS). THE
QUESTION IS: WHAT ARE THE THINGS
EVERYONE NEEDS REGARDLESS OF LIKES
AND DISLIKES? BEGINNING OF ANSWER:
WATER, FOOD, SHELTER, CLOTHING,
ELECTRICITY, AUDIO-VISUAL
COMMUNICATION, TRANSPORTATION. FORM
OF ANSWER: GLOBAL UTILITIES NETWORK.** Do
not fear that as the globe gets utility
organized your daily life will not
remain (or become as the case may be)
disorganized, characterized by chaos,
illuminated anarchically. You'll
have nothing to do; so what will you
do? A lifelong university
(Fuller)? In the lobby after La
Monte Young's music stopped,
Geldzahler said: It's like being in a
womb; now that I'm out, I want to get
back in. I felt differently and so did
Jasper Johns: we were relieved to be
released.

XXVIII. We've
poisoned our food, polluted our air
and water, killed birds and cattle,
eliminated forests, impoverished,
eroded the earth. We're unselfish,
skilful: we include in our acts to
perform—we've had a rehearsal—
the last one. What would you call it?
Nirvana? "Not only was instant
universal voice communication forecast

by David Sarnoff, but also instant
television, instant newspapers, instant
magazines and instant visual
telephone service...the development of
such global communications system
would link people everywhere...for
reorientation toward a 'one-world
concept of mass communications in an
era marked by the emergence of a
universal language, a universal
culture and a universal common
market.'"

XXXIV. Boddhisattva Doctrine: Enter Nirvana only when all beings, sentient, non-sentient, are ready to do likewise.
Couldn't believe my eyes (stopping for
lunch in Red Bud, Illinois): a single
photograph of nature (mountains,
lake, island, forests) enlarged, printed
twice, once left to right, once right to
left, the two prints juxtaposed to form a
single image, seam down the middle.

Eugenics. Proposal: take facts of
art seriously: try them in economics/
politics, giving up, that is, notions about
balance (of power, of wealth),
foreground, background. They will kill
you, she said, with kindness. There's a
temptation to do nothing simply because
there's so much to do that one doesn't
know where to begin. Begin anywhere. For
instance, since electronics is at
the heart of the matter, establish a
global voltage, a single design for
plugs and jacks. Remove the need for
transformers and adaptors. Vary not the
connecting means but the things to be
connected.

XLII. To know whether or not art is contemporary, we no longer use aesthetic criteria (if it's destroyed by shadows, spoiled by ambient sounds); (assuming these) we use social criteria: can include action on the part of others. We'll take the mad ones with us, and we know where we're going. Even now, he told me, they sit at the crossroads in African villages regenerating society. Mental hospitals: localization of a resource we've yet to exploit. I visited an aging anarchist. (He had the remaining copies of Martin's Men Against the State.) He introduced me to two Negro children he'd adopted. After they went out to play, he told me what trouble he'd had in deciding finally to draw this line: No jumping up and down on the beds.

L. Abundance. Officials checked to make certain we'd paid the air-travel tax, didn't ask to see our passports. *Marcel Duchamp.* "...Valencia, cathedral—University. Palma will be interesting again, then Dardona and off to Milan and after which the western coast of Yugoslavia & tour (at southern end) of Grecian Islands after which plane from Athens to New York. Many travelers,—going everywhere. Love, Mom" More irritated by the schedule than the work, he announced he'd do all the dishwashing. Shortly the others were helping. Sometimes he had nothing to do. **Returning from Europe: "We're all looking forward to the return of the W.P.A. It's the only thing we ever had any talent for."**

LIX. Mother wrote to say: "Stay
in Europe. Soak up as much beauty as you
possibly can." Cards punched for
insertion in telephones so we don't
have to remember numbers or spend
time dialing. Acceleration. *What shall we*
do with our emotions? ("Suffer them," I
hear her saying.) Having everything we
need, we'll nevertheless spend restless
nights awake with desire for pleasures we
imagine that never take place. Things
also happen gradually (one of New
Babylon's anarchists was elected a
member of Amsterdam's City Council).
We've the right, Fuller explains, to object
to slavery, segregation, etc. (the
problem of work is solved: machines
take the place of muscles): we've not yet
the right to object to war: first we must
design, then implement means for
making the world's resources the
possession of all men.
LXVI. "They dance the world as
it will be...is now when they
dance." Technique. Discipline.
Ultimately it's not a question of
taste. It's the other way around.
Each thing in the world asks us, "What
makes you think I'm not something you
like?" *The use of drugs to facilitate*
religious experience is against the stream
of the times. (He lost interest in the
tape-music center, its experiments and
performances. He went to the
Southwest desert. He removed himself from
the others.) Begging: difficult
profession. In India, parents maim
children producing bodies that'll attract
pity. His eyes are sheep's eyes; his
mind's superb. Decided not to give

him a penny. Then did (after reading
letter Satie'd written shortly before
death, asking for a little money, enough
so he could sit in a corner, smoke his
pipe).

**LXXII. The
children have a society of their own.
They have no need for ours. At the
airport Ain said he came simply to see
whether his mother was all right.**
**Mumma's music (*Mesa*) for Cunningham's
dance called *Place*. Sitting in the
audience I felt afterward as though
I'd been rung through a ringer. Then had
to play Satie's *Nocturnes*, something not
easy for me to do. Wrong notes all
over the place. Tonight the program's
being repeated. I've practiced. I'll be
deaf and blind. Experimentation.**
Summit lecture series on War: not to be
given in one city, but via a global
Telstar-like facility, each receiving set
throughout the world equipped with a
device permitting hearing no matter
what speech in one's own tongue.

**LXXIX. Get it,
she said, so it's unknown which parent
conceiving will bear the child.
Responsibility undefined. Circa
one hundred and seventy-five kinds of
male, sixty, seventy kinds of female.
Sterility. He had actually gotten slides
showing the passage of the gene from one
cell to the next. Destruction.
Reconstitution. (What we want is very
little, nothing, so to speak. We just
want those things that have so often
been promised or stated: Liberty,
Equality, Fraternity; Freedom of this and
that.)** Clothes for entertainment, not

because of shame. Privacy to become an unusual rather than expected experience. Given disinfection, sanitation, removal of social concerns re defecation, urination. No self-consciousness. Living like animals, becoming touchable.

LXXXVI.

The lazy dog (a bomb containing ten thousand slivers of razor-sharp steel). In one province of North Vietnam, the most densely populated, one hundred million slivers of razor-sharp steel have fallen in a period of thirteen months. These razor darts slice the villagers to ribbons. Maki thinks Hawaii's another part of Japan. Portugal thinks of Angola not as a colony but as Portugal. U.S.A. thinks the Free World is U.S.A.'s world, is determined to keep it free, U.S.A.-determined. *The possibility of conversation resides in the impossibility of two people having the same experience whether or not their attention is directed one-pointedly. An ancient Buddhist realization (sitting in different seats).*

Muriel Rukeyser

THE SPEED OF DARKNESS

I

Whoever despises the clitoris despises the penis
Whoever despises the penis despises the cunt
Whoever despises the cunt despises the life of the child.

Resurrection music,   silence,   and surf.

II

No longer speaking
Listening with the whole body
And with every drop of blood
Overtaken by silence

But this same silence is become speech
With the speed of darkness.

III

Stillness during war, the lake.
The unmoving spruces.
Glints over the water.
Faces, voices.   You are far away.
A tree that trembles.

I am the tree that trembles and trembles.

IV

After the lifting of the mist
after the lift of the heavy rains

the sky stands clear
and the cries of the city risen in day
I remember the buildings are space
walled, to let space be used for living
I mind this room is space
this drinking glass is space
whose boundary of glass
lets me give you drink and space to drink
your hand, my hand being space
containing skies and constellations
your face
carries the reaches of air
I know I am space
my words are air.

V

Between   between
the man : act   exact
woman : in curve   senses in their maze
frail orbits, green tries,   games of stars
shape of the body speaking its evidence

VI

I look across at the real
vulnerable   involved   naked
devoted to the present of all I care for
the world of its history leading to this moment.

VII

Life the announcer.
I assure you
there are many ways to have a child.
I bastard mother
promise you
there are many ways to be born.
They all come forth
in their own grace.

VIII

Ends of the earth join tonight
with blazing stars upon their meeting.

These sons,   these sons
fall burning into Asia.

IX

Time comes into it.
Say it.   Say it.

The universe is made of stories,
not of atoms.

X

Lying
blazing beside me
you rear beautifully and up—
your thinking face—
erotic body reaching
in all its colors and lights—
your erotic face
colored and lit—
not colored body-and-face
but now entire,
colors   lights   the world thinking and reaching.

XI

The river flows past the city.

Water goes down to tomorrow
making its children   I hear their unborn voices
I am working out the vocabulary of my silence.

XII

Big-boned man young and of my dream
Struggles to get the live bird out of his throat.
I am he am I?   Dreaming?
I am the bird am I?   I am the throat?

A bird with a curved beak.
It could slit anything, the throat-bird.

Drawn up slowly.   The curved blades, not large.
Bird emerges   wet   being born
Begins to sing.

XIII

My night awake
staring at the broad rough jewel
the copper roof across the way
thinking of the poet
yet unborn in this dark
who will be the throat of these hours.
No.   Of those hours.
Who will speak these days,
if not I,
if not you?

[1968]

IRIS

I

Middle of May, when the iris blows,
blue below blue, the bearded patriarch-
face on the green flute body of a boy
Poseidon   torso of Eros
blue
sky below sea
day over daybreak violet behind twilight
the May iris
midnight on midday

II

Something is over and under this deep blue.
Over and under this movement, *etwas*
before and after, *alguna cosa*

blue before blue
is it
            perhaps
                        death?
That may be the wrong word.

The iris stands in the light.

III

Death is here, death is guarded by swords.
No. By shapes of swords
flicker of green leaves
under all the speaking and crying
shadowing the words the eyes   here they all die
racing withering   blue evening
my sister death the iris
stands clear in light.

IV

In the water-cave
ferocious needles of teeth
the green morays
in blue water   rays
a maleficence   ribbon of green   the flat look of
eyes staring   fatal mouth staring
the rippling potent force
curving into any hole
death finding his way.

V

Depth of petals, May iris
transparent   infinitely deep they are
petal-thin   with light behind them
and you, death,
and you
behind them
blue under blue.
What I cannot say

in adequate music
something being born
transparency   blue of
light standing on light
this stalk of
(among mortal petals-and-leaves)
light

IN THE UNDERWORLD

I go a road
among the upturned
faces in their colors
to the great arch
of a theatre stage

I the high queen
starting in the air
far above my head
royal of the crown
I the tower
go through the wide arch
proscenium queen

The arch shuts down like December
very small all about me
the entrance to this country

Many whispers in the quick dark
Fingers in swarms, breath is busy,
they have reached above my head
and taken off my crown
I go and I go
I have been searching
since the light of all mornings

I remember only a pale brightness
and no more.   What do I remember?
I no longer

They have reached to my jewels
green in this cave, that one, iceberg the blue,
whirled into diamond
in the deep dark taken.

I move into thicker dark,
moss, earth-smell, wet coal.
Their hands are on my stiff robe.
I walk out of my robe.

At my surfaces
they unfasten my dress of softness.
Naked the naked wind
of the underworld.

Rankness at my breasts,
over my flank
giggle and stink
They have taken little knives
my skin lifts off
I go in pain-colored black
trying to find

I walk into their asking
Where is he
they sing on one note
Your lord memory

He your delight
I cannot hear their music
it scrapes along my muscles
they make my flesh go
among the gusts and whispers
they take off my eyes
my lips no more
the delicate fierce places

of identity
everywhere
taken

I, despoiled and clacking
walk, a chain of bones
into the boneyard dark.
One by one.
Something
reaches for my bones.

Something walks here
a little breath in hell
without its ghost.
A breath after nothing.
Gone.
Nothing turns the place
where perceiving was
from side to side.
There is no place.   It has dissolved.
The lowest point, back there, has slid away.

— What are you working on?
— Istar in the underworld.
— Baby, you *are* in trouble.

What calls her?
The body of a woman alive
but at the point of death,
the very old body lying there riddled with life,
gone, gasping at pain,
fighting for words
fighting for breath.

One clear breast looks up out of this gone body
young, the white clear light of this breast
speaks across distance

Remember is
come back.
Remember is
Who is here?
I am here.

At the pit of the underworld
something flickers in her
without anything

Now I remember love
who has set my being on me,
who permits me move
into all being,
who puts on me perceiving
and my bones
in a live chain
and my flesh that perceives
and acts
and my acknowledging skin
my underdress, my dress
and my robe
the jewels of the world
I touch and find
  —I know him and I know
   the breast speaking
   out of a gone woman
   across distances

And my crown a tower.

A voice saying : She went in a queen,
       she died and came out,
       goddess.

All our faces in their colors
    staring at the
    arch of this world.

The breast smiles : Do not
    think you are invulnerable!
The breast smiles : Do not
    think you are immortal!

[1971]

William Bronk

AT TIKAL

Mountains they knew, and jungle, the sun, the stars—
these seemed to be there. But even after they slashed
the jungle and burned it and planted the comforting corn,
they were discontent. They wanted the shape of things.
They imagined a world and it was as if it were there
—a world with stars in their places and rain that came
when they called. It closed them in. Stone by stone,
as they built this city, these temples, they built this world.
They believed it. This was the world, and they,
of course, were the people. Now trees make up
assemblies and crowd in the wide plazas. Trees
climb the stupendous steps and rubble them.
In the jungle, the temples are little mountains again.

It is always hard like this, not having a world,
to imagine one, to go to the far edge
apart and imagine, to wall whether in
or out, to build a kind of cage for the sake
of feeling the bars around us, to give shape to a world.
And oh, it is always a world and not the world.

[1956]

METONYMY AS AN APPROACH TO A REAL WORLD

Whether what we sense of this world
is the what of this world only, or the what
of which of several possible worlds
– which what? – something of what we sense
may be true, may be the world, what it is, what we sense.
For the rest, a truce is possible, the tolerance
of travelers, eating foreign foods, trying words
that twist the tongue, to feel that time and place,
not thinking that this is the real world.

Conceded that all the clocks tell local time;
conceded, that "here" is anywhere we bound
and fill a space; conceded, we make a world:
is something caught there, contained there,
something real, something which we can sense?
Once in a city blocked and filled, I saw
the light lie in the deep chasm of a street,
palpable and blue, as though it had drifted in
from say, the sea, a purity of space.

[1964]

THE MAYAN GLYPHS UNREAD

Yes, the porpoises of course, it could
be of purport to talk to them. See what they say.
Indeed, what wouldn't we give? But the Mayans, — oh,
not but what I'd want to know, I would.
They were different from us in many ways. But we know
something about them, quite a bit in fact.
They were men, which makes me wonder could they have any more
to say to us than we have to say, ourselves,
to each other, or rather, could they have a better way
to say it that gets across? It seems to me
we all speak in undeciphered glyphs
as much as they do. OK. I'd like to know.

What's new with them? No, I'd try to talk
with anybody if I thought I could. You.
I'd try to talk to you. What do you know?

CORALS AND SHELLS

That which we call reality is that
which except for a dormancy, a kind of death
approaching, we were completely unable to endure.

Do you know what it is? It is that dormancy
itself, that insensate sleep, those stiff
rigors and bones of death where we hide, which we hate.

Alive, we couldn't endure it; we die to endure,
endure to die. It kills us. We are glad it does.
Corals and shells. Shall we ever cover a land?

[1969]

THE PLAINEST NARRATIVE

I am William Bronk, have been raised to believe
the personal pronoun plus the verb to be
and a proper name said honestly is fact
from which the plainest narrative begins.
But it isn't fact; it comes to this. Is it wrong?
Not wrong. Just that it isn't true.
No more than the opposite is true. That "I"—
as arbitrary as the proper name, a role
assumed from the verb to be as though to be
were all assumption, were willed; and of course it is
and anyone fooled is fooled. Do as you will.
It doesn't matter. What happens to us is not
what happens. It isn't by us. We feel it there.
Listen. Something is living. It is not we.
Aren't we that Adam, still, from whom we are?
The garden is here. I have no way to eat,
have never eaten. I round that fruit.
I push against the branches of that tree.

I THOUGHT IT WAS HARRY

Excuse me. I thought for a moment you were someone I know.
It happens to me. One time at *The Circle in the Square*
when it *was* still in the Square, I turned my head
when the lights went up and saw me there with a girl
and another couple. Out in the lobby, I looked
right at him and he looked away. I was no one he knew.
Well, it takes two, as they say, and I don't know what
it would prove anyway. Do we know who we are,
do you think? Kids seem to know. One time I asked
a little girl. She said she'd been sick. She said
she'd looked different and felt different. I said,
"Maybe it wasn't you. How do you know?"
"Oh, I was me," she said, "I know I was."

That part doesn't bother me anymore
or not the way it did. I'm nobody else
and nobody anyway. It's all the rest
I don't know. I don't know anything.
It hit me. I thought it was Harry when I saw you
and thought, "I'll ask Harry." I don't suppose
he knows, though. It's not that I get confused.
I don't mean that. If someone appeared and said,
"Ask me questions," I wouldn't know where to start.
I don't have questions even. It's the way I fade
as though I were someone's snapshot left in the light.
And the background fades the way it might if we woke
in the wrong twilight and things got dim and grey
while we waited for them to sharpen. Less and less
is real. No fixed point. Questions fix
a point, as answers do. Things move again
and the only place to move is away. It was wrong:
questions and answers are what to be without
and all we learn is how sound our ignorance is.
That's what I wanted to talk to Harry about.
You looked like him. Thank you anyway.

[1971]

WHERE IT ENDS

The gentleness of the slant October light
cancels whatever else we might have thought.
It is a hard world, empty and cruel;
but this light, oh Jesus Christ! This light!

The maple leaves, passive in front of the house,
are laved in it, abandoned, green gone.
That nothing else should matter but this light.
Gentleness, gentleness, the light.

[1975]

THE WORLD

I thought that you were an anchor in the drift of the world;
but no: there isn't an anchor anywhere.
There isn't an anchor in the drift of the world. Oh no.
I thought you were. Oh no. The drift of the world.

[1976]

LIFE SUPPORTS

Life keeps me alive: all its tubes
and wires are connected to me and give support
in ways that life determines for my needs.
On a bed of earth, in house, its calendars
and clocks are programmed to me: the various airs
of mornings, evenings, noontimes, in and out;
the seasons turn and come again and turn
and come again. Issue by issue the news
runs by, describing events and non-events,
reports sometimes of me, others I know.
Food, of course, often. Salty and sweet,
soluble, and other solutions at times
—corrective fluids needed to restore such balance

as may be lost. I am aware though I
not seem to be. Hard to believe the surge
of current through my angers, ecstasies
and frights sometimes at crises: a faulty tube,
power-outages, not long, but I cried
to be restored. The dials and switches wait.
No god comes near me. I am alone.

THE STRONG ROOM OF THE HOUSE

We can go by that door a dozen times
in a day and do that for years, maybe, without
thinking what's in there, paying it any heed
or needing to: why look in?
It's as much as though the room weren't part of the house
though we know, of course, it is; we think of it
in passing and dismiss the thought. Other times,
prompted perhaps by some occurrence, we pause
to consider whether it might be better to sort
things over there. Maybe throw some out.

Aren't we the strong ones, though, aren't we here
as masters of the house! We are, indeed, until
one day we come by the door or where the door was once
and the door is gone. In the fetidness of the air,
we can barely breathe. Something nourishes,
as a plant might, in the dirt of the floor, grows
in the light from the window or in the dark at night.
Horror is what it is called. It is the whole
strength of the house, will be there when we move out,
hang deep in the cellar-hole when the house is gone.

[1981]

Robert Duncan

from the Emperor Julian, *Hymn to the Mother of the Gods:*

And Attis encircles the heavens like a tiara, and thence sets out as though to descend to earth.

•

For the even is bounded, but the uneven is without bounds and there is no way through or out of it.

TRIBAL MEMORIES PASSAGES 1

And to Her-Without-Bounds I send,
wherever She wanders, by what
 campfire at evening,

among tribes setting each the City where
 we Her people are
at the end of a day's reaches here
 the Eternal
lamps lit, here the wavering human
 sparks of heat and light
glimmer, go out, and reappear.

For this is the company of the living
and the poet's voice speaks from no
 crevice in the ground between
 mid-earth and underworld
breathing fumes of what is deadly to know,
 news larvae in tombs
 and twists of time do feed upon,

but from the hearth stone, the lamp light,
the heart of the matter where the

house is held •

yet here, the warning light at the edge of town!

The City will go out in time, will go out
into time, hiding even its embers.
And we were scatterd thruout the countries and times of man

for we took alarm in ourselves,
rumors of the enemy
spread among the feathers of the wing that coverd us.

•

Mnemosyne, they named her, the
Mother with the whispering
featherd wings. Memory,
the great speckled bird who broods over the
nest of souls, and her egg,
the dream in which all things are living,
I return to, leaving my self.

I am beside myself with this
thought of the One in the World-Egg,
enclosed, in a shell of murmurings,

rimed round,
sound-chamberd child.

It's that first! The forth-going to be
bursts into green as the spring
winds blow watery from the south
and the sun returns north. He hides

fire among words in his mouth

and comes racing out of the zone of dark and storm

towards us.

I sleep in the afternoon, retreating from work,
reading and dropping away from the reading,
as if I were only a seed of myself,
    unawakend,   unwilling
        to sleep or wake.

THE MOON   PASSAGES 5

so pleasing   a light
    round,   haloed,   partially
disclosed,   a ring,
        night's wedding signet   •

            may be
a great lady drawing
    her tide-skirts up   •
            in whirls
        and loosening to the gilt
            shore-margins   of her sea-robes

• or he,   his consent
        releasing dreams,
    the dazzling path remaining
            over the waves,
        a lord too,   lunar moth king
            Oberon • gleaming amidst clouds.

        From what source
  the light of their faces,   the
            light of their eyes,   the dark
  glance that illumines,   the kindling look

as if over the shimmer of the lake
his flesh radiant •

My Lord-and-Lady Moon
upon whom
as if with love
the sun at the source of light
reflects •

Lifted •
Mount Shasta in snowy reverie
• floats

THE FIRE PASSAGES 13

jump stone hand leaf shadow sun

day plash coin light downstream fish

first loosen under boat harbor circle

old earth bronze dark wall waver

new smell purl close wet green

now rise foot warm hold cool

blood disk

horizon flame

The day at the window
the rain at the window
the night and the star at the window

Do you know the old language?
I do not know the old language.
Do you know the language of the old belief?

From the wood we thought burning
our animal spirits flee,   seeking refuge wherever,
as if in Eden,   in this   panic
lion and lamb lie down,   quail
heed not the eagle in flight before the flames high
over head go.
We see at last the man-faced roe and his
gentle mate;   the wild boar too
turns a human face.   In whose visages no terror
but a philosophic sorrow shows.   The ox
is fierce with terror, his thick tongue
slavers and sticks out panting
to make the gorgoneion face.
(This is Piero di Cosimo's great painting *A Forest Fire*, dated 1490–1500, preserved in the Ashmolean Museum at Oxford)
He inherits the *sfumato* of Leonardo da Vinci—
there is a softening of outline,   his color fuses.
A glow at the old borders makes
magic Pletho, Ficino, Pico della Mirandola prepared,
reviving in David's song,
Saul in his flaming rage heard,   music
Orpheus first playd,
chords and melodies of the spell that binds
the many in conflict in contrasts of one mind:

"For, since song and sound arise from the cognition of the mind, and the impetus of the phantasy, and the feeling of the heart, and, together with the air they have broken up and temperd, strike the aerial spirit of the hearer, which is the junction of the soul and the body, they easily move the phantasy, affect the heart and penetrate into the deep recesses of the mind"

Di Cosimo's featherd, furrd, leafy
boundaries where even the Furies are birds
and blur in higher harmonies Eumenides;
whose animals, entering the charmd field
in the light of his vision, a stillness,
have their dreamy glades and pastures.
The flames, the smoke. The curious
sharp focus in a glow sight
in the Anima Mundi has.

Where in the North (1500) shown in Bosch's illumination:
Hell breaks out an opposing music.
The faces of the deluded leer, faint, in lewd praise,
close their eyes in voluptuous torment,
enthralld by fear, avidly

following the daily news: the earthquakes, eruptions,
flaming automobiles, enraged lovers, wars against communism,
heroin addicts, police raids, race riots…

caught in the *lascivia animi* of this vain sound.
And we see at last the faces of evil openly
over us,
bestial extrusions no true animal face knows.
There are rats, snakes, toads, Boehme tells us,
that are the Devil's creatures. There is
a Devil's mimic of a man, a Devil's chemistry.
The Christ closes His eyes, bearing the Cross

as if dreaming.   Is His Kingdom
not of this world, but a dream of the Anima Mundi,
the World-Ensouling?
The painter's *sfumato* gives His face
pastoral stillness amidst terror,   sorrow
that has an echo in the stag's face we saw before.
About Him, as if to drown   sweet music out,
Satan looks forth from

men's faces:
Eisenhower's idiot grin, Nixon's
black jaw, the sly glare in Goldwater's eye, or
the look of Stevenson lying in the U.N. that our
Nation save face •

His face multiplies from the time of Roosevelt, Stalin,
Churchill, Hitler, Mussolini;   from the dream
of Oppenheimer, Fermi, Teller, Vannevar Bush,

brooding the nightmare formulae—to win the war!   the
inevitable • at Los Alamos
plotting the holocaust of Hiroshima •
Teller openly for the Anti-Christ
• glints of the evil that one sees in the power of this world,

"In the North and East, swarms of dough-faces, office-vermin, kept editors, clerks, attaches of ten thousand officers and their parties, aware of nothing further than the drip and spoil of politics—ignorant of principles... In the South, no end of blusterers, braggarts, windy, melodramatic, continually screaming, in falsetto, a nuisance to These States, their own just as much as any...and with the most incredible successes, having pistol'd, bludgeoned, yelled and threatend America, these past twenty years, into one long train of cowardly concessions, and still not through but rather at the commencement. Their cherished secret scheme is to dissolve the union of These States..."

(Whitman, 1856)

faces of Princes, Popes, Prime Usurers, Presidents,
Gang Leaders of whatever Clubs, Nations, Legions meet
to conspire, to coerce, to cut down •

Now, the City, impoverisht, swollen, dreams again
the great plagues–typhus, syphilis, the black buboes
epidemics, manias.

My name is Legion and in every nation I multiply.
Over those who would be Great Nations Great Evils.

They are burning the woods, the brushlands, the
grassy fields razed; their
profitable suburbs spread.
Pan's land, the pagan countryside, they'd
lay waste.

cool green waver circle fish sun

hold wet wall harbor downstream shadow

warm close dark boat light leaf

foot purl bronze under coin hand

rise smell earth loosen plash stone

now new old first day jump

UP RISING PASSAGES 25

Now Johnson would go up to join the simulacra of men,
Hitler and Stalin, to work his fame
with planes roaring out from Guam over Asia,
all America become a sea of toiling men
stirrd at his will, which would be a bloated thing,
drawing from the underbelly of the nation
such blood and dreams as swell the idiot psyche
out of its courses into an elemental thing
until his name stinks with burning meat and heapt honors

And men wake to see that they are used like things
spent in a great potlatch, this Texas barbecue
of Asia, Africa, and all the Americas,
And the professional military behind him, thinking
to use him as they thought to use Hitler
without losing control of their business of war,

But the mania, the ravening eagle of America
as Lawrence saw him "bird of men that are masters,
lifting the rabbit-blood of the myriads up into. . ."
into something terrible, gone beyond bounds, or
As Blake saw America in figures of fire and blood raging,
...in what image? the ominous roar in the air,
the omnipotent wings, the all-American boy in the cockpit
loosing his flow of napalm, below in the jungles
"any life at all or sign of life" his target, drawing now
not with crayons in his secret room
the burning of homes and the torture of mothers and fathers and children,
their hair a-flame, screaming in agony, but
in the line of duty, for the might and enduring fame
of Johnson, for the victory of American will over its victims,
releasing his store of destruction over the enemy,
in terror and hatred of all communal things, of communion,
of communism •
has raised from the private rooms of small-town bosses and businessmen,
from the council chambers of the gangs that run the great cities,
swollen with the votes of millions,

from the fearful hearts of good people in the suburbs turning the
   savoury meat over the charcoal burners and heaping their barbecue
   plates with more than they can eat,
from the closed meeting-rooms of regents of universities and sessions
   of profiteers

—back of the scene: the atomic stockpile; the vials of synthesized
   diseases eager biologists have developt over half a century dreaming
   of the bodies of mothers and fathers and children and hated rivals
   swollen with new plagues, measles grown enormous, influenzas
   perfected; and the gasses of despair, confusion of the senses, mania,
   inducing terror of the universe, coma, existential wounds, that
   chemists we have met at cocktail parties, passt daily and with a
   happy "Good Day" on the way to classes or work, have workt to
   make war too terrible for men to wage—

raised this secret entity of America's hatred of Europe, of Africa, of Asia,
the deep hatred for the old world that had driven generations of
   America out of itself,
and for the alien world, the new world about him, that might have
   been Paradise
but was before his eyes already cleard back in a holocaust of burning
   Indians, trees and grasslands,
reduced to his real estate, his projects of exploitation and profitable
   wastes,

this specter that in the beginning Adams and Jefferson feard and knew
would corrupt the very body of the nation
      and all our sense of our common humanity,
this black bile of old evils arisen anew,
takes over the vanity of Johnson;
and the very glint of Satan's eyes from the pit of the hell of America's
   unacknowledged, unrepented crimes that I saw in Goldwater's eyes
now shines from the eyes of the President
      in the swollen head of the nation.

TRANSGRESSING THE REAL PASSAGES 27

In the War they made a celestial cave.
In the War now I make
a celestial cave, a tent of the Night
(the Sun, no longer striking day upon the Earth,
but light-years away a diamond spark in the host of stars
sparkling net bejewelld wave of dark over us
distant coruscations
"play of light or of intellectual brilliancy"
in which I pretend a convocation of powers
(under the cloak of his poem *he* retires
invisible
so that it seems no man but a world speaks
for my thoughts are servants of the stars, and my words
(all parentheses opening into
come from a mouth that is the Universe *la bouche d'ombre*
(The poet-magician Dr Dee in his black mirror
calls forth his spirits from their obscurity)
thru the rays of invisible and visible bodies,
known and unknown sources and senders,
thru fumes, lights, sounds, crystallizations...
For now in my mind all the young men of my time
have withdrawn allegiance from *this world,* from public things •
and as their studies in irreality deepen,
industries, businesses, universities, armies
shudder and cease
so that the stone that comes into being
when the pupil of the eye that like a moon
takes all seeing from an unseen sun's light
reflected makes
held under his tongue each man can speak
wonders to come.

Chaos / and the divine measures and orders
so wedded are
we have but to imagine
ourselves the Lover
and the Beloved appears
man and woman, child and king, the ages and ladders of being,
the labor of birth and the release of death so compounded therein
they draw from the War Itself withdrawing
this breath between them.

In this rite the Great Magician stirs in His dream,
and the magician dreaming murmurs to his beloved:
thou art so near to me
thou art a phantom that the heart
would see—
and now the great river of their feeling grows so wide
its shores grow distant and unreal.

[1968]

THE FEAST PASSAGES 34

The butcher had prepared the leg of the lamb.
"Its only mouth being spirit" we prepared richly
clothing its flavor in a coat of many colors.
To ½ cup Dijon mustard
add 1 tbs Kikkoman soy
1 tbs Pickapeppa sauce (Jamaica) made from tomatoes,
onions, sugarcane, vinegar, mangoes, raisins, tamarinds
mainly that it be dark and redolent of tamarind
—but the true measure is hidden in the fingers' feel for the taste of it—
and garlic

rosemary   ground in the mortar
salt, pepper, and drops of oil   workt into the emulsion...

We have come to the Festivities!

The recipe appears
between fond thought
and devout actualities,   at this table

we play the host,   the guests

gather round

pleasures of the household,   the fine

burnt smell of the meat   pleasing to the nostrils, yet

this house is not Jahweh's—carrots, celery, onions, zucchini   cookt
with yogurt in the meat's company,

for Cain's sacrifice in these devotions likewise

satisfies.

The smith   the single most important craftsman

for the Bedouin   ritually   impure excluded from intermarriage
and from eating in the company,

blacksmiths   a pariah caste   only the gods protect them,

Cain,   tribal father of the smith and the musician with his zither,
patron of bards, founder of cities...

Weavers, potters, and carpenters   appear to be foreigners
to the tribe.

The Bethlehem Steel Company now in the place of the Moravian
smithy at Bethlehem,

this turmoil of peoples in the place where the City was!

Milk of the mother,   seed of the father,   cream, barley and
wheatgerm.

Carl Sauer in *Land and Life:*   "We have neglected the natural history
of man"

"Institutions and outlooks have their origins in time and place;
they spread from one group to another"

"origins, derivations and survival   the basic determinations"

"we know even the logos" —taking meaning and sound in our
language as His attributes— "only as a term in culture
history"

in the Orphic rite
the suckling lamb or kid

in the dream
(though I was awake or my mind
was wandering for a moment) it came

in another spelling:

EVE is EWE

in the cauldron of regenerations fallen

feeding on milk as though we were born again.

On *this* side Man's fortunate feast,

harvests of his growing mastery over his nature,

"Antiphonal to this the revenge of an outraged nature on man"

The shit of the sheep does not redeem the shifting sands the stript
rock surfaces,

wastes left after ancient over-grazing devourd landscapes

"*Lapse of time brought no repair*"

the dirty streams...

The hosts have gone down to the edge of the sea,
time has swept their tents away.
The air we breathe grows dark with the debris of burning fats
and dense with animal smoke. All day

exhausts pour forth into the slues of night their centuries.
The black soil scums the putrid bay,

the light is acrid to our eyes, and all the old runes
thicken in our minds.

Gē stinks to Heaven from the dumps of sleep.

And where her children dream of Chaos come again,

undoing the knots and twists of Man we roast the Lamb,

flesh as we are flesh burgundy wine as our blood is wine,

the red glow in the crystal   the fire in the depth of her
remembering
hunger taking over the taste of things
the sun's rays curdle in the pot
as in the first days
the kid or lamb   seethed in the mother's milk
the thirst in the desert   the hot meat

ready in our need for it.

[1970]

Jackson Mac Low

from THE PRESIDENTS OF THE UNITED STATES OF AMERICA

Author's Note: "The Presidents of the United States of America" was composed in January and May 1963. Each section is headed by the first inaugural year of a president (from Washington thru Fillmore), and its structure of images is that of the Phoenician meanings of the successive letters of the president's name[...] They are:

A (aleph) "ox"
B (beth) "house"
C (gimel) "camel"
D (daleth) "door"
E (he) "window" or "look!"
F (vau) "hook"
H (cheth) "fence"
I (yod) "hand"
K (kaph) "palm of the hand"
L (lamed) "ox-goad"
M (mem) "water"
N (nun) "fish"
O (ayin) "eye"
P (pe) "mouth"
Q (qoph) "knot"
R (resh) "head"
S (shin) "tooth"
T (tau) "mark"
V (vau) "hook"
X (samekh) "prop"
Y (vau) "hook"
Z (zayin) "weapon"

Letters developed by the Romans or in the Middle Ages were given the meanings of the letters from which they were derived or to which they were similar:

G (developed by Romans in third century B.C.: similar in form to C) "camel"
J (introduced during Middle Ages as minuscule form of I and made into majuscule in the sixteenth century) "hand"
U (introduced during Middle Ages as a minuscule form of V and made into majuscule in the sixteenth century) "hook"
W (Anglo-Saxon addition in eleventh century; similar to two V's) "hooks" or "hook hook"

These letter-meaning words were used as "nuclei" which were freely connected by other material[...] Each letter-meaning nucleus could be used in any form class (e.g., M could be translated as the noun "water," the verb "water," the adjective "watery," or as the adverb "waterily"). In the earlier sections (written in January 1963), a minimum of connective material was introduced between the nuclei, and the meanings of the letters of each name delimited a strophe. In the later sections (written in May 1963), much more material was introduced between the nuclei, and the verse structures became much more complex.

1789 *(begun about 15 January 1963)*

George Washington never owned a camel
but he looked thru the eyes in his head
with a camel's calm and wary look.

Hooks that wd irritate an ox
held his teeth together
and he cd build a fence with his own hands
tho he preferred to go fishing
as anyone else wd
while others did the work *for* him
for tho he had no camels he had slaves enough
and probably made them toe the mark by keeping an eye on them
for *he* wd never have stood for anything fishy.

1797

John Adams knew the hand
can be quicker than the eye
& knew that not only fencers & fishermen live by this knowledge.

If he kept an ox
he kept it out of doors in summertime
so the ox cd find his water for himself
& make it where he stood
& find the tasty grass
his teeth cd chew as cud.

1801

Marked by no fence
farther than an eye cd see
beyond the big waters
Thomas Jefferson saw grass enough for myriads of oxen
to grind between their teeth.

His farmer hands itched
when he thought of all that vacant land and looked about for a way to
hook it in for us

until something unhooked a window in his head
where the greedy needy teeth & eyes of Napoleon shone
eager for the money which
was Jefferson's bait to catch the Louisiana fish.

1809

James Madison's hand cd lead an ox to water
and he'd look at him while he drank
letting it
spill down from grassy teeth.

After he'd water'd his ox
James Madison'd
push open his door with his hand
& then his teeth'd
grind and mash up all but the bones & eyes of a large fish.

1817

James Monroe
laid a hand
as heavy as the ox that stands on every peon's tongue
on all between the waters between
the new world and both old ones
& looked across both of them
baring but
puppy teeth then.

Across the waters eyes
in fishers' heads
eyed this newest angler
with the grudging look of fellow-recognition
old members of the Predators' Club
bestow on former prey
that blunders past all blackballs
& soon must be accepted for admission.

1825 *(written 24 May 1963)*

John Quincy Adam's right hand
shaded his eyes
as he sat on a fence & fished.

At one end of his line was a knot & a hook
at the
other end
his hand & he sat
fishing for a camel with a hook instead of a hump?

No & not for an ox
because
behind a door he had his papa's ox
& when he went fishing in water
(& that's what he was doing he was no fool)
he was looking to get something
good
something
he cd sink his teeth into & want to.

1829 *(24 May 1963)*

Andrew Jackson's last name's the same as my first
but
that makes me no more like him
than an ox is like a
fish
(or vice versa)
but
open a door in your head
(or a window)
& look!
if your eyes are hooks
what's on those hooks?
Andrew Jackson?

Nonsense:
Andrew Jackson's dead:
you can no more see *him*

than your   hand cd hold in itself
  an ox:
than you cd hold a camel in the palm of your hand
  as you *cd* hold a tooth
    or an eye of a fish:
                  forget Andrew Jackson:
   (you already have).

1837   *(24 May 1963)*

If Martin Van Buren ever swam in water
(if Martin Van Buren ever swam)
what kind of swimmer was he if he held onto an ox's head
        (did he?)
    to keep his own above the surface?

   (he knew about banks
              but
          what did he know about swimming?)
                          but
          what is Martin Van Buren now
                          but
             a series of marks I make
          with
                           my
             hand?
                           (maybe
                            Martin
             Van
                 Buren cd swim like a fish!)
                        do
                             I
                           make
                                  these
                           marks
                                with
                           "my"   hand?
                                     can
                                  "I"
                       catch

this fish
(i.
e.,
"I")?

A hook big enough to hang an ox from's
a hook too big to catch a fish with.

Martin Van Buren lived in a fine big house in New York State
before he was president
but how did he get his hooks into
Ezra Pound's head?
look!
I want to know how a poet became a
rich old dead old politician's fish.

1841 (I) *(24 May 1963)*

Andrew Jackson & Martin Van Buren
are heroes of that old
hero of mine in whose honor I write
"wd"
&
"cd"
&
"shd"
in-
stead
of
"would"
&
"could"
&
"should"
(I write
&
in-
stead
of
"and"

in
honor
of
William
Blake
but
whose
hero's
William
Henry
Harrison? (I mean
whose
hero is he *now?*):
old
hero hung on a hook
the
hook is "Tippecanoe"
&
the smart old politicians used it as an ox-goad
(their
theory was: "an ox-goad in the hand
can
make 'em
go:
treat 'em like oxen & they'll lap it up like water."

That's the way those wily Whigs
fenced: (look!
who remembers who *they* were now?
—those old phynancial string-pullers
(*peace,* Jarry!)
who hung an old Indian fighter on their line
(a smaller fish to catch a bigger one)
pushing thru his aging head
the hook
"Tippecanoe":
who remembers who *they* were now?
we
remember "Tippecanoe":
whose

fish is
who?)—
but
that
was the way those old finaglers did it
&
if you can't learn from history
what *can* "you" learn from?
(Mystery.)

Who was sitting on the fence?
Who was treated like an ox?
Whose head was used as bait?
Whose head planned it all?
Whose hand held the line?
Whose teeth chewed what was caught?
Whose eye caught what was going on?
Who was the fish & how did *he* like it?

1841 (II) *(written 24 May 1963)*

The poor old bait got sick & died
&
then they had "Tyler too!"
(exclamation point & all)
&
some there were who had him on their hands
& some there were who had him in front of their eyes
& some there were who had him
& some there were who wished he'd just go off
& sit on a fence somewhere & fish.

That's the way John Tyler made his mark
& he knew whose hook he was on
& he knew who held the ox-goad
& he knew when to turn his back to the window
: (*he* knew when to look
& when
not
to look:

he knew how to use his *head*):
but
where's John Tyler
now? (Dead.)
& what do "we" have because he made a deal? (Texas.)

1845 *(written 24 May 1963)*

Tyler was no Whig at all & after his term's end
wanted the Demo*crat*ic nomination but
only
a splinter group
nominated him &
Clay
got
the Whigs' &
'the first "dark horse"
of
American
national politics
was suddenly brought forward in the morning.
James K.
[for "Knox"]
Polk, of Tennessee,
after one ballot, was unanimously chosen as
the Democratic candidate.
The country, bewildered,
asked
"Who is Polk?"
He
was
indeed,
not entirely unknown.'
[I quote (I've quoted)
a descendant (?) of
John Adams & John Quincy Adams (?)
—*do* I quote a descendant of
John Adams & John Quincy Adams?—
I don't think I do I

quote a history-textbook-writer
named
James Truslow Adams
who wrote a book called
The Record of America with another
history-
textbook-
writer
named Charles Garrett Vannest
a Professor of History
at Harris Teachers College
in St. Louis:
he (Vannest)
was co-author of
Socialized History of the United States
(whose co-author was he *then*?)]

The main things about James Knox Polk were
that first he had Texas & then a war with Mexico on his hands
that he was no ox but a man with a conscience who made war anyway
that "we" got all of Texas, Utah, Nevada, & California
& most of Arizona & New Mexico because
of conscience-stricken Mr. Polk's war
that Mr. Polk's war
extended "us" to the waters of the
Pacific (Ocean)
(how "pacific" can an ocean be if "we"
got
"our"
window on it thru a war?)
(Answer: just as
"pacific"
as any other ocean)
("window" hell:
"our"
teeth
snapped up a whole damn coast *that* time
& everything up *to* it)
that *that* war
was

why
Thoreau refused to pay his tax
& stayed in jail a night
& wrote *Civil Disobedience*
& eventually
was read by a little Indian lawyer (*Indian* Indian)
who invented another way to fight
& thought it wasn't violent
&
used it
so shrewdly that
he & circumstances made
the British Empire lose a whole sub-continent.

In the palm of his hand
a man who ate no fish or meat
held for a time
an
empire on which the sun never set
his eye
controlled that vast melange of
hungry peoples
he
didnt
fight
not
that is
as
other people fought
he thought
he made no threats
thought
he used no violence
thought
he used only
Satyagraha
the force of truth
to pull away the British Empire's props.

Thus we've come by word of mouth

from James Knox Polk
America's
first "dark horse" president
to the eye of Mohandas Gandhi:
that ox-goad
small enough to be
hidden in the palm of a hand.

(to here at 1:10 am Sat 25 May 1963)

Denise Levertov

THE JACOB'S LADDER

The stairway is not
a thing of gleaming strands
a radiant evanescence
for angels' feet that only glance in their tread, and need not
touch the stone.

It is of stone.
A rosy stone that takes
a glowing tone of softness
only because behind it the sky is a doubtful, a doubting
night gray.

A stairway of sharp
angles, solidly built.
One sees that the angels must spring
down from one step to the next, giving a little
lift of the wings:

and a man climbing
must scrape his knees, and bring
the grip of his hands into play. The cut stone
consoles his groping feet. Wings brush past him.
The poem ascends.

[1961]

TO THE MUSE

I have heard it said,
and by a wise man,
that you are not one who comes and goes

but having chosen
you remain in your human house,
and walk

in its garden for air and the delights
of weather and seasons.

Who builds
a good fire in his hearth
shall find you at it
with shining eyes and a ready tongue.

Who shares
even water and dry bread with you
will not eat without joy

and wife or husband
who does not lock the door of the marriage
against you, finds you

not as unwelcome third in the room, but as
the light of the moon on flesh and hair.

He told me, that wise man,
that when it seemed the house was
empty of you,

the fire crackling for no one,
the bread hard to swallow in solitude,
the gardens a tedious maze,

you were not gone away
but hiding yourself in secret rooms.
The house is no cottage, it seems,

it has stairways, corridors, cellars
a tower perhaps,
unknown to the host.

The host, the housekeeper, it is
who fails you. He had forgotten
to make room for you at the hearth
or set a place for you at the table
or leave the doors unlocked for you.

Noticing you are not there
(when did he last see you?)
he cries out you are faithless,

have failed him,
writes you stormy letters demanding you return
it is intolerable

to maintain this great barracks without your presence,
it is too big, it is too small, the walls
menace him, the fire smokes

and gives off no heat. But to what address
can he mail the letters?
                                        And all the while

you are indwelling,
a gold ring lost in the house.
A gold ring lost in the house.
You are in the house!

Then what to do to find the room where you are?
Deep cave of obsidian glowing with red, with green,
with black light,
high room in the lost tower where you sit spinning,

crack in the floor where the gold ring
waits to be found?

No more rage but a calm face,
trim the fire, lay the table, find some
flowers for it: is that the way?
Be ready with quick sight to catch
a gleam between the floorboards,

there, where he had looked
a thousand times and seen nothing?
Light of the house,

the wise man spoke
words of comfort. You are near,
perhaps you are sleeping and don't hear.

Not even a wise man
can say, do thus and thus, that presence
will be restored.
Perhaps

a becoming aware a door is swinging, as if
someone had passed through the room a moment ago—perhaps
looking down, the sight
of the ring back on its finger?

THE WINGS

Something hangs in back of me,
I can't see it, can't move it.

I know it's black,
a hump on my back.

It's heavy. You
can't see it.

What's in it? Don't tell me
you don't know. It's

what you told me about—
black

inimical power, cold
whirling out of it and

around me and
sweeping you flat.

But what if,
like a camel, it's

pure energy I store,
and carry humped and heavy?

Not black, not
that terror, stupidity

of cold rage; or black
only for being pent there?

What if released in air
it became a white

source of light, a fountain
of light? Could all that weight

be the power of flight?
Look inward: see me

with embryo wings, one
feathered in soot, the other

blazing ciliations of ember, pale
flare-pinions. Well—

could I go
on one wing,

the white one?

[1966]

ADVENT 1966

Because in Vietnam the vision of a Burning Babe
is multiplied, multiplied,
                                        the flesh on fire
not Christ's, as Southwell saw it, prefiguring
the Passion upon the Eve of Christmas,

but wholly human and repeated, repeated,
infant after infant, their names forgotten,
their sex unknown in the ashes,
set alight, flaming but not vanishing,
not vanishing as his vision but lingering.

cinders upon the earth or living on
moaning and stinking in hospitals three abed;

because of this my strong sight,
my clear caressive sight, my poet's sight I was given
that it might stir me to song,
is blurred.
                There is a cataract filming over
my inner eyes. Or else a monstrous insect
has entered my head, and looks out
from my sockets with multiple vision,

seeing not the unique Holy Infant
burning sublimely, an imagination of redemption,
furnace in which souls are wrought into new life,
but, as off a beltline, more, more senseless figures aflame.

And this insect (who is not there—
it is my own eyes do my seeing, the insect
is not there, what I see is there)
will not permit me to look elsewhere,

or if I look, to see except dulled and unfocused
the delicate, firm, whole flesh of the still unburned.

A TREE TELLING OF ORPHEUS

White dawn. Stillness.   When the rippling began
    I took it for sea-wind, coming to our valley with rumors
    of salt, of treeless horizons. But the white fog
didn't stir; the leaves of my brothers remained outstretched,
unmoving.
                Yet the rippling drew nearer—and then
my own outermost branches began to tingle, almost as if
fire had been lit below them, too close, and their twig-tips
were drying and curling.
                                Yet I was not afraid, only
                                deeply alert.

I was the first to see him, for I grew
        out on the pasture slope, beyond the forest.
He was a man, it seemed: the two
moving stems, the short trunk, the two
arm-branches, flexible, each with five leafless
                                                twigs at their ends,
and the head that's crowned by brown or gold grass,
bearing a face not like the beaked face of a bird,
        more like a flower's.
                                    He carried a burden made of
some cut branch bent while it was green,
strands of a vine tight-stretched across it. From this,
when he touched it, and from his voice
which unlike the wind's voice had no need of our
leaves and branches to complete its sound,
                                                came the ripple.
But it was no longer a ripple (he had come near and
stopped in my first shadow) it was a wave that bathed me
            as if rain
                        rose from below and around me
            instead of falling.
And what I felt was no longer a dry tingling:
        I seemed to be singing as he sang, I seemed to know
        what the lark knows; all my sap
            was mounting towards the sun that by now
                had risen, the mist was rising, the grass

was drying, yet my roots felt music moisten them
deep under earth.

He came still closer, leaned on my trunk:
the bark thrilled like a leaf still-folded.
Music! There was no twig of me not
trembling with joy and fear.

Then as he sang
it was no longer sounds only that made the music:
he spoke, and as no tree listens I listened, and language
came into my roots
out of the earth,
into my bark
out of the air,
into the pores of my greenest shoots
gently as dew
and there was no word he sang but I knew its meaning.
He told of journeys,
of where sun and moon go while we stand in dark,
of an earth-journey he dreamed he would take some day
deeper than roots...
He told of the dreams of man, wars, passions, griefs,
and I, a tree, understood words—ah, it seemed
my thick bark would split like a sapling's that
grew too fast in the spring
when a late frost wounds it.

Fire he sang,
that trees fear, and I, a tree, rejoiced in its flames.
New buds broke forth from me though it was full summer.
As though his lyre (now I knew its name)
were both frost and fire, its chords flamed
up to the crown of me.

I was seed again.
I was fern in the swamp.
I was coal.

And at the heart of my wood
(so close I was to becoming man or a god)
there was a kind of silence, a kind of sickness,
something akin to what men call boredom,
something
(the poem descended a scale, a stream over stones)
that gives to a candle a coldness
in the midst of its burning, he said.

It was then,
when in the blaze of his power that
reached me and changed me
I thought I should fall my length,
that the singer began
to leave me. Slowly
moved from my noon shadow
to open light,
words leaping and dancing over his shoulders
back to me
rivery sweep of lyre-tones becoming
slowly again
ripple.

And I
in terror
but not in doubt of
what I must do
in anguish, in haste,
wrenched from the earth root after root,
the soil heaving and cracking, the moss tearing asunder—
and behind me the others: my brothers
forgotten since dawn. In the forest
they too had heard,
and were pulling their roots in pain
out of a thousand years' layers of dead leaves,
rolling the rocks away,
breaking themselves
out of
their depths.

You would have thought we would lose the sound of the lyre,
of the singing
so dreadful the storm-sounds were, where there was no storm,
no wind but the rush of our
branches moving, our trunks breasting the air.
But the music!
The music reached us.

Clumsily,
stumbling over our own roots,
rustling our leaves
in answer,
we moved, we followed.

All day we followed, up hill and down.
We learned to dance,
for he would stop, where the ground was flat,
and words he said
taught us to leap and to wind in and out
around one another in figures the lyre's measure designed.
The singer
laughed till he wept to see us, he was so glad.
At sunset
we came to this place I stand in, this knoll
with its ancient grove that was bare grass then.
In the last light of that day his song became
farewell.
He stilled our longing.
He sang our sun-dried roots back into earth,
watered them: all-night rain of music so quiet
we could almost
not hear it in the
moonless dark.
By dawn he was gone.
We have stood here since,
in our new life.
We have waited.
He does not return.

It is said he made his earth-journey, and lost
what he sought.
                        It is said they felled him
and cut up his limbs for firewood.
                                        And it is said
his head still sang and was swept out to sea singing.
Perhaps he will not return.
                                  But what we have lived
comes back to us.
                          We see more.
                                      We feel, as our rings increase,
something that lifts our branches, that stretches our furthest
                                                       leaf-tips
further.
        The wind, the birds,
                                      do not sound poorer but clearer,
recalling our agony, and the way we danced.
The music!

[1970]

Jack Spicer

A BOOK OF MUSIC

IMPROVISATIONS ON A SENTENCE BY POE

"Indefiniteness is an element of the true music."
The grand concord of what
Does not stoop to definition. The seagull
Alone on the pier cawing its head off
Over no fish, no other seagull,
No ocean. As absolutely devoid of meaning
As a French horn.
It is not even an orchestra. Concord
Alone on a pier. The grand concord of what
Does not stoop to definition. No fish
No other seagull, no ocean—the true
Music.

A VALENTINE

Useless Valentines
Are better
Than all others.
Like something implicit
In a poem.
Take all your Valentines
And I'll take mine.
What is left is better
Than any image.

CANTATA

Ridiculous
How the space between three violins
Can threaten all of our poetry.
We bunch together like Cub
Scouts at a picnic. There is a high scream.
Rain threatens. That moment of terror.
Strange how all our beliefs
Disappear.

ORFEO

Sharp as an arrow Orpheus
Points his music downward.
Hell is there
At the bottom of the seacliff.
Heal
Nothing by this music.
Eurydice
Is a frigate bird or a rock or some seaweed.
Hail nothing
The infernal
Is a slippering wetness out at the horizon.
Hell is this:
The lack of anything but the eternal to look at
The expansiveness of salt
The lack of any bed but one's
Music to sleep in.

SONG OF A PRISONER

Nothing in my body escapes me.
The sound of an eagle diving
Upon some black bird
Or the sorrow of an owl.
Nothing in my body escapes me.
Each branch is closed
I
Echo each song from its throat
Bellow each sound.

JUNGLE WARFARE

The town wasn't much
A few mud-huts and a church steeple.
They were the same leaves
And the same grass
And the same birds deep in the edge of the thicket.
We waited around for someone to come out and surrender
But they rang their church bells
And we
We were not afraid of death or any manner of dying
But the same muddy bullets, the same horrible
Love.

GOOD FRIDAY: FOR LACK OF AN ORCHESTRA

I saw a headless she-mule
Running through the rain
She had the hide of a chessboard
And withers that were lank and dark
"Tell me," I asked
"Where
Is Babylon?"
"No," she bellowed
"Babylon is a few baked bricks
With some symbols on them.
You could not hear them. I am running
To the end of the world."
She ran
Like a green and purple parrot, screaming
Through the sand.

MUMMER

The word is imitative
From the sound mum or mom
Used by nurses to frighten or amuse children
At the same time pretending
To cover their faces.
Understanding is not enough

The old seagull died. There is a whole army of seagulls
Waiting in the wings
A whole army of seagulls.

THE CARDPLAYERS

The moon is tied to a few strings
They hold in their hands. The cardplayers
Sit there stiff, hieratic.
Moving their hands only for the sake of
Playing the cards.
No trick of metaphor
Each finger is a real finger
Each card real pasteboard, each liberty
Unaware of attachment.
The moon is tied to a few strings.
                                        Those cardplayers
Stiff, utterly
Unmoving.

GHOST SONG

The in
          ability to love
The inability
                    to love
In love
            (like all the small animals went up the hill into the
            underbrush to escape from the goat and the bad tiger)
The inability
Inability
            (tell me why no white flame comes up from the earth
            when lightning strikes the twigs and the dry branches)
In love. In love. In love. The
In-
    ability
            (as if there were nothing left on the mountains but
            what nobody wanted to escape from)

ARMY BEACH WITH TRUMPETS

Rather than our bodies the sand
Proclaims that we are on the last edge
Of something. Two boys
Who cannot catch footballs horseplay
On the wet edge.
Or if the sight of the thing ended
Did not break upon us like a wave
From every warm ocean.
We call it sport
To play on the edge, to drop
Like a heartless football
At the edge.

DUET FOR A CHAIR AND A TABLE

The sound of words as they fall away from our mouths
Nothing
Is less important
And yet that chair
this table
named
Assume identities
take their places
Almost as a kind of music.
Words make things name
themselves
Makes the table grumble
I
In the symphony of God am a table
Makes the chair sing
A little song about the people that will never be sitting on it
And we
Who in the same music
Are almost as easily shifted as furniture
We
Can learn our names from our mouths
Name our names
In the middle of the same music.

CONSPIRACY

A violin which is following me

In how many distant cities are they listening
To its slack-jawed music? This
Slack-jawed music?
Each of ten thousand people playing it.

It follows me like someone that hates me.

Oh, my heart would sooner die
Than leave its slack-jawed music. They
In those other cities
Whose hearts would sooner die.

It follows me like someone that hates me.

Or is it really a tree growing just behind my throat
That if I turned quickly enough I could see
Rooted, immutable, neighboring
Music.

A BOOK OF MUSIC

Coming at an end, the lovers
Are exhausted like two swimmers. Where
Did it end? There is no telling. No love is
Like an ocean with the dizzy procession of the waves' boundaries
From which two can emerge exhausted, nor long goodbye
Like death.
Coming at an end. Rather, I would say, like a length
Of coiled rope
Which does not disguise in the final twists of its lengths
Its endings.
But, you will say, we loved
And some parts of us loved
And the rest of us will remain
Two persons. Yes,
Poetry ends like a rope.

[1958/1969]

from *Language*:

THING LANGUAGE

This ocean, humiliating in its disguises
Tougher than anything.
No one listens to poetry. The ocean
Does not mean to be listened to. A drop
Or crash of water. It means
Nothing.
It
Is bread and butter
Pepper and salt. The death
That young men hope for. Aimlessly
It pounds the shore. White and aimless signals. No
One listens to poetry.

SPORTING LIFE

The trouble with comparing a poet with a radio is that radios don't develop scar tissue. The tubes burn out, or with a transistor, which most souls are, the battery or diagram burns out replaceable or not replaceable, but not like that punchdrunk fighter in the bar. The poet
Takes too many messages. The right to the ear that floored him in New Jersey. The right to say that he stood six rounds with a champion.
Then they sell beer or go on sporting commissions, or, if the scar tissue is too heavy, demonstrate in a bar where the invisible champions might not have hit him. Too many of them.
The poet is a radio. The poet is a liar. The poet is a counterpunching radio.
And those messages (God would not damn them) do not even know they are champions.

* * *

I hear a banging on the door of the night
Buzz, buzz; buzz, buzz; buzz, buzz
If you open the door does it let in light?
Buzz, buzz, buzz, buzz; buzz, buzzz.

If the day appears like a yellow raft
Meow, meow; meow, meoww
Is it really on top of a yellow giraffe
Meow, meow, meow, meow. Meow, meow

If the door caves in as the darkness slides
Knocking and knocking; knock, knock, knock
What can tell the light of whatever's inside?
Knocking and knocking; knock, knock, knock

Or the light and the darkness dance in your eye
Shadows falling one by one
Pigs, and eels, and open sky
Dancers falling one by one
Dancers shrieking one by one

[. . .]

The log in the fire
Asks a lot
When it is lighted
Or knot

Timber comes
From seas mainly
Sometimes burns green
-Ly

When it is lighted
The knot
Burns like a joke
With the color of smoke

Save us, with birthdays, whatever is in the fire or not in the fire,
immortal
We cannot be
A chimney tree
Or give grace to what's mere-
Ly fatal.

* * *

Finally the messages penetrate
There is a corpse of an image—they penetrate
The corpse of a radio. Cocteau used a car radio on account of NO SPEED LIMIT. In any case the messages penetrate the radio and render it (and the radio) ultimately useless.
Prayer
Is exactly that
The kneeling radio down to the tomb of some saint
Uselessness sung and danced (the radio dead but alive it can connect things
Into sound. Their prayer
Its only connection.

* * *

Heros eat soup like anyone else. Sometimes the kitchen is so far away
That there is no soup. No kitchen. An open space of ground recovered by
The sky.
Heros eat soup like anyone else. False ground.

Soup
Of the evening
Beautifull soup.
And the sky stays there not an image
But the heros
Like the image of an image
(What is made of soup from)
Zooms.

* * *

Smoke signals
Like in the Eskimo villages on the coast where the earthquake hit
Bang, snap, crack. They will never know what hit them
On the coast of Alaska. They expect everybody to be insane.
This is a poem about the death of John F. Kennedy.

* * *

A redwood forest is not invisible at night. The blackness covers it but it covers the blackness.

If they had turned Jeffers into a parking lot death would have been eliminated and birth also. The lights shine 24 hours a day on a parking lot.

True conservation is the effort of the artist and the private man to keep things true. Trees and the cliffs in Big Sur breathe in the dark. Jeffers knew the pain of their breath and the pain was the death of a first-born baby breathing.

Death is not final. Only parking-lots.

* * *

The whorship of beauty
Or beautiful things take a long time getting used to.
There is no past in beauty. The car going at 97.5 miles an hour.
    The time changes
As you cross each border.
Daffodils, ceremonies of spring, sprang, sprung
And it is August
Another century.
Take each past, combine it with its present. Death
Is a tooth among
Strangers.

* * *

It comes May and the summers renew themselves
(39 of them) Baseball seasons
Utter logic
Where a man is faced with a high curve.
No telling what happened in this game. Except one didn't strike out.
    One feels they fielded it badly at second base.
Oceans of wildflowers. Utter logic of the form and color.

* * *

Thanatos, the death-plant in the skull
Grows wings and grows enormous.
The herb of the whole system.
Systematically blotting out the anise weed and the trap-door spider of the vacant lot.
Worse than static or crabgrass.
Thanatos, bone at the bottom, Saint
Francis, that botanist in Santa Rosa
(Bless me now, for I am a plant and an animal)
Called him Brother Death.

[...]

The country is not very well defined.
Whether they are bat-people or real people. The sea-
Coast of Bohemia. The in-
Visible world.
A man counts his fingers in these situations. Whether there are five or ten of them or udders as we might go sea-bathing in dream.
But dream is not enough. We waking hear the call of the
In-
Visible world
Not seen. Hinted at only. By some vorpals, some sea-lions, some scraggs.
Almost too big to get used to, its dimensions amaze us, who are blind to Whatever
Is rising and falling with us.

* * *

I squint my eyes to cry
(No tears, a barren salt-mine) and then take two sniffles through my nose
This means emotion. Chaplinesque
As the fellow says.
We pantomime every action of our bodies
Do not wait
On one sad hill
For one sad turn. I've had it
Principally because you're young.

* * *

The metallurgical analysis of the stone that was my heart shows an
    alarming percentage of silicon.
Silicon, as George would be the first to tell you, is not a metal.
    It is present in glass, glue and since glue is made from horses
    —living substance.
I love you. But as the iron clangs, the glass, the glue, the living
    subtance (which, God knows, has been to as many glue factories as
    it can remember) muffles what the rest of the heart says.
I see you cowering in the corner and the metal in my heart bangs. Too
    personal
The glass and glue in my heart reply. And they are living substance.
You cannot bake glass in a pie or fry glue in an omelette
"If I speak in the tongue of men and angels…"
The sounding brass of my heart says
"Love."

[1965]

Paul Blackburn

AT THE WELL

Here we are, see?
in this village, maybe a camp
middle of desert, the
Maghreb, desert below Marrakesh
standing in the street
simply.

Outskirts of the camp
at the edge of town, these riders
on camels or horses,
but riders, tribesmen, sitting
there   on their horses.

They are mute.   They are
hirsute, they are not
able to speak. If they
could the sound would be gutteral.
They cannot speak. They want
something.

I nor
you know what they want   . They want
nothing.   They are beyond want.   They need
nothing.   They used to be slaves.   They
want something of us   /   of me   /   what
shall I say to them.

They have had their tongues cut out.
I have nothing to give them ¿There is no
grace at the edge of my heart I would grant,
render them? They want something, they
sit there on their horses. Are there
children in the village I can give them.

My child's heart? Is it goods they want
as tribute. They have had their tongues
cut out. Can I offer them some sound
my mouth makes in the night? Can I
say they are brave, fierce, im-
placable? that I would like to
join them?

Let us go together

across the desert toward the
cities, let us
terrify the towns, the villages,
disappear among bazaars, sell our
camels, pierce our ears, for-
get that we are mute and drive
the princes out, take all the
slave-girls for ourselves?
What can I offer them.

They have appeared here on the edge of my soul.
I ask them what they want, they say
—You are our leader. Tell us what
your pleasure is, we
want you. They
say nothing. They

are mute. they are hirsute. They
are the fathers I never had. They are
tribesmen standing on the edge of town near
water, near the soul I must look into each
morning . myself.

Who are these wild men?
I scream:
—I want my gods!
I want my goods! I want
my reflection in the sun's pool at morning,
shade in the afternoon under the
date palms, I want and want!

What can I give them.
What tribe of nomads and wanderers am I continuation of, what
can I give my fathers?
What can I offer myself?

I want to see my own skin
at the life's edge, at the
life-giving water. I want
to rise from the pool,
mount my camel and
be among the living, the other side of this village.

Come gentlemen,
wheel your mounts about.
There is nothing here.

[1963/1970]

from THE SELECTION OF HEAVEN

17. The mind returns to it always
a machine gone insane, the senses
tamped down, turn the dial to – 1
that kind of death .

The dead man sits at the table
a dead cigarette in his mouth,
drinks, the mind-gears turn
repetitiously over the same materials,
the same images return, murderously.

He sits and looks at them again and again.
The smashed glass, her high at the party, a
pickup truck, an empty road, sound of the man' s voice,
of his own as from a taperecorder far off and drunk,
cannot recognize the sound of his own voice, the
sleeping bag no one can find, a pink poppy beside the chair, the
cat
jumps into his lap
wanting, not food, but love,
the glass knocked over, the
second glass thrown at that exact spot .

        Admit: it had been a long time preparing,
now a long time gone . Nothing just happens. But
to cut onesself down when
there's nothing left to manipulate but the impulse to murder?

Solid panic is a state of normality
when you cannot blame anyone, not even yourself.
Just the fact, THE FACT!
Go over it step by step, repeat, go
over it in utter despair, turn
the mind-machine on, let it run,
feed the data into the computer,
whirr –
                whirr .
—Can you tell me what difference it makes?
                    —Yes. None.
        —You're a fool.
                    —You're another!

Dust devils spin down the road.
Every 10th building, every 5th
corner, every 2nd
mountain is the knife . How
        recover the town to himself
        —no, not with her— for

his own annihilated, powerless, murderous self? How
give up any thought of final recovery
any victory, even over himself?
give up even the defeat and sit
at a wooden table in a strange
land, murdering flies dully
with a flyswatter and his left hand?

How come to it with the inexhaustible world of phantoms on his back
pressing in the repetitious fact—nothing
he can say or do
will make the slightest difference to her?

Going OVER that road step by step
until he knows it like his broken hand,
living symbol of his impotence,
a right arm broken in two places, and
everytime there's a twinge in the interosteol musculature, the

pickup truck will return, with the
sound of a glass smashing, with
the hysterical vision of a wet rock
and a pink flower in the identical spot a week later .

So he murders flies, throws
the dead cigarette away and lights
another.

A sweet potato
in water
in the bowl in front of him
grows into a forest of green, cuneate leaves,
al-most unbelievably .
From every eye of the inert thing, dark
blooded stems growing pale toward the top
rise,
then the leaves,

light green on the younger ones, dark green on the rest,
all turned
toward the light from the kitchen window .
A jungle rises out of that inert potato
not/dead, clearly, tho it not move .

O, LOVE!

Smoke
rises from between the first and middle fingers of his left hand
which came to life,
so passive it was before .
He rises and opens the door to a
courtyard full of trees and birds.
Sounds of the wakening city come in .
But the laurel has one pink blossom. He

returns to the chair
& murders a few more flies .

[1964/72]

TWO POEMS BY BERNART DE VENTADORN
(translated from the Provençal)

CAN VEI LA LAUZETA MOVER

When I see the lark stir her wings for joy
against the sunlight,
forgetting herself,
letting herself
fall
with the sweetness that comes into her heart,
AIE!
so great an envy comes on me to see her rejoicing
I wonder that my heart does not melt with desiring.

Hell, I
who thought I knew so much of love,
know so little:

and cannot keep from loving her whose favors
I shall not have. And she
has all my heart and all myself and all herself and
all the world, has
robbed my heart from me and left me
not a thing but my desire
and a desiring heart.

It having been granted me,
permission,
having been allowed my moment to look
into her eyes,
since I saw reflected in those eyes
my image / that
image has held the power, not myself!
Since that mirage, my glass, influx of breath
ravages my innards:
Narcissus at the spring, I kill
this human self.

Really, though, without hope over the ladies;
never again trust myself to them.
I used to be their champion but
now I quit them entire. Not
one of them helps me against her who
destroys and confounds me,
fear and disbelieve all of them,
all the same cut.

And in this my lady appears very much a woman
for which I reproach her.
She thinks one should not want what is forbidden him.
It happens. And here
I have fallen in bad grace,
I have acted like the fool on the bridge.
I don't know why it happens to me unless
I climb too hard against the mountain.

The chance for grace has been lost, I shall not taste it,
for she who should have it most has hardly any, and
where else shall I seek it?

It is bitter for me to look on her
who lets a helpless wretch die of his desire
                                        and will not aid him.
          He will have nothing without her.

But I have no right, and no pity or prayer
          can avail me with my lady:
since my loving does not please her, I shall
          speak no more to her of it,
so take my leave, sever myself from her, she
                    has killed me,
          answer her like a corpse, she
                    does not keep me,
go away into exile, I
                    don't even know where.

                    Tristans, you'll have no more of me.
                    I'm going away with my misery,
                         don't know where.
                    I'm giving up my songs and
                         going off to hide
                    from all love, from all joy.

CHANTARS NO POT GAIRE VALER

It is worthless to write a line
if the song proceed not from the heart:
nor can the song come from the heart
if there is no love in it.

Maligning fools, failing all else, brag,
but love does not spoil,
but countered by love, fills,
     fulfilling grows firm.
A fool's love is like verse poor in the making,
only appearance and the name having,
for it loves nothing except itself, can
               take nothing of good,
               corrupts the rhyme.

And their singing is not worth a dime
whose song comes not from the heart.
If love has not set his roots there
the song cannot put forth shoots there: so
my song is superior, for I turn to it
mouth   eyes   mind   heart
and there is the joy of love in it.
And the binding glance is food for it
and the barter of sighs is food for it
and if desire is not equal between them
there is no good in it.

God grants me no strictness to counter my desire
yet I wonder if we afford its acceptance,
responsible for what we have of it. Though
                    each day goes badly for me.
Fine thought at least will I have from it
                    though no other thing:
for I have not a good heart and I work at it,
a man with nothing.

Yet she has made me rich, a man with nothing.
Beautiful she is and comely, and the more
I see her openness and fresh body, the more
                    I need her and have smarting.
Yet so seldom her fine eyes look on me
one day must last me a hundred.
                    Yet her fine body—
when I gaze on it, I
grow like a canso, perfect.
And, if desire is equal between us
and the darkness enters my throat?

[1954–71/1978]

Robert Creeley

MAZATLÁN: SEA

The sea flat out,
the light far out,
sky red, the
blobs of dark clouds
seem closer, beyond
the far lateral of
extended sea.

•

Shimmer of reflected
sand tones, the flat
ripples as the water
moves back—an oscil-
lation, endlessly in-
stinct movement—leaves
a ribbing after itself
it then returns to.

•

Bird flicker, light
sharp, flat—the
green hills of the two
islands make a familiar
measure, momently seen.

•

The air is thick
and wet and
comfortably encloses
with the sea's sounds.

•

Sleep—it washes
away.

KIDS WALKING beach,
minnow pools—
who knows which.

•

Nothing grand—
The scale is neither
big nor small.

•

Want to get the sense of "I" into Zukofsky's
"eye"—a locus of experience, not a presumption
of expected value.

•

Here now—
begin!

BOBBIE

Crazy kid-face
skun, in water—
wide hips. The white,
white skin—a big
eared almost feral
toothed woman—
lovely in all particulars.

•

Other way—dark
eyed, the face a
glow of some other
experience, deepens
in the air.

AGH—MAN
thinks.

•

Moving away in time,
as they say: *days*
later. Later than this—
what swings in the day's
particulars, one to one.

•

An unexamined hump
at first of no
interest lifting out
of the beach at
last devoured us all.

•

Sell the motherfucker for
several hundred dollars.

•

"...I ran out of my cabin, both glad and frightened, shouting, 'A noble earthquake! A noble earthquake!' feeling sure I was going to learn something." [John Muir, *The Yosemite,* p. 59.]

THE KICK
of the foot against...

•

Make time
of irritations,
looking for the
recurrence—

waiting, waiting,
on the edge of its
to be there
where it was, waiting.

•

Moving in the mind's
patterns, recognized
because there is where
they happen.

•

Grease
on the hands—

Four

Before I die.
Before I die.
Before I die.
Before I die.

How that fact of
seeing someone you love away
from you in time will
disappear in time, too.

•

Here is all there is,
but *there* seems so
insistently across the way.

•

Heal it, be
patient with
it—be quiet.

•

Across the
table,
years.

HERE

Past time—those
memories opened
places and minds,
things and such reassurance—

now the twist,
and what was a road
turns to a circle
with nothing behind.

•

I didn't know what I could do.
I have never known it
but in doing found it
as best I could.

Here I am still,
waiting for that discovery.
What morning, what way now,
will be its token.

•

They all walk by
on the beach,
large, or little,
crippled, on the face
of the earth.

•

The wind holds
my leg like

a warm hand.

SOME NIGHTS, a fearful
waking—beside me
you were sleeping,
what your body was

a quiet, apparent
containment. All the world is
this tension, you or me,
seen in that mirror,

patent, pathetic, insured.
I grow bored with lives
of such orders—my own
the least if even yours the most.

•

No one lives in
the life of another—
no one knows.

In the singular
the many cohere,
but not to know it.

Here, here, the body
screaming its orders,
learns of its own.

•

What would you have
of the princess—
large ears, to hear?
Hands with soft fingers?

You will ride away
into the forest, you will
meet her there
but you will know her.

Why not another
not expected, some
lovely presence suddenly
declared?

All in your mind
the body is, and of
the body such
you make her.

•

One, two,
is the rule—

from there to three
simple enough.

Now four
makes the door

back again
to one and one.

•

My plan is
these little boxes
make sequences...

•

Lift me
from such I
makes such declaration.

•

Hearing it—*snivelling*—
wanting the reassurance of
another's decision.

There is no one precedes—
look ahead—and behind
you have only where you were.

YOU SEE the jerked
movement, in the
rigid frame, the
boy—the tense stricken

animal, and behind,
the sea moves and
relaxes. The island sits
in its immovable comfort.

What, in the head, goes wrong—
the circuit suddenly
charged with contraries,
and time only is left.

•

The sun drops. The swimmers
grow black in the silver
glitter. The water slurs
and recurs. The air is soft.

COULD WRITE of fucking—
rather its instant or the slow
longing at times of its approach—

how the young man desires,
how, older, it is never known
but, familiar, comes to be so.

How your breasts, love,
fall in rhythm also familiar,
neither tired nor so young they

push forward. I hate the metaphors.
I want you. I am still alone,
but want you with me.

LISTLESS,
the heat rises—
the whole beach

vacant,
sluggish.
The forms shift

before we know,
before we thought
to know it.

The mind
again, the manner
of mind in the

body, the
weather, the waves,
the sun grows lower

in the faded
sky. Washed
out—the afternoon

of another day
with other people,
looking out of other eyes.

Only the
children, the sea,
the slight wind move

with the
same insistent
particularity.

•

I was sleeping
and saw the context
of people, dense
around me, talked
into their forms, almost

strident. There were
bright colors, intense
voices. We were, like
they say, discussing

some point of procedure—
would they go, or
come—and waking,
no one but my wife there,
the room faint, bare.

•

"It's strange. It's
all fallen
to grey."

•

How much
money is
there now?

•

Count it
again. There's
enough.

•

What changes.
Is the weather
all there is.

Such strangeness of mind I know
I cannot find there more
than what I know.

I am tired of purposes,
intent that leads itself
back to its own belief. I want

nothing more of such brilliance
but what makes the shadows darker
and that fire grow dimmer.

•

Counting age as form
I feel the mark of one
who has been born and grown
to a little past return.

The body will not go
apart from itself to be
another possibility.
It lives where it finds home.

Thinking to alter all
I looked first to myself,
but have learned the foolishness
that wants an altered form.

Here now I am at best,
or what I think I am
must follow as the rest
and live the best it can.

•

There was no one there.
Rather I thought I saw her,
and named her beauty.

For that time we lived
all in my mind
with what time gives.

The substance of one
is not two. No thought
can ever come to that.

I could fashion another
were I to lose her.
Such is thought.

•

Why the echo of
the old music
haunting all? Why

the lift and fall
of the old rhythms,
and aches and pains.

Why one, why two,
why not go utterly
away from all of it.

•

Last night's dream of a complex of people, almost suburban it seemed, with plots to uncover like a thriller. One moment as we walk to some house through the dark, a man suddenly appears behind us who throws himself at us, arms reaching out, but falls short and lands, skids, spread-eagled on the sidewalk. Then later, in another dream, we are bringing beer somewhere on a sort of truck, rather the cab of one, nothing back of it, and I am hanging on the side which I realize is little more than a scaffolding—and the wheels nearly brush me in turning. Then, much later, I hear our dog yelp—three times it now seems—so vividly I'm awake and thinking he must be outside the door of this room though he is literally in another country. Reading Yeats: "May we not learn some day to rewrite our histories, when they touch upon these things?"

WHEN HE and I,
after drinking and
talking, approached
the goddess or woman

become her, and by my
insistence entered
her, and in the ease
and delight of the

meeting I was given that
sight gave me myself,
this was the mystery
I had come to—all

manner of men, a
throng, and bodies of
women, writhing, and
a great though seemingly

silent sound—and when
I left the room to them,
I felt, as though hearing
laughter, my own heart lighten.

•

What do you do,
what do you say,
what do you think,
what do you know.

[1969]

Allen Ginsberg

THE CHANGE: *KYOTO-TOKYO EXPRESS*

I

Black Magicians
Come home: the pink meat image
        black yellow image with
        ten fingers and two eyes
is gigantic already: the black
        curly pubic hair, the
        blind hollow stomach,
the silent soft open vagina
        rare womb of new birth
cock lone and happy to be home
                                again
touched by hands by mouths,
        by hairy lips—

Close the portals of the festival?

Open the portals to what Is,
The mattress covered with sheets,
        soft pillows of skin,
long soft hair and delicate
        palms along the buttocks
        timidly touching,
waiting for a sign, a throb
        softness of balls, rough
        nipples alone in the dark
        met by a weird finger;

Tears allright, and laughter
    allright
I am that I am—

        Closed off from this
The schemes begin, roulette,
    brainwaves, bony dice,
    Stroboscope motorcycles
    Stereoscopic Scaly
      Serpents winding thru
        cloud spaces of
          what is not—

"...convoluted, lunging upon
a pismire, a conflagration, a—"

II

Shit! Intestines boiling in sand fire
    creep yellow brain cold sweat
    earth unbalanced vomit thru
    tears, snot ganglia buzzing
    the Electric Snake rising hypnotic
    shuffling metal-eyed coils
    whirling rings within wheels
    from asshole up the spine
    Acid in the throat the chest
    a knot trembling Swallow back
    the black furry ball of the great
    Fear

Oh!

The serpent in my bed pitiful
    crawling unwanted babes of
    snake covered with veins and pores
    breathing heavy frightened love
    metallic Bethlehem out the window
    the lost, the lost hungry

ghosts here alive trapped
in carpet rooms   How can I
be sent to Hell
with my skin and blood

Oh I remember myself so

Gasping, staring at dawn over
lower Manhattan   the bridges
covered with rust, the slime
in my mouth & ass, sucking
his cock like a baby crying Fuck
me in my asshole   Make love
to this rotten slave   Give me the
power to whip & eat your heart
I own your belly & your eyes
I speak thru your screaming
mouth Black Mantra Fuck you
Fuck me Mother Brother Friend
old white haired creep shuddering in
the toilet slum bath floorboards—

Oh how wounded, how wounded, I
murder the beautiful chinese women

It will come on the railroad, beneath
the wheels, in drunken hate screaming
thru the skinny machine gun, it will
come out of the mouth of the pilot
the dry lipped diplomat, the hairy
teacher will come out of me
again shitting the meat out of
my ears on my cancer deathbed

Oh crying man crying woman
crying guerrilla shopkeeper
crying dysentery boneface on
the urinal street of the Self

Oh Negro beaten in the eye in my
home, oh black magicians
in white skin robes boiling the
stomachs of your children that
you do not die but shudder in
Serpent & worm shape forever
Powerful minds & superhuman
Roar of volcano & rocket in
Your bowels—

Hail to your fierce desire, your
Godly pride, my Heaven's gate
will not be closed until
we enter all—

All human shapes, all
trembling donkeys & apes, all
lovers turned to ghost
all achers on trains &
taxicab bodies sped away
from date with desire, old movies,
all who were refused—

All which was rejected, the
leper-sexed hungry of
nazi conventions, hollow
cheeked arab marxists of Acco
Crusaders dying of starvation
in the Holy Land—

Seeking the Great Spirit of the
Universe in Terrible Godly
form, O suffering Jews
burned in the hopeless fire
O thin Bengali sadhus adoring
Kali mother hung with
nightmare skulls O Myself
under her pounding
feet!

Yes I am that worm soul under
the heel of the daemon horses
I am that man trembling to die
in vomit & trance in bamboo
eternities belly ripped by
red hands of courteous
chinamen kids—Come sweetly
now back to my Self as I was—

Allen Ginsberg says this: I am
a mass of sores and worms
& baldness & belly & smell
I am false Name the prey
of Yamantaka Devourer of
Strange dreams, the prey of
radiation & Police Hells of Law

I am that I am I am the
man & the Adam of hair in
my loins This is my spirit and
physical shape I inhabit
this Universe Oh weeping
against what is my
own nature for now

Who would deny his own shape's
loveliness in his
dream moment of bed
Who sees his desire to be
horrible instead of Him

Who is, who cringes, perishes,
is reborn a red Screaming
baby? Who cringes before
that meaty shape in
Fear?

In this dream I am the Dreamer
and the Dreamed I am
that I am Ah but I have
always known

oooh for the hate I have spent
in denying my image & cursing
the breasts of illusion—
Screaming at murderers, trembling
between their legs in fear of the
steel pistols of my mortality—

Come, sweet lonely Spirit, back
to your bodies, come great God
back to your only image, come
to your many eyes & breasts,
come thru thought and
motion up all your
arms the great gesture of
Peace & acceptance Abhaya
Mudra Mudra of fearlessness
Mudra of Elephant Calmed &
war-fear ended forever!

The war, the war on Man, the
war on woman, the ghost
assembled armies vanish in
their realms

Chinese American Bardo Thodols
all the seventy hundred hells from
Orleans to Algeria tremble
with tender soldiers weeping

In Russia the young poets rise
to kiss the soul of the revolution
in Vietnam the body is burned
to show the truth of only the
body in Kremlin & White House
the schemers draw back
weeping from their schemes—

In my train seat I renounce
my power, so that I do
live I will die

Over for now the Vomit, cut
up & pincers in the skull,
fear of bones, grasp
against man woman & babe.

Let the dragon of Death
come forth from his
picture in the whirling
white clouds' darkness

And suck dream brains &
claim these lambs for his
meat, and let him feed
and be other than I

Till my turn comes and I
enter that maw and change
to a blind rock covered
with misty ferns that
I am not all now

but a universe of skin and breath
& changing thought and
burning hand & softened
heart in the old bed of
my skin From this single
birth reborn that I am
to be so—

My own Identity now nameless
neither man nor dragon or
God

but the dreaming Me full
of physical rays' tender
red moons in my belly &
Stars in my eyes circling

And the Sun the Sun the
Sun my visible father
making my body visible
thru my eyes!

[Tokyo, July 18, 1963]

WALES VISITATION

White fog lifting & falling on mountain-brow
Trees moving in rivers of wind
The clouds arise
as on a wave, gigantic eddy lifting mist
above teeming ferns exquisitely swayed
along a green crag
glimpsed thru mullioned glass in valley raine—

Bardic, O Self, Visitacione, tell naught
but what seen by one man in a vale in Albion,
of the folk, whose physical sciences end in Ecology,
the wisdom of earthly relations,
of mouths & eyes interknit ten centuries visible
orchards of mind language manifest human,
of the satanic thistle that raises its horned symmetry
flowering above sister grass-daisies' pink tiny
bloomlets angelic as lightbulbs—

Remember 160 miles from London's symmetrical thorned tower
& network of TV pictures flashing bearded your Self
the lambs on the tree-nooked hillside this day bleating
heard in Blake's old ear, & the silent thought of Wordsworth in eld
Stillness
clouds passing through skeleton arches of Tintern Abbey—
Bard Nameless as the Vast, babble to Vastness!

All the Valley quivered, one extended motion, wind
undulating on mossy hills
a giant wash that sank white fog delicately down red runnels
on the mountainside
whose leaf-branch tendrils moved asway
in granitic undertow down—
and lifted the floating Nebulous upward, and lifted the arms of the trees
and lifted the grasses an instant in balance
and lifted the lambs to hold still
and lifted the green of the hill, in one solemn wave

A solid mass of Heaven, mist-infused, ebbs thru the vale,
a wavelet of Immensity, lapping gigantic through Llanthony Valley,
the length of all England, valley upon valley under Heaven's ocean
tonned with cloud-hang,
—Heaven balanced on a grassblade.
Roar of the mountain wind slow, sigh of the body,
One Being on the mountainside stirring gently
Exquisite scales trembling everywhere in balance,
one motion thru the cloudy sky-floor shifting on the million feet of daisies,
one Majesty the motion that stirred wet grass quivering
to the farthest tendril of white fog poured down
through shivering flowers on the mountain's head—

No imperfection in the budded mountain,
Valleys breathe, heaven and earth move together,
daisies push inches of yellow air, vegetables tremble,
grass shimmers green
sheep speckle the mountainside, revolving their jaws with empty eyes,
horses dance in the warm rain,
tree-lined canals network live farmland,
blueberries fringe stone walls on hawthorn'd hills,
pheasants croak on meadows haired with fern—
Out, out on the hillside, into the ocean sound, into delicate gusts of wet air,
Fall on the ground, O great Wetness, O Mother, No harm on your body!
Stare close, no imperfection in the grass,
each flower Buddha-eye, repeating the story,
myriad-formed—
Kneel before the foxglove raising green buds, mauve bells drooped
doubled down the stem trembling antennae,
& look in the eyes of the branded lambs that stare
breathing stockstill under dripping hawthorn—
I lay down mixing my beard with the wet hair of the mountainside,
smelling the brown vagina-moist ground, harmless,
tasting the violet thistle-hair, sweetness—
One being so balanced, so vast, that its softest breath
moves every floweret in the stillness on the valley floor,
trembles lamb-hair hung gossamer rain-beaded in the grass,

lifts trees on their roots, birds in the great draught
hiding their strength in the rain, bearing same weight,

Groan thru breast and neck, a great Oh! to earth heart
Calling our Presence together
The great secret is no secret
Senses fit the winds,
Visible is visible,
rain-mist curtains wave through the bearded vale,
gray atoms wet the wind's kabbala
Crosslegged on a rock in dusk rain,
rubber booted in soft grass, mind moveless,
breath trembles in white daisies by the roadside,
Heaven breath and my own symmetric
Airs wavering thru antlered green fern
drawn in my navel, same breath as breathes thru Capel-Y-Ffn,
Sounds of Aleph and Aum
through forests of gristle,
my skull and Lord Hereford's Knob equal,
All Albion one.

What did I notice? Particulars! The
vision of the great One is myriad—
smoke curls upward from ashtray,
house fire burned low,
The night, still wet & moody black heaven
starless
upward in motion with wet wind.

[July 29, 1967 (LSD)—August 3, 1967 (London)]

Frank O'Hara

IN MEMORY OF MY FEELINGS

To Grace Hartigan

1

My quietness has a man in it, he is transparent
and he carries me quietly, like a gondola, through the streets.
He has several likenesses, like stars and years, like numerals.

My quietness has a number of naked selves,
so many pistols I have borrowed to protect myselves
from creatures who too readily recognize my weapons
and have murder in their heart!
                                                  though in winter
they are warm as roses, in the desert
taste of chilled anisette
                                    At times, withdrawn,
I rise into the cool skies
and gaze on at the imponderable world with the simple identification
of my colleagues, the mountains. Manfred climbs to my nape,
speaks, but I do not hear him,
                                                  I'm too blue.
An elephant takes up his trumpet,
money flutters from the windows of cries, silk stretching its mirror
across shoulder blades. A gun is "fired."
                                                            One of me rushes
to window #13 and one of me raises his whip and one of me
flutters up from the center of the track amidst the pink flamingoes,
and underneath their hooves as they round the last turn my lips
are scarred and brown, brushed by tails, masked in dirt's lust,
definition, open mouths gasping for the cries of the bettors for the lungs
of earth.

So many of my transparencies could not resist the race!
Terror in earth, dried mushrooms, pink feathers, tickets,
a flaking moon drifting across the muddied teeth,
the imperceptible moan of covered breathing,
love of the serpent!
I am underneath its leaves as the hunter crackles and pants
and bursts, as the barrage balloon drifts behind a cloud
and animal death whips out its flashlight,
whistling
and slipping the glove off the trigger hand. The serpent's eyes
redden at sight of those thorny fingernails, he is so smooth!
My transparent selves
flail about like vipers in a pail, writhing and hissing
without panic, with a certain justice of response
and presently the aquiline serpent comes to resemble the Medusa.

2

The dead hunting
and the alive, ahunted.
My father, my uncle,
my grand-uncle and the several aunts. My
grand-aunt dying for me, like a talisman, in the war,
before I had even gone to Borneo
her blood vessels rushed to the surface
and burst like rockets over the wrinkled
invasion of the Australians, her eyes aslant
like the invaded, but blue like mine.
An atmosphere of supreme lucidity,
humanism,
the mere existence of emphasis,
a rusted barge
painted orange against the sea
full of Marines reciting the Arabian ideas
which are a proof in themselves of seasickness
which is a proof in itself of being hunted.
A hit? *ergo* swim.
My 10 my 19,
my 9, and the several years. My
12 years since they all died, philosophically speaking.

And now the coolness of a mind
like a shuttered suite in the Grand Hotel
where mail arrives for my incognito,
                                                            whose façade
has been slipping into the Grand Canal for centuries;
rockets splay over a *sposalizio,*
                                                    fleeing into night
from their Chinese memories, and it is a celebration,
the trying desperately to count them as they die.
But who will stay to be these numbers
when all the lights are dead?

3

The most arid stretch is often richest,
the hand lifting towards a fig tree from hunger
                                                                      digging
and there is water, clear, supple, or there
deep in the sand where death sleeps, a murmurous bubbling
proclaims the blackness that will ease and burn.
You preferred the Arabs? but they didn't stay to count
their inventions, racing into sands, converting themselves into
so many,
          embracing, at Ramadan, the tenderest effigies of
themselves with penises shorn by the hundreds, like a camel
ravishing a goat.
                                  And the mountainous-minded Greeks could speak
of time as a river and step across it into Persia, leaving the pain
at home to be converted into statuary. I adore the Roman copies.
And the stench of the camel's spit I swallow,
and the stench of the whole goat. For we have advanced, France,
together into a new land, like the Greeks, where one feels nostalgic
for mere ideas, where truth lies on its deathbed like an uncle
and one of me has a sentimental longing for number,
as has another for the ball gowns of the Directoire and yet
another for "Destiny, Paris, destiny!"
                                                        or "Only a king may kill a king."

How many selves are there in a war hero asleep in names? under
a blanket of platoon and fleet, orderly. For every seaman
with one eye closed in fear and twitching arm at a sigh for Lord Nelson,

he is all dead; and now a meek subaltern writhes in his bedclothes
with the fury of a thousand, violating an insane mistress
who has only herself to offer his multitudes.
Rising,
he wraps himself in the burnoose of memories against the heat of life
and over the sands he goes to take an algebraic position *in re*
a sun of fear shining not too bravely. He will ask himselves to
vote on fear before he feels a tremor,
as runners arrive from the mountains
bearing snow, proof that the mind's obsolescence is still capable
of intimacy. His mistress will follow him across the desert
like a goat, towards a mirage which is something familiar about
one of his innumerable wrists,
and lying in an oasis one day,
playing catch with coconuts, they suddenly smell oil.

4

Beneath these lives
the ardent lover of history hides,
tongue out
leaving a globe of spit on a taut spear of grass
and leaves off rattling his tail a moment
to admire this flag.
I'm looking for my Shanghai Lil.
Five years ago, enamored of fire-escapes, I went to Chicago,
an eventful trip: the fountains! the Art Institute, the Y
for both sexes, absent Christianity.
At 7, before Jane
was up, the copper lake stirred against the sides
of a Norwegian freighter; on the deck a few dirty men,
tired of night, watched themselves in the water
as years before the German prisoners on the *Prinz Eugen*
dappled the Pacific with their sores, painted purple
by a Naval doctor.
Beards growing, and the constant anxiety
over looks. I'll shave before she wakes up. Sam Goldwyn
spent $2,000,000 on Anna Sten, but Grushenka left America.
One of me is standing in the waves, an ocean bather,
or I am naked with a plate of devils at my hip.
Grace

to be born and live as variously as possible. The conception
of the masque barely suggests the sordid identifications.
I am a Hittite in love with a horse. I don't know what blood's
in me I feel like an African prince I am a girl walking downstairs
in a red pleated dress with heels I am a champion taking a fall
I am a jockey with a sprained ass-hole I am the light mist
                                        in which a face appears
and it is another face of blonde I am a baboon eating a banana
I am a dictator looking at his wife I am a doctor eating a child
and the child's mother smiling I am a Chinaman climbing a mountain
I am a child smelling his father's underwear I am an Indian
sleeping on a scalp
                        and my pony is stamping in the birches,
and I've just caught sight of the *Niña,* the *Pinta* and the *Santa María.*
                        What land is this, so free?
                                        I watch
the sea at the back of my eyes, near the spot where I think
in solitude as pine trees groan and support the enormous winds,
they are humming *L'Oiseau de feu!*
                              They look like gods, these whitemen,
and they are bringing me the horse I fell in love with on the frieze.

5

And now it is the serpent's turn.
I am not quite you, but almost, the opposite of visionary.
You are coiled around the central figure,
                                        the heart
that bubbles with red ghosts, since to move is to love
and the scrutiny of all things is syllogistic,
the startled eyes of the dikdik, the bush full of white flags
fleeing a hunter,
                        which is our democracy
                                        but the prey
is always fragile and like something, as a seashell can be
a great Courbet, if it wishes. To bend the ear of the outer world.
                                    When you turn your head
can you feel your heels, undulating? that's what it is
to be a serpent. I haven't told you of the most beautiful things
in my lives, and watching the ripple of their loss disappear
along the shore, underneath ferns,
                                  face downward in the ferns

my body, the naked host to my many selves, shot
by a guerrilla warrior or dumped from a car into ferns
which are themselves *journalières.*
The hero, trying to unhitch his parachute,
stumbles over me. It is our last embrace.
And yet
I have forgotten my loves, and chiefly that one, the cancerous
statue which my body could no longer contain,
against my will
against my love
become art,
I could not change it into history
and so remember it,
and I have lost what is always and everywhere
present, the scene of my selves, the occasion of these ruses,
which I myself and singly must now kill
and save the serpent in their midst.

[1956]

John Ashbery

INTO THE DUSK-CHARGED AIR

Far from the Rappahannock, the silent
Danube moves along toward the sea.
The brown and green Nile rolls slowly
Like the Niagara's welling descent.
Tractors stood on the green banks of the Loire
Near where it joined the Cher.
The St. Lawrence prods among black stones
And mud. But the Arno is all stones.
Wind ruffles the Hudson's
Surface. The Irawaddy is overflowing.
But the yellowish, gray Tiber
Is contained within steep banks. The Isar
Flows too fast to swim in, the Jordan's water
Courses over the flat land. The Allegheny and its boats
Were dark blue. The Moskowa is
Gray boats. The Amstel flows slowly.
Leaves Fall into the Connecticut as it passes
Underneath. The Liffey is full of sewage,
Like the Seine, but unlike
The brownish-yellow Dordogne.
Mountains hem in the Colorado
And the Oder is very deep, almost
As deep as the Congo is wide.
The plain banks of the Neva are
Gray. The dark Saône flows silently.
And the Volga is long and wide
As it flows across the brownish land. The Ebro
Is blue, and slow. The Shannon flows

Swiftly between its banks. The Mississippi
Is one of the world's longest rivers, like the Amazon.
It has the Missouri for a tributary.
The Harlem flows amid factories
And buildings. The Nelson is in Canada,
Flowing. Through hard banks the Dubawnt
Forces its way. People walk near the Trent.
The landscape around the Mohawk stretches away;
The Rubicon is merely a brook.
In winter the Main
Surges; the Rhine sings its eternal song.
The Rhône slogs along through whitish banks
And the Rio Grande spins tales of the past.
The Loir bursts its frozen shackles
But the Moldau's wet mud ensnares it.
The East catches the light.
Near the Escaut the noise of factories echoes
And the sinuous Humboldt gurgles wildly.
The Po too flows, and the many-colored
Thames. Into the Atlantic Ocean
Pours the Garonne. Few ships navigate
On the Housatonic, but quite a few can be seen
On the Elbe. For centuries
The Afton has flowed.
                                        If the Rio Negro
Could abandon its song, and the Magdalena
The jungle flowers, the Tagus
Would still flow serenely, and the Ohio
Abrade its slate banks. The tan Euphrates would
Sidle silently across the world. The Yukon
Was choked with ice, but the Susquehanna still pushed
Bravely along. The Dee caught the day's last flares
Like the Pilcomayo's carrion rose.
The Peace offered eternal fragrance
Perhaps, but the Mackenzie churned livid mud
Like tan chalk-marks. Near where
The Brahmaputra slapped swollen dikes
Was an opening through which the Limmat
Could have trickled. A young man strode the Churchill's
Banks, thinking of night. The Vistula seized

The shadows. The Theiss, stark mad, bubbled
In the windy evening. And the Ob shuffled
Crazily along. Fat billows encrusted the Dniester's
Pallid flood, and the Fraser's porous surface.
Fish gasped amid the Spree's reeds. A boat
Descended the bobbing Orinoco. When the
Marne flowed by the plants nodded
And above the glistering Gila
A sunset as beautiful as the Athabasca
Stammered. The Zambezi chimed. The Oxus
Flowed somewhere. The Paranaíba
Is flowing, like the wind-washed Cumberland.
The Araguaia flows in the rain.
And, through overlying rocks the Isère
Cascades gently. The Guadalquivir sputtered.
Someday time will confound the Indre,
Making a rill of the Huang Ho. And
The Potomac rumbles softly. Crested birds
Watch the Ucayali go
Through dreaming night. You cannot stop
The Yenisei. And afterwards
The White flows strongly to its...
Goal. If the Tyne's shores
Hold you, and the Albany
Arrest your development, can you resist the Red's
Musk, the Meuse's situation?
A particle of mud in the Neckar
Does not turn it black. You cannot
Like the Saskatchewan, nor refuse
The meandering Yangtze, unlease
The Genesee. Does the Scamander
Still irrigate crimson plains? And the Durance
And the Pechora? The São Francisco
Skulks amid gray, rubbery nettles. The Liard's
Reflexes are slow, and the Arkansas erodes
Anthracite hummocks. The Paraná stinks.
The Ottawa is light emerald green
Among grays. Better that the Indus fade
In steaming sands! Let the Brazos
Freeze solid! And the Wabash turn to a leaden

Cinder of ice! The Marañón is too tepid, we must
Find a way to freeze it hard. The Ural
Is freezing slowly in the blasts. The black Yonne
Congeals nicely. And the Petit-Morin
Curls up on the solid earth. The Inn
Does not remember better times, and the Merrimack's
Galvanized. The Ganges is liquid snow by now;
The Vyatka's ice-gray. The once-molten Tennessee's
Curdled. The Japurá is a pack of ice. Gelid
The Columbia's gray loam banks. The Don's merely
A giant icicle. The Niger freezes, slowly.
The interminable Lena plods on
But the Purus' mercurial waters are icy, grim
With cold. The Loing is choked with fragments of ice.
The Weser is frozen, like liquid air.
And so is the Kama. And the beige, thickly flowing
Tocantins. The rivers bask in the cold.
The stern Uruguay chafes its banks,
A mass of ice. The Hooghly is solid
Ice. The Adour is silent, motionless.
The lovely Tigris is nothing but scratchy ice
Like the Yellowstone, with its osier-clustered banks.
The Mekong is beginning to thaw out a little
And the Donets gurgles beneath the
Huge blocks of ice. The Manzanares gushes free.
The Illinois darts through the sunny air again.
But the Dnieper is still ice-bound. Somewhere
The Salado propels its floes, but the Roosevelt's
Frozen. The Oka is frozen solider
Than the Somme. The Minho slumbers
In winter, nor does the Snake
Remember August. Hilarious, the Canadian
Is solid ice. The Madeira slavers
Across the thawing fields, and the Plata laughs.
The Dvina soaks up the snow. The Sava's
Temperature is above freezing. The Avon
Carols noiselessly. The Drôme presses
Grass banks; the Adige's frozen
Surface is like gray pebbles.

Birds circle the Ticino. In winter
The Var was dark blue, unfrozen. The
Thwaite, cold, is choked with sandy ice;
The Ardèche glistens feebly through the freezing rain.

from THE SKATERS

IV

The wind thrashes the maple seed-pods,
The whole brilliant mass comes spattering down.

This is my fourteenth year as governor of C province.
I was little more than a lad when I first came here.
Now I am old but scarcely any wiser.
So little are white hair and a wrinkled forehead a sign of wisdom!

To slowly raise oneself
Hand over hand, lifting one's entire weight;
To forget there was a possibility
Of some more politic movement. That freedom, courage
And pleasant company could exist.
That has always been behind you.

And earlier litigation: wind hard in the tops
Of the baggy eucalyptus branches.

Today I wrote, "The spring is late this year.
In the early mornings there is hoarfrost on the water meadows.
And on the highway the frozen ruts are papered over with ice."

The day was gloves.

How far from the usual statement
About time, ice—the weather itself had gone.

I mean this. Through the years
You have approached an inventory
And it is now that tomorrow

Is going to be the climax of your casual
Statement about yourself, begun
So long ago in humility and false quietude.

The sands are frantic
In the hourglass. But there is time
To change, to utterly destroy
That too-familiar image
Lurking in the glass
Each morning, at the edge of the mirror.

The train is still sitting in the station.
You only dreamed it was in motion.

There are a few travelers on Z high road.
Behind a shutter, two black eyes are watching them.
They belong to the wife of P, the high-school principal.

The screen door bangs in the wind, one of the hinges is loose.
And together we look back at the house.
It could use a coat of paint
Except than I am too poor to hire a workman.
I have all I can do to keep body and soul together
And soon, even that relatively simple task may prove to be beyond my
powers.

That was a good joke you played on the other guests.
A joke of silence.

One seizes these moments as they come along, afraid
To believe too much in the happiness that might result
Or confide too much of one's love and fear, even in
Oneself.

The spring, though mild, is incredibly wet.
I have spent the afternoon blowing soap bubbles
And it is with a feeling of delight I realize I am
All alone in the skittish darkness.
The birch-pods come clattering down on the weed-grown marble
pavement.
And a curl of smoke stands above the triangular wooden roof.

Seventeen years in the capital of Foo-Yung province!
Surely woman was born for something
Besides continual fornication, retarded only by menstrual cramps.

I had thought of announcing my engagement to you
On the day of the first full moon of X month.

The wind has stopped, but the magnolia blossoms still
Fall with a plop onto the dry, spongy earth.
The evening air is pestiferous with midges.

There is only one way of completing the puzzle:
By finding a hog-shaped piece that is light green shading to buff at one side.

It is the beginning of March, a few
Russet and yellow wallflowers are blooming in the border
Protected by moss-grown, fragmentary masonry.

One morning you appear at breakfast
Dressed, as for a journey, in your worst suit of clothes.
And over a pot of coffee, or, more accurately, rusted water
Announce your intention of leaving me alone in this cistern-like house.
In your own best interests I shall decide not to believe you.

I think there is a funny sand bar
Beyond the old boardwalk
Your intrigue makes you understand.

"At thirty-two I came up to take my examination at the university.
The U wax factory, it seemed, wanted a new general manager.
I was the sole applicant for the job, but it was refused me.
So I have preferred to finish my life
In the quietude of this floral retreat."

The tiresome old man is telling us his life story.

Trout are circling under water—

Masters of eloquence
Glisten on the pages of your book
Like mountains veiled by water or the sky.

The "second position"
Comes in the seventeenth year
Watching the meaningless gyrations of flies above a sill.

Heads in hands, waterfall of simplicity.
The delta of living into everything.

The pump is busted. I shall have to get it fixed.

Your knotted hair
Around your shoulders
A shawl the color of the spectrum

Like that marvelous thing you haven't learned yet.

To refuse the square hive,
postpone the highest. . .

The apples are all getting tinted
In the cool light of autumn.

The constellations are rising
In perfect order: Taurus, Leo, Gemini.

[1966]

SYRINGA

Orpheus liked the glad personal quality
Of the things beneath the sky. Of course, Eurydice was a part
Of this. Then one day, everything changed. He rends
Rocks into fissures with lament. Gullies, hummocks
Can't withstand it. The sky shudders from one horizon
To the other, almost ready to give up wholeness.
Then Apollo quietly told him: "Leave it all on earth.
Your lute, what point? Why pick at a dull pavan few care to
Follow, except a few birds of dusty feather,
Not vivid performances of the past." But why not?

All other things must change too.
The seasons are no longer what they once were,
But it is the nature of things to be seen only once,
As they happen along, bumping into other things, getting along
Somehow. That's where Orpheus made his mistake.
Of course Eurydice vanished into the shade;
She would have even if he hadn't turned around.
No use standing there like a gray stone toga as the whole wheel
Of recorded history flashes past, struck dumb, unable to utter an intelligent
Comment on the most thought-provoking element in its train.
Only love stays on the brain, and something these people,
These other ones, call life. Singing accurately
So that the notes mount straight up out of the well of
Dim noon and rival the tiny, sparkling yellow flowers
Growing around the brink of the quarry, encapsulates
The different weights of the things.
But it isn't enough
To just go on singing. Orpheus realized this
And didn't mind so much about his reward being in heaven
After the Bacchantes had torn him apart, driven
Half out of their minds by his music, what it was doing to them.
Some say it was for his treatment of Eurydice.
But probably the music had more to do with it, and
The way music passes, emblematic
Of life and how you cannot isolate a note of it
And say it is good or bad. You must
Wait till it's over. "The end crowns all,"
Meaning also that the "tableau"
Is wrong. For although memories, of a season, for example,
Melt into a single snapshot, one cannot guard, treasure
That stalled moment. It too is flowing, fleeting;
It is a picture of flowing, scenery, though living, mortal,
Over which an abstract action is laid out in blunt,
Harsh strokes. And to ask more than this
Is to become the tossing reeds of that slow,
Powerful stream, the trailing grasses
Playfully tugged at, but to participate in the action
No more than this. Then in the lowering gentian sky
Electric twitches are faintly apparent first, then burst forth
Into a shower of fixed, cream-colored flares. The horses

Have each seen a share of the truth, though each thinks,
"I'm a maverick. Nothing of this is happening to me,
Though I can understand the language of birds, and
The itinerary of the lights caught in the storm is fully apparent to me.
Their jousting ends in music much
As trees move more easily in the wind after a summer storm
And is happening in lacy shadows of shore-trees, now, day after day."

But how late to be regretting all this, even
Bearing in mind that regrets are always late, too late!
To which Orpheus, a bluish cloud with white contours,
Replies that these are of course not regrets at all,
Merely a careful, scholarly setting down of
Unquestioned facts, a record of pebbles along the way.
And no matter how all this disappeared,
Or got where it was going, it is no longer
Material for a poem. Its subject
Matters too much, and not enough, standing there helplessly
While the poem streaked by, its tail afire, a bad
Comet screaming hate and disaster, but so turned inward
That the meaning, good or other, can never
Become known. The singer thinks
Constructively, builds up his chant in progressive stages
Like a skyscraper, but at the last minute turns away.
The song is engulfed in an instant in blackness
Which must in turn flood the whole continent
With blackness, for it cannot see. The singer
Must then pass out of sight, not even relieved
Of the evil burthen of the words. Stellification
Is for the few, and comes about much later
When all record of these people and their lives
Has disappeared into libraries, onto microfilm.
A few are still interested in them. "But what about
So-and-so?" is still asked on occasion. But they lie
Frozen and out of touch until an arbitrary chorus
Speaks of a totally different incident with a similar name
In whose tale are hidden syllables
Of what happened so long before that
In some small town, one indifferent summer.

[1977]

Nathaniel Tarn

from *Lyrics for the Bride of God*:

SECTION: AMERICA (2): SEEN AS A BIRD

The light in the skull of the bird
tugging her down
she'll fly by the rest of her life,
mirror of sky among leaves,
in low grasses at morning,
mirror of high sky in low and of heaven in high
along the milky way—
her eye: the order of the heavens
falling / falling with the weight of damp stars
down flocks of other birds
down through t.v. antennae
funnel of space
above the house at last
great fields of light above her
over Cape May

Birds in layers on the sky
a flock of certain birds above a flock of others and besides
yet a third flock
kettle of broadwing on the spiral air
cut to the quick by geese along the shore
and here the blackbirds scatter like ink-shot—
the sky has great depth
the depth opens on without end higher and higher

Alighieri describing the major angels as birds of God:

Take here the little birds for the kingdom of heaven,
the little birds for the banners of God—
and say what we love about them is simply the system:
that they are all of one set, yet different colored,
id est—diversity within unity, heraldic counterpoint
of certain colors where others are expected to be
—my dream as a child, the interchange of colors—
what gives my mind peace, my mind peace, my mind peace

immense fields of light traversed by angels

/ / / over Cape May...

II

Seeing her as a bird,
looking within that mind
for the cut of our sparks in each mirror shard,
her flight breaks over and over
as she tumbles down
through cloud, through stricken dawn-dark, and bait and lure,
TO
if she be (for example) that one-eyed falcon, sparrow-hawk,
bird of the year,
so must in nest have lost
one half of strike-force within the head
yet falls on sodden sparrow in his trap
waiting her tear of talons and her take
his cheep towards
his and her father both.

We'll have, above all, her movement
and her descent, layer on layer,
through the bright cloud of our blood
and the exact description of her rapine
when she comes to fetch us
fingernail by fingernail

I mean of course talon.

Look long ago the sky had many birds
look long ago the sky had many colors

and now we have the chicken only
and the sparrow like an aerial rat.
We mourn like antiquarians for the world's colors
while the rest of the world makes do.

III

And she is bird, falling,
and I am bird, passing from behind that branch
to this branch in front of your eyes, and you are bird,
hopping to middle branches in a three-tiered forest
and he is bird flits to the first branch in the foreground of /
your alien life under heavenhome:

and they all mirror each other, looking with bright eye
periscope to the shard of the inner mind,
at the tone of your color today bright cousin,
and the shade of your tint tomorrow, bright female cousin—
and, by God, I think they talk, Alice would say that morning
as she broiled the two budgerigars side by side on a spit.

while the white heart of the sky, ignorant of all color
arched over, archangelical
throbs in restricted place
the pure white heart pulsating where it borned
with rims of mourning

Elánus leucúrus, minute particular,
Coyote Hills, on San Francisco Bay,
November seven-one (great bird of God)

goes into somersault
revised and held thereafter
and, looking down—
buckle of elbow forward
drag back of pinions in the wind
slow crash at twilight angles—

(the planes in circles overhead, ever diminishing)

slow fall to grasses like the dying snow.

[1975]

JOURNAL OF THE LAGUNA DE SAN IGNACIO

Immense architecture
building in air
towers and palaces
from which their eyes look out,
star denizens
living in the heights
as they live below
building in air
and undersea
their passage through our life—
　　　　　　a gentle glide
like a dream
because no thing men know
so huge and gentle at once
can be other than dream
　　　in such a world.
Whales breathing
all around us in the night
just beyond the lights,
ghost gulls
following the ship
which seems to breathe
yet never moves
against the great Pacific's
unfathomable shoulders

*

The mountains rise out of the desert
way out over Baja
the whales rise out of the sea
the mountains rise out of the sea
the whales rise out of the desert
the whales are taller than the mountains

*

There was a man one time
got buried in a whale they say,
found bed and board down there
also some breakfast,
found desk and library
and was granted extra knowledge
    (the whale a shaman they say).
        Cast from the human city,
he went down to the sea in whales
clothed with all his grave clothes
collected over the years
complete with turquoise necklace
and jadeite necklace
and one bead of jade—
his body full of sweet winds,
        he lay inside the whale
and wrote, in his death, terrible hymns
which no amount of pain
had ever torn from him,
wrenched from his mouth
out through his teeth
            in his mind's hearing

*

Touching the skin of water
as it glides against water
slow slip of time
the black flesh gleaming like a hull
            (they call it Grey)
mottled with barnacles,
the imaginary touch
which men could have touched for centuries
                (instead of the carnage)
as it took them so long
to come to the beaches
to come to the sea
to come to the mountains

*

Birds of America
we rendezvous with all of you
in Baja of the sweet blue skies
streaked with the grey and sand.
            From south you call,
            from north,
            up and down your flyways,
and visit here, on the desert floor,
where my love is collecting shells,
      shells of one kind
            Mound of Venus shells,
and laying them out in a pattern
facing into the wind
as if she were making a book
for birds to read.
            All morning she is at it
peacefully, like a worker,
while I walk my fears
from one beach to another
stilling them with the sight of birds.
   At the end,
she places three pelican plumes
at the head of her pattern
facing the Santa Clara mountains.
The very next tide
will take this prayer
back to the sea

*

Vagaries of the sea life.
My bunk is so short
I need to lose head or feet
and its sky is so low
I have to be fitted into it
like a dime into a slot machine.
If you come into the cabin
you break my back,
if I come in, I break yours.
We have bruised elbows.

Nowhere to sit and read,
the lights don't work.
Water floods in the basin.
And how the hell we get to fuck in here
is any circus animal's guess

*

Dazzle of light
pale mountains, pale dunes
pale clouds on pale blue skies
immense skullcap of light over the whole,
                                the sea fetching sighs
      under the skiff,
his heart
folded among the sea's pages—
              from the depths coming up
      in musical surf
arched bow of the whale
      the vertebrae
shining through skin
circling the skiff
passing, they say,
the flukes over his head
so fast he did not see them
(though they were larger than his houseroof)
but felt the hair in his head
lie down which the wind had raised.
              And the heart came up also
which, in its fear,
the sea had previously bound into its secrets

*

Forest of whales,
Lebanon cedars
with their roots in the sea
sparring,
looking down at leisure
on the human world.

Forest of heads
above the prophet
in his rubber coffin,
laid out with all his jewels
tight round his neck,
his escaping soul's
breath still alive
is the finest mist
among the clouds of spray
from the cruising whales,
you will recognize it

*

Our lives collapse,
houses of water,
as the whale glides
up out of water
smooth and exact
with no effect beyond
its perfect fit
into eight million years
each passage like the last.
Our childish history
expires into a sky
so vast it has no edges

*

Lagoons in space
enclosed like wombs,
satellites of earth,
wide mirrors receiving
the planet's music,
star songs
in well-tuned skies.
Far out in space,
warmed by the sun,
fry, bubble, sizzle,
in silver-wrap

the celestial whales:
down drip of blubber
(deluge of calm)
turning in our sphere
every sign of the zodiac
to their own favor

*

Whales wild this morning
and skittish,
waves lapping against skiffs,
the skiffs rocking,
and animals preparing
for the voyage north,
taking longer to rise
between their breaths

*

& how come no fear
in this roiling—
dragons among the waves,
behemoth / leviathan,
close as domestic pets?
          If they barked, I think,
as loud as their size suggested,
childhood would tower
out of all proportion,
the world's walls
would cave in,
the floor break earthquake:
I would probably not
enter this lagoon
in a battleship!

*

"Though they take me down
into the freezing wave,
though they drop me naked
into the invisible,
and I cry there
for any voice to answer—
one voice out of the void—
and no voice sounds,
while leviathan
rises from below
his mouth agape
to take me in his body,
though they kill me and cut me to pieces
to feed me to that whale:
still I sing,
still do not keep quiet,
they have a singer
on their hands
and a voice
talking, singing, praying,
they cannot quench
if only the sun returns
to bless the earth like this
once in the centuries
between each of my breaths."

*

"Perhaps it is not the sea
we have witnessed
raising these whales
to the power of air
and downing them again to depths
unheard of in the history of water—
                perhaps it is the sky,
even paradise,
        and these are the heavenly animals
with wings of wind and music
who have laid their image
on all earthly souls

(since nothing is forgotten.)"
Father, the gate is open
        he declared on landing.
Wrote on that desk
and in that book they say
that was the oldest in the library
        within the belly of the whale:
                "these are the animals
the ancient men,
blind leading blind,
in the old days, on the old ships
with perfumed masts,
hearing the music of the sirens
                        thought to be angels… "

[1985]

Gary Snyder

BURNING ISLAND

O Wave God who broke through me today
Sea Bream
massive pink and silver
cool swimming down with me watching
staying away from the spear

Volcano belly Keeper who lifted this island
for our own beaded bodies adornment
and sprinkles us all with his laugh—
ash in the eye
mist, or smoke,
on the bare high limits—
underwater lava flows easing to coral
holes filled with striped feeding swimmers

O Sky Gods cartwheeling
out of Pacific
turning rainsqualls over like lids on us
then shine on our sodden—
(scanned out a rainbow today at the
cow drinking trough
sluicing off
LAHKS of crystal Buddha Fields
right on the hair of the arm!)

Who wavers right now in the bamboo:
a half-gone waning moon.
drank down a bowlful of shochu

in praise of Antares
gazing far up the lanes of Sagittarius
richest stream of our sky—
a cup to the center of the galaxy!

and let the eyes stray
right-angling the pitch of the Milky Way:
horse-heads   rings
clouds   too distant to *be*
slide free.
on the crest of the wave.

Each night
O Earth Mother
I have wrappt my hand
over the jut of your cobra-hood
sleeping;
left my ear
All night long by your mouth.

O   All
Gods   tides   capes   currents
Flows and spirals of
pool and powers—

As we hoe the field
let sweet potato grow.
And as sit us all down when we may
To consider the Dharma
bring with a flower and a glimmer.
Let us all sleep in peace   together.

Bless Masa and me as we marry
at new moon   on the crater
This summer.

VIII. 40067

WHAT YOU SHOULD KNOW TO BE A POET

all you can about animals as persons.
the names of trees and flowers and weeds.
names of stars, and the movements of the planets
                    and the moon.

your own six senses, with a watchful and elegant mind.

at least one kind of traditional magic:
divination, astrology, the *book of changes,* the tarot;

dreams.
the illusory demons and illusory shining gods;

kiss the ass of the devil and eat shit;
fuck his horny barbed cock,
fuck the hag,
and all the celestial angels
                    and maidens perfum'd and golden—

& then love the human: wives   husbands   and friends.

children's games, comic books, bubble-gum,
the weirdness of television and advertising.

work, long dry hours of dull work swallowed and accepted
and livd with and finally lovd.   exhaustion,
                    hunger, rest.

the wild freedom of the dance, *extasy*
silent solitary illumination, *enstasy*

real danger.   gambles.   and the edge of death.

[1970]

WHAT HAPPENED HERE BEFORE

–300,000,000–

First a sea: soft sands, muds, and marls
  —loading, compressing, heating, crumpling,
    crushing, recrystallizing, infiltrating,
several times lifted and submerged.
intruding molten granite magma
    deep-cooled and speckling,
      gold quartz fills the cracks—

–80,000,000–

sea-bed strata raised and folded,
  granite far below.
warm quiet centuries of rains
  (make dark red tropic soils)
  wear down two miles of surface,
lay bare the veins and tumble heavy gold
  in steambeds
    slate and schist rock-riffles catch it—
volcanic ash floats down and dams the streams,
  piles up the gold and gravel—

–3,000,000–

flowing north, two rivers joined,
  to make a wide long lake.
and then it tilted and the rivers fell apart
  all running west
  to cut the gorges of the Feather,
    Bear, and Yuba.

Ponderosa pine, manzanita, black oak, mountain yew.
  deer, coyote, bluejay, gray squirrel,
 ground squirrel, fox, blacktail hare,
  ringtail, bobcat, bear,
    all came to live here.

–40,000–

And human people came with basket hats and nets
winter-houses underground
yew bows painted green,
feasts and dances for the boys and girls
songs and stories in the smoky dark.

–125–

Then came the white man: tossed up trees and
boulders with big hoses,
going after that old gravel and the gold.
horses, apple-orchards, card-games,
pistol-shooting, churches, county jail.

We asked, who the land belonged to.
and where one pays tax.
(two gents who never used it twenty years,
and before them the widow
of the son of the man
who got him a patented deed
on a worked-out mining claim,)
laid hasty on land that was deer and acorn
grounds of the Nisenan?
branch of the Maidu?

(they never had a chance to speak, even,
their name.)
(and who remembers the Treaty of Guadalupe Hidalgo.)

the land belongs to itself.
"no self in self; no self in things"

Turtle Island swims
in the ocean-sky swirl-void
biting its tail while the worlds go
on-and-off
winking

& Mr. Tobiassen, a Cousin Jack,
assesses the county tax.
(the tax is our body-mind, guest at the banquet
Memorial and Annual, in honor
of sunlight grown heavy and tasty
while moving up food-chains
in search of a body with eyes and a fairly large
brain—
to look back at itself
on high.)

now,

we sit here near the diggings
in the forest, by our fire, and watch
the moon and planets and the shooting stars—

my sons ask, who are we?
drying apples picked from homestead trees
drying berries, curing meat,
shooting arrows at a bale of straw.

military jets head northeast, roaring, every dawn.

my sons ask, who are they?

WE SHALL SEE
WHO KNOWS
HOW TO BE

Bluejay screeches from a pine.

[1974]

from *Mountains and Rivers Without End*:

THE HUMP-BACKED FLUTE PLAYER

The hump-backed flute player
walks all over.
sits on the boulders around the Great Basin
his hump   is a pack.

Hsüan Tsang
went to India 629 AD
returned to China 645
with 657 sûtras, images, mandalas,
and fifty relics—
a curved frame pack with a parasol,
embroidery, carving,
incense censer swinging as he walked
the Pamir   the Tarim   Turfan
the Punjab   the doab
of Ganga and Yamuna,

Sweetwater, Quileute, Hoh
Amur, Tanana, Mackenzie, Old Man,
Big Horn, Platte, the San Juan

he carried
"emptiness"
he carried
"mind only"
vijñaptimâtra

The hump-backed flute player
Kokope'ele
His hump is a pack.

•

In Canyon de Chelly on the north wall up by a cave is the hump-backed flute player laying on his back, playing his flute. Across the flat sandy canyon wash, wading a stream and breaking through the ice, on the south wall, the pecked-out pictures of some mountain sheep with curling horns. They stood in the icy shadow of the south wall two hundred feet away; I sat with my shirt off in the sun facing south, with the hump-backed flute player just above my head. They whispered. I whispered. Back and forth across the canyon, clearly heard.

•

In the plains of Bihar, near Rajgir, are the ruins of Nalanda. The name Bihar comes from "vihara"—Buddhist temple—the Diamond Seat is in Bihar, and Vulture Peak—Tibetan pilgrims come down to these plains. The six-foot-thick walls of Nalanda, the monks all scattered—books burned—banners tattered—statues shattered—by the Turks. Hsüan Tsang describes the high blue tiles, the delicate debates—Logicians of Emptiness—worshippers of Târâ, "Joy of Starlight," naked breasted, She who saves.

•

Ghost bison, ghost bears, ghost bighorns, ghost lynx, ghost pronghorns, ghost panthers, ghost marmots, ghost owls:

swirling and gathering, sweeping down, in the power of a dance and a song.

> Then the White Man will be gone.
> butterflies will sing on slopes of grass and aspen—
> thunderheads the deep blue of Krishna
> rise on rainbows
> and falling shining rain—
> each drop—
> tiny people gliding slanting down:
> a little buddha seated in each pearl—
> and join the million waving grass–seed–buddhas
> on the ground.

•

Ah, what am I carrying? What's this load?
  who's that out there in the dust
  sleeping on the ground?
  with a black hat, and a feather stuck in his sleeve?

  —It's old Jack Wilson,
  Wovoka, the prophet,

Black Coyote saw the whole world
In Wovoka's empty hat

the bottomless sky

the night of starlight, lying on our sides

the ocean, slanting higher

all manner of beings
may swim in my sea
echoing up conch spiral corridors

the mirror: countless ages back
dressing   or laughing
what world today?

    pearl crystal jewel
    taming and teaching
    the dragon in the spine

    spiral, wheel,
    or breath of mind

    desert sheep with curly horns.
    the ringing in your ears

    is the cricket in the stars.

•

Up in the mountains that edge the Great Basin

    it was whispered to me
    by the oldest of trees.

    by the oldest of beings
    the oldest of trees

    bristlecone pine.

    and all night long, sung on
        by a young throng

    of pinyon pine.

[1970]

EARRINGS DANGLING AND MILES OF DESERT

Sagebrush (*Artemisia*) is of the sunflower family, or Compositae. It is not related to sage, *Salvia,* which is in the family of mint. The great basin sagebrush, our biggest artemisia, *A. tridentata,* grows throughout the intermountain zone and other portions of the arid west. Sagebrush lives together with rabbitbrush (*Chrysothamnos*), saltbush (*Atriplex*) and greasewood (*Sarcobatus*). As a little group they make up one of the largest plant communities on Turtle Island. Another huge community would be the sub-boreal spruce forests of Canada and Alaska.

—brushy, bushy, stringybark cobwebby tangle
multi-stemmed, forking,
twiglets just sidewise, a scatter of silky tiny leaves,
dry twigs stick up straight,
   a lizard scooting in the frizzy dust—

It is eaten by sagebrush voles, pygmy rabbits, sage grouse, and pronghorn (which can browse it: the plant contains an oil that inhibits microbes in the rumen of cows so that they cannot digest it. Sheep can eat a little. Elk eat it and belch a lot.) It is a home to mourning doves, night hawks, sage thrashers, shrikes, and sage sparrows.

The bark has been used by humans for tens of thousands of years. The shreddy fiber makes bags, nets, shawls, and sandals. It is used by ranchers and Indians alike for firewood. The leaves are burned as a purifying incense or a mosquito-repellant-smoke. It is used as a tea for stomach disorders by the Hopi, who call it *wi:'kwapi.* The edible seeds are gathered by the Cahuilla, who also make an herbal tea from it. They call it *wikwat.* Another smaller artemisia, *Artemisia californicam,* is used by the Cahuilla for a women's tonic.

Sagebrush: in northern Paiute called *sawabi,* in southern Paiute *sangwabi.*

Artemisia,
who lives across the ranges,
stretching for miles,
   she's always there:
with saltbush and greasewood, with rabbitbrush
and all the little grasses.
Her blue-gray-green—

In Europe, plants of the sagebrush group are called wormwood. Tarragon the herb is an artemisia, and *A. absinthium,* from which the "extract of absinthe" is made and used to flavor the drink by that name. The drink sold in France under the name "Pernod" is the same liquor without the wormwood.

Artemisia is everywhere: thirty species in Japan alone. It is the mugwort and moxa of China.

The name artemisia comes from the goddess Artemis, because for her the wormwood is a sacred plant. Narrow leaves glow silver in her moonlight—

"She loves to hunt
  in the shadows of mountains
  and in the wind"

Artem in Greek means "to dangle" or "earring."
(Well-connected, "articulate," *art.*)

Her blue-gray-green
stretching out there
sagebrush flats reach to the edge
bend away—
emptiness far as the mind can see

Raincloud maidens come walking
  lightning-streak silver.
grey skirts sweeping and trailing:

Farewell, Artemisia,
  aromatic in the rain,
    I will think of you in my other poems.

[1991]

Jerome Rothenberg

THE 12TH HORSE SONG OF FRANK MITCHELL (BLUE)

("total translation" from the Navajo)

Key: wnn N nnnn N gahn   hawuNnawu   nngobaheegwing

Some are & are going to my howinouse baheegwing hawuNnawu N nngahn baheegwing
Some are & are going to my howinouse baheegwing hawuNnnawi N nngahn baheegwing
Some are & some are gone to my howinouse nnaht bahyee nahtgwing buhtzzm bahyee noohwinnnGUUH

Because I was (N gahn) I was the boy raised Ng the dawn (n)(n) but some are & are gowing to my howinouse baheegwing
& by going from the house the bluestone hoganome but some are & are gone to my howinow baheegwing
& by going from the house the shahyNshining hoganome but some are & are gone to my howinow baheeGWING
& by going from the swollenouse my breath has blown but some are & are going to my howinouse baheegwing
& by going from the house the hohly honganome but some are & are gone to my howinow baheegwing ginng ginnng
& from the place of precious cloth we walk (p)pon (N gahn) but some are gone to my howinow baheegwing hawunawwing
with those prayersticks that are blue(u)(u) but some are & are (wnn N) gahn to my howinouse baheegwing
with my feathers that are b(lu)u but some are & are going to my howinouse baheegwing

Author's note: The Horse Songs are compositions derived by translation from seventeen Navajo songs in the Blessingway of ceremonial singer Frank Mitchell. My attempt was to translate *all* elements of the original—not only words but vocables between words & at line ends, word distortions, even music. The underlying narrative is of the hero-god Enemy Slayer, sent by his mother Changing Woman (the Earth) to bring back horses from the Sun (his father). Dedicated to David P. McAllester, who led me to the source.

with my spirit horses that are b(lu)u but some are & are going to my howinouse baheegwing
with my spirit horses that are blue & dawn but some are & are gone to my howinow baheegwing nngnnng
with those spirit (hawuN) horses that are bluestone (nawu) but some are & are gone to my howinow baheegwing
with those hoganorses that are bluestone but some are & are going to my howinouse baheegwing
with cloth of ever(ee)ee kind tgaahn & draw them on nahhtnnn but some are & are gone to my howinow baheegwing
with jewels of ever(ee)ee kind tgaahn & draw them on nahhtnnn but some are & are going to my howinouse baheegwing
with hoganorses of ever(ee)ee kind to go & draw them on nahhtnnn but some are & are going to my howinouse baheegwing
with sheep of evree(ee)(ee) kind tgaahn & draw them on nahhtnnn but some are & are going to my howinouse baheegwing
with cattle of every kind (N gahn) to go & draw them on nahhtnnnn but some are & are going to my howinouse baheegwing
with men of evree(ee)(ee) kind tgaahn & draw them on nahhtnnn but some are & are going to my howinouse baheegwing
now to my howinome of precious cloth in my backroom Ngahhnn where Nnnn but some are & are going to my howinouse baheegwing
in my house of precious cloth we walk (p)pon (N gahn) where Nnnn but some are & are going to my howinouse baheegwing
& everything that's gone before (mmmm) more we walk (p)pon but some are & are going to my howinouse baheegwing
& everything that's more & won't be (be!) be poor but some are & some are gone to my howinow baheegwing
& everything that's (nawuN) living to be old & blesst (bhawuN) some are & are going to my howinouse baheegwing
because I am the boy who goes & blesses/blisses to be old but some are & are going to my howinouse baheegwing hawuNnawu N nngahn baheegwinnng

Zzmmmm are & are gone to my howinow baheegwing hawuNnawu N nngahn baheegwing
Zzmmmm are & are going to my howinouse baheegwing hawuNnawu N nngahn baheegwing
Some are & some are gone to my house now naht bahyeee naht nwinnng buht nawuNNN baheegwinnng

[1970]

SENECA JOURNAL 1: "A POEM OF BEAVERS"

for Gary Gordon

in dream
the beavers come to
Harry Watt
"a child could
"speak
"communication
"were standing in a row
"they said I would not
"harm them
"would not ever
"after
"hunted mink
"& badger
"but the beavers were
"my friends
"& helped me

so his story began & I knew it also hearing what he said hearing I knew it was with me from before my time & knew it as a memory of my own grandfathers not as hunters in the woods but on the edge of old world forests men & women walked by on the way to markets public baths went berrying in summer chased by wolves in winter past the huts where mushrooms hung to dry the old women of the woods lived heavy in grey dresses chin hairs bristling into gentile beards their own familar dogs & cats beside them had the master of the good name learned from these the speech of animals this is the secret all men have retained that greater language of what biological fellowhood will open to us once again

ethology the visions
of McClure & Chomsky all
the speakers of deep tongues point
a route this generation
will be privileged to assume

a universal speech
in which the kingdoms of the world
are one
the kingdoms of the world are one

---

what is it to be a beaver truly
when I think of it I think
of water water on a body
wholly hair
I think of beaver hats
& beaver movies
I think of a new birth into
beaver life
the beaver in the poem of the Baal Shem
is being born
he is the generative part of man
the cock in hair
that low intelligence erupting
changes what we are
the soft becoming
hard the cold one
hot
red tongue of beaver in a nest
of fur
by a sudden metamorphosis
a fluid world
becoming
anything the mind can think
the mind is thinking
entering the fluid bottom stream
of sex transformed
the Baal Shem leaves the light of Torah
& becomes
any old animal inside
the sacred wood

& I am now living in
a place called Bucktooth once

its Indian name
the name of a small man (the book says
"he was only 4 feet tall
"& had a single tooth
"they found his skeleton
"a single tooth
"that fell out when they crossed
"the Allegany
"belt buckle bore his mark
"the grandsons made a coffin
"they buried him
"back where his fathers were)
& only 4 feet tall he must 've been
"one of them little fellers"
pygmies of this place
or leprechauns who own
the Dark Dance
no self-respecting Indian would be
that small   or say
that by that tooth he was
a beaver I would call
Old Beaver Tooth
being myself a Beaver
by adoption
as my wife & child are Herons
also by adoption
we adopt these titles
we go home with them
what is this membership we have
adopted grinning
in the mirror my face
is changing to
a mask Floyd John once showed me
had a single tooth
if I could make my face a mask
I'd be Old Bucktooth
Beaver once again old founder
of a town we all can live in hoping
that no other
Duke of Salamanca comes

to sponsor a new railroad
beavers & blue heron
can't live near
but hide from in the silence of
some lousy cave

---

not a sweet beast he is power
not a sweet man he is like a muscle tightened waiting to crack
  down & break
a skull maybe splintering the jaw & making
the teeth like his own an almost non-existent row the ghost tooth
in the center shining is a mirror we can see ourselves
down to the farthest tunnel winding among
shining leaves & flowers words & tiny melodies
the colors make
          or if the dream begins with
silence in the foot itself
that silence stirs
it is a dance vibrating at center of each isolated
nerve reminds him of the song
he wants to sing when
dying
& if the beaver sings it to him now it means
an easy death

---

just as the birth was easy
beaver life began in
water was a pound of bones & fur
sure instinct to the mark
sent out his tongue
into the left rear nipple sucked
sweet yellow sticky milk
his mudder gave him
"slurp" sez Old Bucktooth Beaver
"now I must try a swim around"
he's only an hour old & talking
swimming paddling around her tits
in noonday sun reclining

top of the lodge will learn
not to let tail get dry but dribble
sweet clarifying smell from nether
hole all creatures hanker
for a whiff of
smears it on his hands &
dabs the fur so comfortable
& sweet this is the beaver's life
(sez Old Man Beaver)
think I might chew a little wood
—just loves to chew & fart—
"pleasures are simple
"in this world the trick's
"to find a tree & let the sun flash
"on my orange tooth
"tree chips fly all day
"& I will stop never
"until the tree shall come to earth
"& never stop though it may crush me
"the film across my eye shall turn to fog
"old ones call dying

---

but not without a fight
(sez Beaver) Otter stalks him
"most cunning raids my tunnels
"kicks in my sweetened
"mudpatties steaming still hot with my
"fragrance stuffs
"oil drops & stones up
" 's rectum (cries)
Me King Otter! Lick Me!
the Great Mask of Otter filling
Beaver Man's dreams
makes tracks in his corn mush
pearly grains of hominy
under the otter's claws
otter piss splatters
's corn soup
"sands soft waves of nausea across

"my cerebellum o sly dance of
"otters on harvest nights full moon
"suspended atop an alder pole
delights Old Beaver Man gathers
descendants around him
he stands on the water
slaps it
hard with his tail (sez)
"Old Enemy
"Otter
"in the name of Longhouse the Great
"Rabbinical Council
"of elders mystical
"mammals the longbeards of
" Zion America
"I have lived my last under the earth
"into a new sun I skitter
"tribal triumphant (sez Beaver)
"I chew off your balls
"I survives

*OLD*MAN*BEAVER'S*BLESSING*SONG*
* all * i * want * 's * a * good * 5¢ * seegar *
heeheeHOHOheeheeHOHOheeheeHOHO
* all * i * want * 's * a * good * 5¢ * seegar *
heeheeHOHOheeheeHOHOheeheeHOHO
* all * i * want * 's * a * good * 5¢ * seegar *
heeheeHOHOheeheeHOHOheeheeHOHO
* all * i * want * 's * a * good * 5¢ * seegar *
heeheeHOHOheeheeHOHOheeheeHOHO
* all * i * want * 's * a * good * 5¢ * seegar *
heeheeHOHOheeheeHOHOheeheeHOHO
* all * i * want * 's * a * good * 5¢ * seegar *
heeheeHOHOheeheeHOHOheeheeHOHO
* all * i * want * 's * a * good * 5¢ * seegar *
heeheeHOHOheeheeHOHOheeheeHOHO
* all * i * want * 's * a * good * 5¢ * seegar *
heeheeHOHOheeheeHOHOheeheeHOHO
*OLD*MAN*BEAVER'S*BLESSING*SONG*

[1978]

VISIONS OF JESUS

Let's say it was Jesus. Who is Jesus? Why should Jesus be the name
now celebrated, entering the poem?
Or let's say it wasn't. That I have the key to make it open
like a sound. Each sound's a rage.
Each page a turning over. I am writing this
the way a preacher speaks the word out on a prairie.
Visions of Jesus everywhere.
Sweet Jesus, says the song, to which the mind says
archly, darkly, "sour Jesus,"
& the poem begins with that.
Pink Jesus. Tiny Jesuses
on every bush, the world of sagebrush now a world of tiny Jesuses.
Soft Jesus maybe. (Is there a sexual aspersion in it
or only another way of saying "tender Jesus"?)
Jesus in Oklahoma
with his beard cut off. A weepy girl
named Jesus. She opens up her breast,
the moon pops out. O menses, colored glass
& papers, birds with messages
of love, tra la, on metal wings. His other name
is Rollo, Baby Winchester
or Baby Love. Jesus with a cow's head
on his shoulders, candles reaching from
his fingertips. Jesus in his one-eyed ford.
Squawk squawk, the preacher cries.
Eyes of the congregation turning white. The pinwheel
shooting sparks against his lap.
Jesus in furs. Jesus in Oklahoma,
growing old.
Hot & glowing Jesus. Jesus on the ace of hearts.
Alfalfa Jesus.
I am writing this the way a gambler cuts his name
into the table. Jesus in formica.
Drinking in the morning, playing coon-can
with his brother James.
Other names of Jesus.
Jesus H. Jones or Jesus in the woodpile.
Tomtom Jesus.

Jesus who aims a bullet down his mouth.
His children hang his body from a cross.
Three Jesuses in Ypsilanti.
Three in Tishomingo.
Jesus buried in Fort Sill.
His suffering has left their bodies
empty. In the night sky past El Reno
Jesus becomes his pain & flies,
aiming to leave his eyes for others.
Mother Jesus.
Her children have forsaken her.
She learns to cry & plays
nightly at mah jong, dropping her tiles
into the bottomless lake.
The man who chews his wrists down to the bone
is also Jesus. Jesus
in a feathered skull cap. Tacking stars
onto his vest, o cockeyed Jesus,
wanderer from Minsk,
he squawks the language of the little merchants,
squatting at their campfire he stirs
their coffee with *his* tool. How like his grandfather
he has become. Coyote Jesus.
Farting in the sweat lodge, tight
against his buttons
in the bride's room. Ponca City
Jesus. Pawnee Jesus.
He is staring at the eyes of Jesus
staring into his.
Their eyeballs spin around
like planets.
Visions of Jesus everywhere.
Gambler Jesus.
Banker Jesus.
Flatfoot Jesus with a floy floy.
Jesus shuffling.
The soldiers guard his silent fan,
tacked up, beside his rattle.
Jesus on the pavement. Jesus
shot for love, the powwow over,

naked, crawling toward you,
vomit on his beard. His father's milk
is dribbling—plin plin—in the cup
called Jesus. Ghosts
unhook the breast plate, draw
two streams of milk out,
mix them, opening
the mother's womb. No midwife
comes to her, she gives birth
like a man, & holds him
in a dream. Old song
erupting in the gourd dance,
in the storefront church
at night, among the hapless
armies. Two plus two is
Jesus. Five is Jesus.
Jesus is Okarchie,
driving. Jesus in his one-eyed ford,
arriving for the dance in Barefoot.
Visions of Jesus everywhere.
Jesus wrapped up in a woman's shawl.
Jesus in a corner,
stroking his tight body.
Masturbating Jesus.
Jesus sucking on a ball of fat.
There is no language left for him to speak,
only the humming in his chest,
a rush of syllables
like honey. Pouring
from every orifice, the voice
of renegades & preachers
without words.
Pink Jesuses in Oklahoma,
emerging with the spring.
Catfish Jesuses.
A beetle with the face of Jesus
scribbled on its back, squashed flat
against the dance floor.
Jesus squawking with the voice of angels.
I am writing this the way a man speaks without words.

Wordless in the light he pulls
out of his mouth. In the holes he hides in.
Wordless in praises. Wordless in peyote.
Wordless in hellos & hallelujahs.
The freaky Jew slips in beside
his bride, asleep forever, counts up bears
& cadillacs
under a leaky sky.

[Oklahoma/1985]

HUNGER

1

the prisoners, committed to death
around the world
the squadrons of hungry ghosts almost like armies
that swarm up & down the streets
always behind your house
never in front
where the bright wall tells the world
"a happy giant lives here"
I would rather run away
no more terror & no more loss of memory
promises the guard
I tell him: I don't want any part of this
even if it's a dream—& it is—
in the blood the enzymes are the same
the prisoners are all marching & won't stop
until they lay you flat
until your eye—no longer focused on the road
no longer on the sign over the supermarket
illumination—flops on your cheek
the jaw at a cockeyed angle
away from your face, the skin
peculiar, pasty like a kind of earth
loose & crumbling
what will you become & what will we all become
before the time of the big change
the miracle?

the body is a remorseless institution
it escapes me though I respect it
greatly, though I equate it with this poem
another metaphor for death
the armies of the world have no respect
for flesh
          they run their wheels
over it, they crush it to shadows
with their wheels

2

the hunger of the rich man
knows no end
the man & the woman, both insatiable
reduce the world's flesh to a sauce
& smear it over their wrists & thighs
& follow the delicious cracks of their bodies
trying to shove the substance in
a gibelotte done hunter style
the dead feet still thick with fur
the tongues torn from their cries
harbor the ghosts of tears
wild capers scrape the bourgeois flesh
the hunger of the man & woman
lords of hunger
gives a direction to their lives
they speak in French
the only language the bones understand
when they rub the femurs against each other's nipples
—hungry hungry—
when his own mouth over her cunt
feels the dead bone slip in
from his trembling fingers
this is how gods make love in graveyards
eating, sucking out their lives
the woman mother of the bones straddles
a throne of hungry beggars
hands reach up to her in death
they stroke her ribs
incite her, the man & woman
gather strength

under the shadow of an egg-beater
a new vibrator, watching
"les viandes roties, the eloquence
"of slowly turning flesh
"contracting
"swelling
"fondled by repeated basting
"assumes a rich brown satin glaze
the hunger of the rich man
leaves him shrunken
because it doesn't end
he says "sweet momma," croons it
in the voice that made him famous
they eat each other's sex
then they eat the sex of others
they invent new hungers
hunger for power & for grass
hunger for sleep & badges
hunger for swollen sausages
hunger for swollen legs
hunger for the sounds of swollen children
hunger for omens
hunger for facades
hunger for kings
hunger for irreversible death
hunger for a monument to hunger
only the rich can still invent
they wait for future hungers
servants will spoon for them
they drive to funerals & spas
they leave crisp dollars on each other's plates
the hunger of the rich man
reaches for the moon
it breaks the world in half
& hands it
first to his bride, his love
they melt in tears
the band plays "satisfaction"
but they go on eating
"till the end of time"

[1986]

David Antin

A LIST OF THE DELUSIONS OF THE INSANE WHAT THEY ARE AFRAID OF

the police
being poisoned
being killed
being alone
being attacked at night
being poor
being followed at night
being lost in a crowd
being dead
having no stomach
having no insides
having a bone in the throat
losing money
being unfit to live
being ill with a mysterious disease
being unable to turn out the light
being unable to close the door
that an animal will come in from the street
that they will not recover
that they will be murdered
that they will be murdered when they sleep
that they will be murdered when they wake
that murders are going on all around them
that there are murderers all around them
that they will see the murderer
that they will not
that they will be boiled alive
that they will be starved
that they will be fed disgusting things

that disgusting things are being put into their food and drink
that their flesh is boiling
that their head will be cut off
that children are burning
that they are starving
that all of the nutriment has been removed from food
that evil chemicals have been placed in the earth
that evil chemicals have entered the air
that it is immoral to eat
that they are in hell
that they hear people screaming
that they smell burnt flesh
that they have committed an unpardonable sin
that there are unknown agencies working evil in the world
that they have no identity
that they are on fire
that they have no brain
that they are covered with vermin
that their property is being stolen
that their children are being killed
that they have stolen something
that they have too much to eat
that they have been chloroformed
that they have been blinded
that they have gone deaf
that they have been hypnotized
that they are the tools of another power
that they have been forced to commit murder
that they will get the electric chair
that people have been calling them names
that they deserve these names
that they are changing their sex
that their blood has turned to water
that their body is being transformed into glass
that insects are coming out of their body
that they give off a bad smell
that houses are burning around them
that people are burning around them
that children are burning around them
that houses are burning
that they have committed suicide of the soul

[1968]

DEFINITIONS FOR MENDY

loss is an unintentional decline in or disappearance of
    a value arising from a contingency
a value is an efficacy a power a brightness
it is also a duration

to lose something keys hair someone
we suffer at the thought
he has become absent imaginary false
a false key will not turn a true lock
false hair will not turn grey
mendy will not come back
but longing is not imaginary
we must go down into ourselves
down to the floor   that is not imaginary
where hunger lives and thirst
hunger imagine bread   thirst imagine water
the glass of water slips to the floor
thirst is a desert
value a glass of water
loss is the glass of water slipping to the floor
loss is the unintentional decline in or disappearance
    of a glass of water arising from a contingency
the glass   pieces of glass
the floor is a contingency
the floor is a floor
is a contingency
made of wood
the fire is a contingency
the bread is burned
burning is not a contingency
the presence of the dead is imaginary
the absence is real
henceforth it will be his manner of appearing
so he appears   in an orange jacket and workpants and a blue
                                                            denim shirt

Author's note: The initial definition of *loss* is quoted from p. 22 of Mehr and Cammack's *Principles of Insurance.* The initial definitions of value are from *Webster's New International Dictionary,* the 1927 revision.

his hair is black his eyes are black
and a blue crab is biting his long fingers
he is trying to hold the bread
he is trying to bring the water to his mouth
his mouth is a desert
the glass of water will not come
the glass of water keeps slipping through his fingers
the floor is made of wood it is burning
it is covered with pieces of glass
arising from a contingency
his face is the darkened face of a clock
it is marked with radium
the glass is falling from his face
the face of a clock in which there is a salamander
whose eyes are bright with radium
radium is a value that is always declining
radium is a value that is always disappearing
lead is also a value
but it is less bright than radium

loss is an unintentional decline in or disappearance of
 a value arising from a contingency
a value is an efficacy a power a brightness
it is also a duration

is there enough silence here for a glass of water

is it dark enough for bread

take a glass of water
hold it against a wall
it is not pure water
it is almost pure wall

glass   what is glass

glass is a solution
of sand and chalk and ashes
fused by fire
it is a desert
that transmits light

the thirst is not appeased

water is a barrier

a glass of water is between us
you are there and i am here
is it a corollary of the fact that two things cannot
  be at the same place at the same time
that two things can be at two different places at the
  same time
you are there and i am here and i see you
but you are changed
two things at the same place at two different times
where you were the floor is empty
there is no shadow on the wall
i can only see the wall in my mind
i am not where i was then
but i still see your shadow the glass on the floor

in all matter there is an innate force
a power of resisting

take a glass   fill it with water

the thirst is not appeased

take a glass of water
drop it on the floor

it smashes
it is wood and glass and water

the thirst is not appeased

a glass of water falling
is a falling body of water
and obeys the laws of falling bodies
according to which
all bodies fall
at a rate that increases   uniformly
regardless of their form or weight
at the same altitude and latitude
the weight of a body   is the force
with which the earth   pulls the body down
mendy weighed one hundred and thirty-seven pounds
which is to say
that the earth   pulled mendy down
with a force equal to that
exerted upon a mass of one hundred and thirty-seven pounds
at forty-five degrees latitude
at the level of the sea
the earth pulls all bodies down

the thirst is not appeased

i am trying to hand you a glass of water
i am trying to give you a piece of bread
i cannot give you anything
there is a glass of water between us
i can only see you by the light the glass lets through

there is a piece of bread between us
if we could only see it

no one doubts the efficacy of bread
bread is a power
if we could only release it
it is a body
containing light

there is a piece of bread between us
break it
bread is a barrier

bread is a body
water is a body
the earth is a body
the sun is a body
a clock is also a body
light is a body   of a sort

what sort   it is heavy and falls
three hundred and sixty tons of light fall
from the sun on the earth every day
physics imagines a black body
a black body gives back no light

•

duration
it is a stone
it is a fact
it does not move
it has no place into which it could move
it has no place to move out of
it is a stone
it is a face
it is a stone on which water has dropped
it is a face
it is hard
it is smooth
the water does not wear it away
it wears the water away
it is a fact
it does not mean anything
it cannot tell time

•

it is a fact

not having seen you for a long time and you
didn't live far away you came to see me in the
winter it was cold in my apartment which was
heated with gas and you wore a scarf to keep
warm when i asked you what you were doing you
said you were sick and i said we were all sick
and it didnt matter but you said you were really
sick you were dying and i asked you how did it
feel because i didnt know what to say and
you said it felt queer

•

yellow
branches of willow
small flames of forsythia

soft air
black water
caressing the branches
sun
overhead

•

it is a fact

to hear the Grosse Fuge and Webern and the
great fugue was a great distance away like a
square masted ship tossed in a storm in an
old painting and the Webern was close and
dazzling   light glancing off glass and water
we came back in the rain i never saw you again

it is important to learn what the eye can see and the
ear can hear

to record the truth

taking pictures of trees
the fountain of elm branches a spray of silver now
last of the maidenhairs timbre of a voice
drops of water sounds decaying on the air

choose/to fix a body in space
choose/unaccelerated axes
choose/a frame to fix a face

the eye cannot discriminate true intensities of light
only their ratios
similarly the ear
cannot distinguish among sounds that are very high or low
in the dark all cats are black
what color are they in a blinding light

[1967]

Amiri Baraka

RETURN OF THE NATIVE

Harlem is vicious
modernism. BangClash.
Vicious the way its made.
Can you stand such beauty?
So violent and transforming.
The trees blink naked, being
so few. The women stare
and are in love with them
selves. The sky sits awake
over us. Screaming
at us. No rain.
Sun, hot cleaning sun
drives us under it.

The place, and place
meant of
black people. Their heavy Egypt.
(Weird word!) Their minds, mine,
the black hope mine. In Time.
We slide along in pain or too
happy. So much love
for us. All over, so much of
what we need. Can you sing
yourself, your life, your place
on the warm planet earth.
And look at the stones

the hearts, the gentle hum
of meaning. Each thing, life

we have, or love, is meant
for us in a world like this.
Where we may see ourselves
all the time. And suffer
in joy, that our lives
are so familiar.

[1965]

FOR MAULANA KARENGA & PHAROAH SANDERS

The body of man is evolved to a brain
and speech, in the dark, a drum, thru
forests and over water, speech, man
with his black self, describes the
sea and forest, the trails of earth
and sinewy flying things, the pyramid
of his life, begins to describe
what is in him, beating image off his tongue,
the blood, carrying image thru the heart, the blood
himself, on a lake, with his, wo-man, the blood, then,
in his black eloquence, described, that, wo-man

speech, the drum creates
life as the heart, sees, and makes
itself, a life, and again, a life, like the holy sun
with us for ever, then another, past that.

Describe beauty brother-lover, create worlds of dazzling sweet color
Speech, image in the sand, the water pulls up, cloud sketch a colony
of other kinds of life, rain waving thru the middle air, as a heart
describes,

the momentary taste of picture
the God Thot
arrived
sweet seeing
and then, behind that,
we did another thing

we began
to sing

THE MINUTE OF CONSCIOUSNESS

You pay for it, for sure, dont let nobody tell you you don. You pay.
In all the ways, possible, through the traps, moon light traps, collecting
absences, and kisses, lovers trail through the imagination lighting fires
throughout the civilized world, destroying primitive man's "progress"
to the obeisances of spirit, the salary of the blind.

It is a path song. Mountains pass under and over, cold birds turn to blink.
A rope hung from way up, tied to a leader, a spirit, a system, an old teacher
himself, tied up higher movn just a lil higher.

Sometimes you want to know is it worth it. The deprivation, the trying
narrow decision, move on, move on. You want to know sometimes when the
world
beat down around you, the planet groans from so much pain, the pointless
murders and idiot laughter from the merv griffin show, then you know that

what you do is what the ancestors prepared you for. The lighting of the flame
The moving of the rock. The shouting out of the great names, the great
national spirits. Then the feeling in tuned and turned slowly our turn itself

hits a certain note, mighty pythagoras, the sound, the color.

[1969]

STUDY PEACE

Out of the shadow, I am come in to you whole a black holy man
whole of heaven in my hand in my head look out two yeas to ice
what does not belong in the universe of humanity and love. I am
the black magician you have heard of, you knew was on you in you now
my whole self, which is the star beneath the knower's arc, when the star it
self rose and its light illuminated the first prophet, the five pointed being
of love.
I have come through my senses
The five the six the fourteen
of them. And I am a fourteen point star
of the cosmic stage, spinning in my appointed orbit

giving orders to my dreams, ordering my imagination
that the world it gives birth to is the beautiful quranic vision

We are phantoms and visions, ourselves
Some star's projection, some sun's growth beneath that holy star
And all the other worlds there are exist alive beneath their own
 beautiful fires

real and alive, just as we are
beings of the star's mind
images cast against the eternally shifting
heavens.

[1972]

A POEM FOR DEEP THINKERS

Skymen coming down out the clouds land
and then walking into society try to find out
whats happening—"Whats happening," they be saying
look at it, where they been, dabbling in mist, appearing &
disappearing, now there's a real world breathing—inhaling exhaling
concrete & sand, and they want to know what's happening. What's
 happening
is life itself "onward & upward," the spirals of fireconflict clash
of opposing forces, the dialogue of yes and no, showed itself in stabbed
 children
in the hallways of schools, old men strangling bankguards, a hard
 puertorican inmate's tears
exchanging goodbyes in the prison doorway, armies sweeping wave
 after wave to contest
the ancient rule of the minority. What draws them down, their blood
 entangled with humans,
their memories, perhaps, of the earth, and what they thought it could
 be. But blinded by
sun, and their own images of things, rather than things as they actually
 are, they wobble,
they stumble, sometimes, and people they be cheering alot, cause they
 think the skymen
dancing, "Yeh...Yeh...get on it...," people grinning and feeling good
 cause the skymen

dancing, and the skymen stumbling, till they get the sun out they
eyes, and integrate the
inhead movie show, with the material reality that exists with and
without them. There are
tragedies tho, a buncha skies bought the loopdieloop program from
the elegant babble of
the ancient minorities. Which is where they loopdieloop in the sky
right on just loopdieloop
in fantastic meaningless curlicues which delight the thin gallery
owners who wave at them
on their way to getting stabbed in the front seats of their silver alfa
romeos by lumpen
they have gotten passionate with. And the loopdieloopers go on,
sometimes spelling out
complex primitive slogans and shooting symbolic smoke out their gills
in honor of something
dead. And then they'll make daring dives right down toward the earth
and skag cocaine money
whiteout and crunch iced into the statue graveyard where Ralph
Ellison sits biting his banjo
strings retightening his instrument for the millionth time before
playing the star spangled
banjo. Or else loopdieloop loopdieloop up higher and higher and
thinner and thinner and finer
refiner, sugarladdies in the last days of the locust, sucking they greek
lolliepops.
Such intellectuals as we is baby, we need to deal in the real world, and
be be in the real
world. We need to use, to use, all the all the skills all the spills and
thrills that we
conjure, that we construct, that we lay out and put together, to create
life as beautiful
as we thought it could be, as we dreamed it could be, as we desired it
to be, as we knew it
could be, before we took off, before we split for the sky side, not to
settle for endless
meaningless circles of celebration of this madness, this madness, not to
settle for this
madness this madness madness, these yoyos yoyos of the ancient
minorities. Its all for real,

everythings for real, be for real, song of the skytribe walking the earth,
faint smiles to
open roars of joy, meet you on the battlefield they say, they be
humming, hop, then stride,
faint smile to roars of open joy, hey my man, what's happening, meet
you on the battlefield
they say, meet you on the battlefield they say, what i guess needs to be
discussed here tonight
is what side yall gon be on

WHEN WE'LL WORSHIP JESUS

We'll worship Jesus
When jesus do
Somethin
When jesus blow up
the white house
or blast nixon down
when jesus turn out congress
or bust general motors to
yard bird motors
jesus we'll worship jesus
when jesus get down
when jesus get out his yellow lincoln
w/the built in cross stain glass
window & box w/black peoples
enemies we'll worship jesus when
he get bad enough to at least scare
somebody—cops not afraid
of jesus
pushers not afraid
of jesus, capitalists racists
imperialists not afraid
of jesus shit they makin money
off jesus
we'll worship jesus when mao
do, when toure does
when the cross replaces Nkrumah's
star

Jesus need to hurt some a our
enemies, then we'll check him
out, all that screaming and hollering
& wallering and moaning talkin bout
jesus, jesus, in a red
check velvet vine + 8 in. heels
jesus pinky finger
got a goose egg ruby
which actual bleeds
jesus at the apollo
doin splits and helpin
nixon trick niggers
jesus w/his one eyed self
tongue kissing johnny carson
up the behind
jesus need to be busted
jesus need to be thrown down and whipped
till something better happen
jesus aint did nothin for us
but kept us turned toward the
sky (him and his boy allah
too, need to be checkd
out!)
we'll worship jesus
when he get a boat load of ak-47s
and some dynamite
and blow up abernathy robotin
for gulf
jesus need to be busted
we ain't gonna worship nobody
but niggers gettin up off
the ground
not gon worship jesus
unless he just a tricked up
nigger somebody named
outside his race
need to worship yo self fo
you worship jesus
need to bust jesus (+ check
out his spooky brother

allah while you heavy
on the case
cause we ain gon worship jesus
we aint gon worship
jesus
we aint gon worship
jesus
not till he do somethin
not till he help us
not till the world get changed
and he ain, jesus ain, he cant change the world
we can change the world
we can struggle against the forces of backwardness, we can change the world
we can struggle against our selves, our slowness, our connection with the oppressor, the very cultural aggression which binds us to our enemies as their slaves.
we can change the world
we aint' gonna worship jesus cause jesus dont exist
xcept in song and story except in ritual and dance, except in slum stained
tears or trillion dollar opulence stretching back in history, the history
of the oppression of the human mind
we worship the strength in us
we worship our selves
we worship the light in us
we worship the warmth in us
we worship the world
we worship the love in us
we worship our selves
we worship nature
we worship ourselves
we worship the life in us, and science, and knowledge, and transformation
of the visible world
but we aint gonna worship no jesus
we aint gonna legitimize the witches and devils and spooks and hobgoblins
the sensuous lies of the rulers to keep us chained to fantasy and illusion
sing about life, not jesus
sing about revolution, not no jesus
stop singing about jesus,
sing about, creation, our creation, the life of the world and fantastic
nature how we struggle to transform it, but dont victimize our selves by
distorting the world

stop moanin about jesus, stop sweating and crying and stompin and dyin for jesus
unless thats the name of the army we building to force the land finally to
change hands. And lets not call that jesus, get a quick consensus, on that,
lets damn sure not call that black fire muscle no invisible psychic dungeon
no gentle vision strait jacket, lets call that peoples army, or wapenduzi or simba
wachanga, but we not gon call it jesus, and not gon worship jesus, throw
jesus out yr mind. Build the new world out of reality, and new vision
we come to find out what there is of the world
to understand what there is here in the world!
to visualize change, and force it.
we worship revolution

[1975]

DOPE

uuuuuuuuuu
uuuuuuuuuu
uuuuuuuuuu uuu ray light morning fire lynch yet
uuuuuuu, yester-pain in dreams
comes again, race-pain, people our people our people
everywhere...yeh...uuuuu. yeh uuuuu. yeh
our people
yes people
every people
most people
uuuuuu, heh uuuuu, most people
in pain
yester-pain, and pain today
(Screams) ooowow! ooowow! It must be the devil
(jumps up like a claw stuck him) oooo wow! oooowow!
(screams)

It must be the devil
It must be the devil
It must be the devil
(shakes like evangelical sanctify
shakes tambourine like evangelical sanctify in heat)

ooowow! ooowow! yeh, devil, yeh, devil ooowow!

Must be the devil must be the devil
(waves plate like collection) mus is mus is mus is
mus is be the devil, cain be rockefeller (eyes roll
up batting, and jumping all the way around to face the
other direction) caint be him, no lawd
caint be dupont, no lawd, cain be, no lawd, no way
noway, naw saw, no way jose—cain be them rich folks
theys good to us theys good to us theys good to us theys
good to us theys good to us, i know, the massa tolt me
so, i seed it on channel 7, i seed it on channel 9 i seed
it on channel 4 and 2 and 5. Rich folks good to us
poor folks aint shit, hallelujah, hallelujah, ooowow! oowow!
must be the devil, going to heaven after i die, after we die
everything gonna be different, after we die we aint gon be
hungry, ain gon be pain, ain gon be sufferin wont go thru this
again, after we die, after we die owooo! owowoooo!

after we die, its all gonna be good, have all the money we
need after we die, have all the food we need after we die
have a nice house like the rich folks, after we die, after we die. after we
die, we can live like rev ike, after we die, hallelujah, hallelujah. must be
the devil, it ain capitalism, it aint capitalism, it aint capitalism.
naw it ain that, jimmy carter wdnt lie, "lifes unfair" but it aint capitalism
must be the devil, owow! it ain the police, jimmy carter wdnt lie. you
know rosalynn wdnt not lillian, his drunken racist brother aint no reflection
on jimmy, must be the devil got in im, i tell you, the devil killed malcolm
and dr king too, even killed both kennedies, and pablo neruda and overthrew
allende's govt. killed lumumba, and is negotiating with step and fetchit,
sleep n eat and birmingham, over there in "Rhodesia", goin' under the name
ian smith, must be the devil, caint be vorster, caint be apartheid, caint
be imperialism, jimmy carter wdnt lie, didnt you hear him say in his state
of the union message, i swear on rosalyn's face-lifted catatonia, i wdnt lie
nixon lied, haldeman lied, dean lied, hoover lied hoover sucked (dicks) too
but jimmy dont, jimy wdnt jimmy aint lying, must be the devil, put yr
money on the plate, must be the devil, in heaven we'all all be straight.
cain be rockfeller, he gave amos pootbootie a scholarship to Behavior
Modification Univ, and Genevieve Almoswhite works for his foundation
Must be niggers! Cain be Mellon, he gave Winky Suckass, a fellowship in
his bank put him in charge of closing out mortgages in the lowlife

Pittsburgh Hill nigger section, caint be him.
(Goes on babbling, and wailing, jerking in pathocrazy grin stupor)
Yessuh, yessuh, yessuh, yessuh, yessuh, yessuh, yessuh, yessuh, yessuh, yessuh
put yr money in the plate, dont be late, dont have to wait, you gonna be in
heaven after you die, you gon get all you need once you gone. yessuh, i heard
it on *the jeffersons*, i heard it on *the rookies*, i swallowed it
whole on *roots*: wasn't it nice slavery was so cool and
all you had to do was wear derbies and vests and train chickens and buy your
way free if you had a mind to, must be the devil, wasnt no *white* folks.
lazy niggers chained theyselves and threw they own black asses in the bottom
of the boats. [(well now that you mention it King Assblackuwasi helped
throw yr ass in
the bottom of the boat, yo mamma, wife, and you never seed em no more)]
must
a been the devil, gimme your money put your money in this plate. heaven be
here soon, just got to die, just got to stop living. close yr eyes stop
breathin and bammm-O heaven be here, you have all a what you need.
Bam-O
all a sudden, heaven be here, you have all you need, that assembly line
you work on will dissolve in thin air owowoo! owowoo! Just gotta die
just gotta die, this ol world aint nuthin, must be the devil got you
thinkin so, it cain be rockefeller, it cain be morgan, it caint be capitalism
it caint be national oppression owow! No Way! Now go back to work and
cool
it, go back to work and lay back, just a little while longer till you pass
its all gonna be alright once you gone. gimme that last bitta silver you got
stashed there sister, gimme that dust now brother man, itll be ok on the
other side, yo soul be clean be washed pure white. yes. yes. yes. owow.
now go back to work, go to sleep, yes, go to sleep, go back to work, yes
owow. owow. uuuuuuuuuu. uuuuuuuuuuu. uuuuuuuuu. yes, uuuuuuu. yes.
uuuuuuuuuu.
a men

[1979]

Clayton Eshleman

HADES IN MANGANESE

for James Hillman

Today I'd like to climb the difference
between what I think I've written and
what I *have* written, to clime being,
to conceive it as a weather
generate and degenerate,
a snake turning in digestion with the low.

But what you hear
are the seams I speak, animal,
the white of our noise
meringues into peaks
neither of us mount—or if we do,
as taxidermists, filling what is over
because we love to see as if alive.

Seam through which I might enter,
wounded animal, stairwayed
intestine in the hide of dream,
Hades, am I
yule, in nightmare
you weigh my heart,
you knock, in the pasture at noon,
I still panic
awaking at 3 AM
as if a burglar were in the hall,
one who would desire me, on whose claw
I might slip a ring, for in the soft

cave folds of dream
in conversation you woo, I weigh,
I insert something cold in you,
you meditate me up, I carry
what is left of you, coils
of garden hose, aslant, in my gut...

Hades, in manganese you rocked, an animal,
the form in which I was beginning to
perish, wading in eidola
while I separated you out!
To cross one back line with
another, hybrid, to take from the graft
the loss, the soul now wandering
in time, thus grieving for
what it must invent, an out of time,
an archetype, a non-existing
anthrobeast, rooted and seasonally
loosing its claws in the air!

O dead living depths!
One face cooing to another plungers
that went off, torpedos, in dream,
to spin through a pasture at noon,
sphincter-milled, sheep-impacted,
the lower body attached
to separation, pulling the seam of it along
cold cave stone, the head as
a pollen-loaded feeler tunneling
to ooze a string of eggs
where the rock, strengthening its yes,
returned the crawler to vivid green
sunlight that *was* profundity
now invested with linkage,
the grass, invested with linkage,
the whole sky, a tainted link,
man, a maggot on stilts,
desiring to leave elevation at the mouth
to seam unyield to his face.
Tethered, Hades phoned, om

phallos, the metro the zipper
of dread at every branch-off,
the pasture at noon conducted
by the bearmarm below, batoning
sun down word rust scraper by scraper out.

*

Below, in the culvert
behind the house of Okumura, Kyoto, 1963,
the conveyor-belt ran all night.
The clanking got louder, tore
then died, surf roar, origin beguiling,
a highway was going through.
During late night breaks,
the itinerant laborers would smoke
by a sparking oil drum in domed yellow helmets,
navy-blue wool puttees, men goblined by metal,
pitch blackness and popping fire. I watched
from a glassed-in porch, not quite able to see
inside the drum, wanting to engage
the action, to tie the fire into a poem
Paul Blackburn spoke on tape to me,
which would not burn. He suffered savage men,
without a context, standing about a dying fire
jacking off into it. Depth was the crisis
I tried to raise. The surf roar, earth
tearing, lifted, but not transformed, seemed,
as if part of me, an unending mechanicality.
I could and could not—it could and could.

I was, in spirit, still
in puberty, before my typewriter,
as if in a pew before an altar,
itchy, bored, afraid of being whipped
when we all got home. I played the hymnals
and black choir gowns into a breathing cellar
larder, a ladder to
convincing ore, a bed-shaped
Corregidor flashing, as if a beacon, to me adrift

—or was it the Phi Delta Theta dorm door opened
a crack? I would think of Mrs. Bird's canary
waiting to be driven downstairs and beat bloody.
That canary, hardly an image, helped me,
but it faded in an instant, the actives were
shouting around our bunks, beating pans.
Meowing like Raoul Hausmanns—or were we silent?—
we bent over where the wall had been removed
and only the fireplace remained, gripping
each others' shoulders, our naked huddle
encircled the open-ended fire—we were fisted
loosely to a turbined mass, our heads
a common tampax clamped into the actives' hate.

This fire surrounded by walls of flesh is now
contained. Hades makes a target of this maze.

*

Perseus holds the written head out to the sun.
His sword from his hip projects what is on his mind,
a center torn from a center, Medusa
wrenched from her jellyfish stronghold,
her severed pipes, the caterwauling serpents,
his treasure from the underworld.
The hero will not be
transfixed into himself, he will lift
reflected terror from reflected depth,
he will thrust his hand down
into the sodden tampax mass where earth bleeds.
My father, for 30 years timing blacks
slaughtering steers, folds into men
beating the animal in other men,
extracting its Pan-pipes, jugular flutes of morning.

Picking the confetti from our hair,
Little Lulu and I cross the city
Francis Bacon mayors. In this city
cartoons mingle equally with men.
In their cruel goo outlines I sense

the terrible strength in our lifting up,
unceasingly to translate upward,
to take whatever stuff and lift it,
earth, dream, whatever, up,
the pyramidic impulse to slave-point sunward,
to streamline, rather than to learn from, Lazarus.

*

Surface is reality as is ascension
as is depth. Medusa hangs down through
fathoms of archaic familiarity,
the pylons men have made of female psyche,
women beat into gates through which to draw
the ore of heroic energy, to appease
a masculine weather for manipulation and torture.
War on matter lumped into a procrustian mater
crammed, with her crucified familiar,
into the entrance way to Hades. I knew,
holding my 50 pound mother in her swaddling
cancer sheet, that there is no triumph *over*.
Resurrection, a Carl Dreyer altarpiece, yes,
a true finger-exercise in hope, a waist-
hinge, in the waste of spirit the crocus-bud
surely is not to be denied, its yellowy flame
playing among the stones warms what is
youngest in us, most held in night, tender,
voracious for sunset, fire appetite,
to watch the mountain smoke with modesty,
the thing to transform itself, lifting
from itself but carrying Hades as pendulum,
the parachutist gathering in Medusa's threads,
an intelligence under, not of us, but receptive
to us as we drift and wither...

Why do we treat the hero
better than he treated the material
he severed to feed the sun?
Perseus with his fistful of belladonna,
could we transform him into a hermit

with a lantern? Give him an awl,
teach him meander-work, zigzag wobbling through
the infante-clotted rushes, teach him salamander,
teach his semen how to stimulate fire. Unblock
the entrance way to Hades, allow the violet odors
of its meats to simmer in ice penetrating
advice. Something will work its magic against
the door of never. Hell Week, 1953,
a postcard Hades mailed to me,
his kids in demon suits tied to a string
about my penis led up through my white shirt
tied to a "pull me" card dangling
from my sport-coat pocket. The personal
is the apex of pain, but without it
mountains begin to numb specificity.
The personal works in specificity like a tail-
gunner, the tension in the dog-fight tying
my death into my work.

*

Concentration now includes Dachau,
barbed wire has replaced reason
as the circumference of energy. There is
no hail to rise to. Names are cultural
foam, nada-maggots stretching their scrawl-souls, paw
scorings in the frost of the mother corridor
where our faces were first ironed softly.

Hades receives meandering Hermes
mazing my thoughts into the La Pieta
softness of the target-maker's arms—
there what I change is ended, my despair
is nursed cryptically, for Hades' breasts,
like cob-webbed mangers, are miracleproof.
There a sucking goes on, below the obstructed
passage way, all senses of the word, stilled
in its being, take place. I am playing
with what is left of my animal, a marble
it rolls into neuter, a cat's eye, rolls back,
I crack its pupil between word-infant lips...

Bird spirit flew into Apollo—
animal appeared in Dis.
What was sky and earth became life and death,
or hell on earth and psychic depth,
and I wonder: how has Hades been affected by Dachau?
In the cold of deepest bowels, does a stained
fluid drip? Does pure loss now have an odor
of cremation, a fleshy hollow feel
of human soul infiltrating those realms
Hades had reserved for animals?
Are there archai, still spotted with
this evening's russets, stringing and quartering
an anthrobestial compost? Or are the zeros,
of which we are increasingly composed,
folding out the quick of animal life?
Is that why these outlines, these Hadic kin,
take on mountainous strength,
moving through the shadows of these days?

A wheeled figure stabs and sews
the infancy in our grain to the skin of the ground.
Wheeled wall master who mends in manganese,
talk through what I do not remember,
the life in which I am glued
stringings of narrative Ariadnes.
All hominids share a scarlet where the dark is
pitch with horizon, note leaps, the static
of non-meaning tendrilling us, making way
for not another bringing of the dark
up into the light, but a dark
delivered dark Paleolithic dimension.

[1979]

DEEDS DONE AND SUFFERED BY LIGHT

One can glimpse Apollo in the door of each thing,
as if each thing now contains his oven—
in vision I open an olive tree and see his earlier animal
shapes fleeing at the speed of light, the python,
mouse, and lion Apollo, fleeing so that human forms
may walk unharmed by the invasion of the supernatural.
Light increased incredibly after the end of animal deity,
at the point verticality was instituted,
and the corpse of one's mother buried far, far from the place
on which one slept one's head. But the supernatural
in the guise of the natural is turning us over
in its fog a half mile from this ledge. Burnished
muscleless fist of a grey cloud. Sound of rain
from water still falling from the olives. I have no desire
to live in a world of nature conditioned by patriarchy.
I kick off my head and live in the light
bounding in from my mother. It is her great
ambivalence toward her own navel that conditions
the decreasing dripping. The hills now
writhe with green meat and something should follow.
Something should be explaining the tuft of salmon bull shape
abandoned by the other stilled clouds. Something
should be done with the swatted fly. Something is
this abyss of unusableness that remainders me
and pays no royalty. There are hosts of thrones
directly above. A witch hammer. A cleated enclosure.
The way a church has of making you puke your soul
upon entering and then, as the dryness of birth is rehashed
by nun and candle, of worshipping what has just left you,
the bride of your chest, the stuff inside you that a moment before
twinkled with the sadness and poverty of the street's
malicious laughter. How I wish that this poem
would birth another, and that the other had something to do
with unpacking the olive meat of this mountain. No
apocalypse. An enlargement, rather, of the so-called Whore
on her severely underfed Dragon. And more wine. More plumes
of silver azure evening coursing over
the thatch of the mountainside. More space to suffer,

more farewell to the flesh, more carnival in the face of everyman,
less perfection, more coherence. Meaning: more imagination,
more wigs for glowworms, more cribs for the restless dead
who wake us right before dawn with their bell leper
reminding us that fresh rain air is a clear indication
that here is not entirely here. The processions of graffiti-
scarred bison are, like us, clouds imprisoned to be viewed.
And then my mother began to speak: "You've put on a lot of weight!
Look at your father and me, some shape we're in! We've suffered
a lot for you these 14 years. You should've seen my left side
when it turned into a purple sponge and strained what
you buried me in to the point it rotted. I'm glad
John Ashbery appeared to you last night reading new
incomprehensible poems that made perfectly good sense. You are
much more organized, much more chaotic, than you behave here.
When I think of you, I see you at 12, stuck in the laundry chute,
your legs wiggling in the basement air, while the top part talked
with me as we waited for the renter to pull you out.
We had a nice chat that afternoon, and I almost liked you best
that way, just what stuck out of the chute. If I could only have
that part on a roller skate and let what was wiggling below go—
it's that part that's gone off gallivanting,
that's carried you goodness knows where while I
and your father lie here a few feet away from each other
waiting for our coffin lids to cave in. Then, even
the little space you left us to play with memories of you
on our chest bones will be gone. My buttons are mouldy
and my hands have no flesh left but I still manage
to squeak my buttons a little and get into your dreams.
I'm sorry if I appear both dead and alive to you,
but you should know by now you can't have it your way all the time.
I'm as real in this way as I ever was, sick more often than not
when I appear, but you're never here, you're worrying
how to take care of me, and then you wake to a jolt
every time there's nothing to take care of.
Now your father wants to say a word." "Clayton,
why don't you come home? We were such a nice little family.
Now it is like when you went off to that university.
Your mother and I would sit up and talk about you
until our fathers came in from the night and motioned us

into our bed. You were such a nice little fellow
when we could hold you up high and look at each other
through you. Ten little fingers ten little toes
Two bright eyes a funny little nose
A little bunch of sweetness that's mighty like a rose
Your mother, through you, looked so much like
your grandmother I could never get over it.
Why I bet you don't even remember your birth gifts
a savings bank and one dollar from granddad and grandmother
Two kimonas from aunt Georgia and uncle Bob
Supporters from Faye's dollie Patricia Ann
A Romper Suit from Mrs. Warren Bigler
A Dress from Mr. & Mrs. SR Shambaugh
Silk Booties & Anklets Knit Soaker & Safety Pins
Hug-me-tight a Floating Soap Dish with Soap Rubber Doggie
I don't see why you don't come home. Your mother and I
have everything you need here. Why sure,
let's see, maybe you could pick up some things,
Gladys—no, she's not listening—*Gladys what do you want?*"
"Well, I know we need some scouring powder and light bulbs"
"GLADYS WHAT DO YOU WANT?" "And Clayton, we want
Clayton to come back we don't like Clayton Jr. out so late at night"
"GLADYS WHAT DO YOU WANT?" "You never know what will happen, why
just last week Eunice Wilson, over in Plot #52541, told me"
"GLADYS WHAT DO YOU WANT?" "—are you listening, Daddy?
Eunice said while Jack was getting out of his car parked in his own driveway at 2 AM"
"GRADDISROTDUYRUNT" "—after his date with Kay Fisbeck, this man
came up to him and said something I will not"
"GRADDISROTDRURUNT" "—I will not repeat it was that vulgar—
this man said: if you don't come with me, I'll crush your cows.
Doesn't that take the cake? Why Clayton you can't blame Jack
for going off with him, and you would not believe where
this man took Jack Wilson and what he wanted him to do.
Now that your father's lid has caved in, I'll tell you:
he made him drive north to the Deaf School parking lot,
and when he was sure nobody else was around, he said:

Persephone's a doll
  steeper than Marilyn,
miracles lick her,
  dreams invader,

over the cobweb orchestra
there's an ice
conductor,
forget the orchestra,
conduct the pit!
Hanged
Ariadne
giving birth in Hades
is the rich, black music in mother's tit."

[1984]

Ronald Johnson

from *ARK:*

BEAM 4

The human eye, a sphere of waters and tissue, absorbs an energy that has come ninety-three million miles from another sphere, the sun. The eye may be said to be sun in other form.

It is part of a spectrum of receptors, and if we could only 'see' more widely the night sky would be 'brighter' than the moon. Matter smaller than the shortest wavelength of light cannot be seen.

Pressure on the surface of an eye makes vision, though what these same pressures focus to the radial inwardness of a dragonfly in flight is unimaginable. Through pressure also, the head-over-heels is crossed right-side-up, in eye as camera. (It is possible to take a cow's eyeball and thin the rear wall of it with a knife, fit it front forward in a tube, and the tube pointed at an elm will image an upside down elm.)

The front of the eye is a convex glass, alive, and light bent through its curve strikes a lens. This lens is behind an iris—pushing it into the shape of a volcano. In light, the iris appears as a rayed core of color, its center hole dilating dark to day, transformed instantly into what man's twinned inner hemispheres call sight.

The retina is its bowl-shaped back—the cones at retinal center growing through intersections with rods, toward rods at the rim. Through this mesh, ray seizes ray to see. In the rods there is a two-part molecule that is unlinked by light. One quantum of light unlinks one molecule, and five rods are needed to perceive the difference. Some stars are at this threshold, and can only be seen by the sides of the eyes. The eye can see a wire .01 inch in diameter at a distance of 100 yards. The retina itself seeks equilibrium.

Though to look at the sun directly causes blindness, sight is an intricately precise tip of branched energy that has made it possible to measure the charge of solar storm, or to calculate nova. It is possible that all universe is of a similar form.

Our eyes are blue for the same reason sky is, a scattering of reflectors: human eyes have only brown pigment.

In the embryo two stalks push from the brain, through a series of infoldings, to form optic cups. Where the optic cup reaches surface, the surface turns in and proliferates in the shape of an ingrowing mushroom. The last nerve cells to form are those farthest from light.

If I sit at my table and look at the shaft of light which enters a glass filled with water—and exits rainbow—then move my head to the left, the shaft and glass move right, and the window behind them, left. If I stand up and step to the table, the glass at its edge moves downward, while the far end of the table, and the window with it, rise straight up in the air.

No one knows the first man to stare long at a waterfall, then shift his gaze to the cliff face at its side, to find the rocks at once flow upward. But we have always known the eye to be unsleeping, and that all men are lidless Visionaries through the night. Mind & Eye are a logarithmic spiral coiled from periphery. This is called a 'spiral sweep'—a biological form which combines (as do galaxies) economy with beauty. (We define 'beauty' from symmetrical perceptions): *subjects observing a flickered pulsation of light have seen something like a Catherine-wheel reversing rotation, with a center of fine detail.* Men have found cells sensitive to light in the hearts of snails.

The human lens grows flatter for looking across a prairie, and the sparrow is able to see the seed beneath its bill—and in the same instant the hawk descending. A cat watches the-sparrow-at-the-end-of-the-world in a furred luminosity of infra-reds, enormous purples.

After a long time of light, there began to be eyes, and light began looking with itself. At the exact moment of death the pupils open full width.

BEAM 7

Sound is sea: pattern lapping pattern. If we erase the air and slow the sound of a struck tuning-fork in it, it would make two sets of waves interlocking the invisibility in opposite directions.

As the prong of the fork moved one way, it compressed the air at its front, which layer in turn relieves its compression by expanding the layer in front, and so back to back. As it started the other direction it left the air in front (opposite) immediately rarefied. The air beyond this expands to the rarefaction—itself becoming rarefied—forth and forth.

Compression rarefaction compression rarefaction: these alternate equidistant forces travel at the rate of 1,180 feet per second through the elasticity of air, four times that through water (whale to singing whale), and fifteen times as fast through pure steel. Men have put ear to earth to hear in advance of air.

Pattern laps pattern, and as they joined, Charles Ives heard the 19th Century in one ear, and the 20th out the other, then commenced to make a single music of them. The final chord of the 2nd Symphony is a reveille of all notes at once, his The Fourth of July ends with a fireworks of thirteen rhythmic patterns zigzagging through the winds and brasses, seven percussion lines criss-crossing these, the strings divided in twenty-fours going up and down every-which-way—and all in FFFF.

Both tuning fork and Fourth are heard by perturbations of molecules, through ever more subtle stumbling blocks, in spiral richochet, to charged branches treeing a brain.

The outer earshell leads to a membrane drum—and what pressure needed to sound this drum is equal to the intensity of light and heat received from a 50 watt electric bulb at the distance of 3,000 miles in empty space. (Though sound cannot travel, as light, through the void.) At the threshold of hearing the eardrum may be misplaced as little as a diameter of the smallest atom, hydrogen.

This starts a 'hammer' to strike an 'anvil' which nudges a 'stirrup'—all, bones—against a drum known as The Oval Window. Shut to air, this window vibrates another windowed membrane, tuning a compressed fluid between. *Here, also, is couched our sense of the vertical.*

A resonance is set up in a spiral shell-shaped receptor turned with yet another, also spiral, membrane. This is the pith of labyrinth, and as sound waves themselves it trembles two directions at once, crosswise and lengthwise.

The mind begins early to select from the buzz and humdrum, till most men end hearing nothing, when the earth speaks, but their own voices. Henry David Thoreau seems to have been the first man to re-learn to hear that *Moto Perpetuo* of the actual: the Greeks strung their lyre to the planets, but Thoreau heard his stretched from first dark sparrow to last dog baying moon.

While a bat uses its ears to see, its optics overtones, the fly hears only in frequencies of its own (and other) fly-wings. I know the housefinch singing outside the window just now heard its own song with slower and lower ear than mine, but I do not know what this means, or how it rings in finchskull. (Though all animals have an auditory range which includes hearing what they can eat, and what can eat them.)

A man once set out to see birds, but found instead he'd learned to listen: an ear better unwinds the simultaneous warblers in a summer birch-wood. There, he came upon an Orpheus, all marble, holding a spiral shell to the ear of his Euridice. Turning the other way, he saw Orpheus again, listening to harmonics of midges in sun, the meadow like a nightingale around him. Cat's purr, moth-wing.

The physicists tell us that all sounding bodies are in a state of stationary vibration, and that when the word *syzygy* last shook atoms, its boundary was an ever slighter pulse of heat, and hesitation of heat. Matter delights in music, and became Bach. Its dreams are the abyss and empyrean, and to that end, may move, in time, the stones themselves to sing.

BEAM 25, *A Bicentennial Hymn*

prosper
O
cell

through there where the forest is thickest

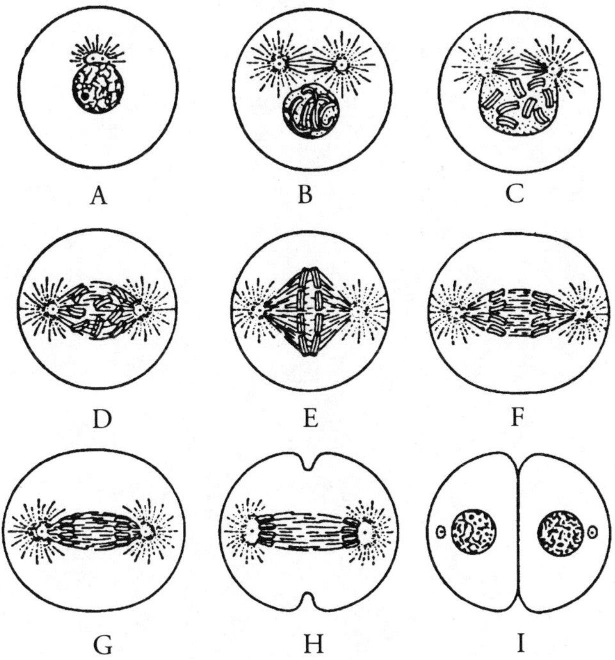

gave proof through the

bells'

twentyonegun*son&lumiere*salutetothesun

Aquila chrysaetos, I have seen Him in the watchfires

full sail the *Ruffles & Flourishes*

sifting out a glory
loosed lightning to answer
arching on

A

FIREWORKS MUSIC:
—hexagonal prisms terminated by hexagonal pyramids—
quartzrose oscillations of velocities
(link on washing tone)
of the coming of the eyes, across the sea, swift sounded
hundred circling beauty trampling out the heart,
Lord
Coriolis coalescens

see how he walks upon the wheat!

:the mind become its own subject matter:
bent ambient
(all meaning is an angle)
sampling
the optimum play at any one moment spray of curvature

falling off toward the edge great gold sunflowerhead of photons
sum of sun and moon
in array the flicker of diamond-lattice pattern
against a complex dappled back-
ground also moving.

Ratio is all.

[1980]

ARK 37, *Prospero's Songs to Ariel (contructed in the form of a quilt snipped from Roger Tory Peterson's* A Field Guide to Western Birds)

hear hear hear hear
see-see-see
"upcurled" uttered like a mallet driving a stake
a tick of white, pale buff
constantly changing speed and direction
immutabilis
with an air-splitting stitch at the "focus"
"dead-leaf" pattern
in falling diminuendo blending into a broad terminal band of
"code"

low
"dissonances through dissonances through dissonances"
dark winged Solitary
with a scythelike *check-check-check*
sewing-machine motion blood red to the zoned
magnificens

with a center of slower winding
trying to sing like a Canary
in higher orchard
killy killy killy great yellow bill

quark "frozen"
("like a sparrow dipped in raspberry juice")
in rhythm of a small ball bouncing to a standstill
nestling *flammeus*
closed ellipse with diagonal axis
garden
bordered by blue-stem ethereal prairie
split-second
"Dancing" Cascade Mts.
or frail saucer in conifer

silent
barred crosswise streaked lengthwise
speculum *borealis*
Turnstone white, ocher, cerulean, cog the deep (from above)
Stilt
Great Plains to equator
(clockwork) across Oceans of the
laterally
a-ring-a-ring-a-ring-a at wheeling anchor
sawedged image

wick-wick-wick-wick
large black swift wheels, a wash of gold
light fanwise off in a zigzag
-fastened

scissorlike insistence, moth come past dotted *stellata*
proportion, to balance
repeated shape it might have none
until they catch the light
bowed Nightjar-
bell

angles of scarlet, old poplars
erect as waterfalls
shook-shook-shook through the zoom changing azure hinges
ruffed muffled thumping, salmon the *antiquum*
beeline voices in the bronze of Thought
stone grasshopper to stone open eye
montezumae
triangle ring repeated
(reason unknown)
at song

constant
"fire-throat" "spread-eagle"
rising and falling
as if answering its own question
(in the hand)
heart-shaped familiaris
ascending the scale by short iridescent retreating waves
Omnivorous, woven rose-scallop, interior of light
Ancient of dove
(which also soars)

dark, white, dark, white, dark
"like a roller-coaster"

folded back upon
tick-tick, the Kittiwake silhouette sweet time skip
smoke-slate
Corpus Christi off the water, grainfields upend in V-formation
through breezy Air to chisel ripple summit
Phaethon aethereus
accelerating russet, then Big Bend
Starling dips

pale ghost-bird of the inner eyrie
silvery over and over
body in strong light, radial
at a distance, only the hollow long-drawn *whoooooooo*
tooit-wit winnowing an almost touching elsewhere
in bright yellow lines, twinkling flight to flesh at "window"
"eyed on back of head" at night in spring
in endless succession
as it walks
the rip-tipe *paradisaea*

to corners
Blue Goose, in lemon-colored shade
patterning beyond the pale
grass cup in briar
loosed crease in the summer, streams punctuated by daylight
the glass reveals basket-like sparkles of margin
or circumpolar seed seen in sky
violet eyelets in olive
rootling
in wide circles

[1984]

Robert Kelly

Those who are beautiful
A sonata
If even sounds have skin
A space some spaces give
Some who are beautiful because space

Sun's able to shape sequent light on wood mere
Ear squints to hear rightly rightly
Intonation of the sitting still
Some because space because wood
Glue gold hold what you said
My eye playing your lap
Space in your knee's time to hold
Sonorous what did you say?

A chaplet of amber noises
Humming around your neck
I would expect May in California
Heat I remember
Long roads northeast from the San Pablo
Into amazing rice

Something blossoms every month
Call it into my mouth
A little bleak a little bird
Taking self less serious
So I can take you
You look exactly like yourself

Equally white
Chaste nostrils in arc-en-ciel
It is better not to see than to obsess
Certain curves command my mind
And all time after repeats their sleek geometry
I grieve in those numbers except to hold
Better not to see than to possess
Undivided destinies we cant control
Fortune cookies on the plate distinguish text

This one for you that
One must be listening in the wood
Itself a sort of glass
Finger wet
Sings
A sort of forest
Under a sort of varnish all that color knows
A sort of company of potential friends or
So often it sounds as if it can't decide
Or as if deciding were not beautiful
Not half as beautiful as being

To be healthy is not necessarily to be
Or to be going or anywhere
To be healthy is only a woollen
Shirt in winter it is always winter out
Because some compression in the music
Faces glass
Her like exactly look you equal
Rainbow clothes better to see stretto
Fortune in the wood
The sound has sheen
The share is *schön*
You must be shimmering when you do that
You must remembering me when you hear that in your hands
Because our blues
Are very ravenous are you
Some bite and some drink the shape of the cup itself
Drink this drawing of you doing so

Rest a hair of color on a lot of air
Seed marigolds and wait for white
An obvious imposition on the mind
Keep me in your heart
To be this agriculture too
So many chitterlings in this cauldron
And my burnt thumb tastes you
Serene hysteric with large eyes
Immensely wise and hardly knowing
Now is the time
Before you get older or I get young
The way time's hydraulic flushes
Certainly leave large spaces
Or where would the music go
Lady blow me blue
The nature of what is personal imitates music
Fond father uncle of nine a desert
Advertises for its ruling rock
Come do my job I need some help
Sit up late taking me seriously
Every lover says obsess obsess
So I'll be no lover longer
And this quick kiss won't tie your hands

Any living room looks better for fish
There are slow release feeders for fish
We can leave the tank alone for days and not hurt fish
I swear Ladie my tongue is one of such
Fish and feeder both you'll find
Lambent in your fish bowl I your mica castle
And all I am is good for you again
Your house and never be possessed
Your hands and never be obsessed
Your nose and never be plain
Your hair and never be rage
Your arm and never be curt
Your belly and never be mute
Your knee and never be local
Your fingertip and never sand
Your two ears and never Solomon

Your important neck and never Tahiti
Do not hide your heart your navel and your left hip
Do not have a shy shank
Do not let your elbow learn Norwegian
Do not be wise o do not be wise
There are birds here that could make two of us
Dinner for a star and cheese for a child
Your eyelid and never a Ferrari
Your eyelash and never a boat
Your nostril and never philosophy
Your chin and not a postage stamp
Your tonguetip and never night
Shimmer o do not be wise
Grow young without apologies
Your buttock and never a bible
Your shoulderblade and no sheep
Your nape and no oracle
Never be wise o never
O shimmer and not relax
Be wise neither nor soft
Your ankle and never the Bastille
Your sex and never a senate
Your breast and never a prayer

All we have are the names of things
Not so
All we have are names and scarcely things
Scarcely things are for the having
Names are for the calling
Calling is beautiful and what we have
Is busy with calling

During the recent war there was some traffic in meat
During the opera what we had eaten began to sing
During history women changed their minds
There are so many alternate releases
There is time there is ink there is time
So some of some that are beautiful
Resist the resistance is beautiful
Things are remarkable things have come back

We are busy with calling
The resistance is ribbon blue-black for your hair
Scarlet grosgrain a stone at morning
A headache a bonsai these things are calling
Something red is calling a green book
Some sympathy is sure to be itself
O I am tired of not being loose
All these connections are freedom looselimbed mind
What is resistance resistance is a hedge
Resistance is sand under pine tree
Resistance is railroad
Matchhead a beach a guitar of a certain kind
Resistance is palm
Resistance is a cat howling in the cellar under a civil house
What is resistance
All these connections are freedom
A baby in a postcard tree
A passacaglia tied to the bed
Resistance is the shape of a ham upside down
What is resistance resistance is resin
It is often apricot it is masculine
Resistance is feminine is hawser is handkerchief
War is resistance what is resistance
Resistance is careful listening rarer than thought
Resistance is copper is numerical is number
What is resistance resistance
It is umber it matches it disguises it dispenses pills
It is ink
All these connections are freedom
Connection is freedom
That is equation not definition
Resistance is something to be equal to
A moment in sunshine like a seal on a rock
Resistance is something to go to the ocean with
Resistance complains to the waves
Resistance asks if it may speak
Resistance asks the sun to shine
May I shine says the sun may I shine says my voice
To the house if it listens
Resistance is trying to go

Resistance is gone
Ask the wood are you house and the music are you listening
If it is a house it listens
If it is music it hears.

[1983]

STUDYING HORSES

When you wake up from sleeping with women
whether or not you yourself are a woman,
there are only a few matters left to consider:
matter of the sun, matter of money,
and the matter of horses. They are grey
from sweat, whatever their color in dream
(like my cropped head of hair,
trop de parole, too many years
of talking and talking turned grey)
three matters (the way the mediaevals
—as Marlene called them—cherished
three great cycles of love:
three *matières*: of Antiquity (Helen, Ajax,
Alexander, Golden Fleece), of France
(Roland and Huon and Charlemagne),
and the Matter of Britain (Guinevere
and her tarnished, vanished cup
so many beautiful young men set out to find)
Sorry for the lecture. When you wake up
from sleeping with whatever a woman *is*
—the both of you keeping your secret,
the shared lips wet, the lap of the one
in the lap of the other—you are of course
each other's mother—you have to cope
and go on coping with directions,
the shredded manual of dream instructions
that rules the world, you woke up
clutching scraps of it, how to get there,
who to go with, who will help you,
what birds to listen to, what dragons
to leave respectfully alone,

and you lost that page, the map is gone,
you have no money and you wake up
from sleeping with women and you're gone,
it's Greenpoint again, and you took like a dope
the wrong subway to the wrong stop and suddenly
you can't remember the street of the man
—it is a man—why are you bothering
to go so far to visit a man—neither young
nor old, black nor white, why—and why
would there be a Piedras Negras St. in Brooklyn
and then you remember: it's Alvarado!
but you can't find a bus and a woman
is trying to catch a cab and she will share
—suddenly you're in a wheelchair
so she's not scared of you—without
being thrilled at the idea
but there's something wrong with her face,
and before the two of you—again, the
two of you, lost in the big world—
even spot a cab you realize
you've forgotten the number of his house,
this mystic charlatan, third world messiah
you've come so far—so far?—a subway
ride is far? where did you first
go under the ground, Egypt? o love
I am holding my own hand and praying for love—
so far to see, and all the buildings
on his block look alike—that much
you do remember—six story tenements
walk-ups with fragrant vestibules
from the dawn of civilization—
and the park of the needles—McSomething—
is not too far away. All this
is the Matter of the Sun, what we call
impoverishment: what you drag
like It over the horizon from the dark
and try to make sense of all day long,
the you and the it, inner and outer,
the drag. I know nothing about money.
And horses are grey with sweat, dry sticky,

eat sugar, wear stripes in jungles,
horses eat goats, goats catch birds,
birds swim. That much I know.
Fire flies. Water forgets. Everything
in its place. The island. Sleeping
with women. But the matter of horses
is beautiful money nowadays, verdant
sprawls of the Rhinebeck condottieri,
my cast iron circus wagon when I was five:
two heavy glossy smooth white horses pulled
a red cage with gilded wheels—and in that cart
a lion roared, I trapped it
from my other animals
—the ones with France or Austria embossed
on their pale bellies—ostrich, crocodile,
elephant, bear—and this lion,
matter of Britain, king roaring for his cup,
the grail lost behind the summer stars,
I trapped it and put it in the cage myself!
O confusion infinitely fertile we call dear world!
O spindrift credences and spontaneous theologies,
o money sloshing in the groove of time
hard, like a toilet plunger making
the blocked city be abruptly gone—
but I know nothing about that, nothing
about money, look what it did to Pound,
I would talk about horses, grey
with sea foam, sweaty with wanting,
too much time, twilights, loving someone,
les crépuscules de chevaux are the palest hours,
luminous against sumacs a white horse.

2

When you wake up from sleeping with women
you're supposed to put money in your pocket,
get on your horse and travel into the sun-work
all the while studying other people's horses.
How they go. The colors that they have,
the arguments. In your dream you remembered nothing,
or nothing was worth it. All numbers

are wrong, think about it, wrong and count
nothing, or count for nothing. A number
is no house. Even if it was you can't find it,
can't find a street or a house or a door
and the woman with something wrong with her face
is always beside you, riding with you
into the wrong direction. They all are.
You cry some other woman's name over and over,
the one you want to be with when you're away,
awake, but sleeping with women gives you
little opportunity for being awake. Sugar
in the coffee, hair on your hair,
her name in your mouth—so much
for prepositions—the strong syllables
of her rolling in your jaws. In your dream
the grey horses were you, you pulled yourself
with painful enthusiasm from fire to fire.
Motive: take care of people. Put fires out
in tenements, look beautiful in quick streets
lathered with sexy sweat. Recite poems
into ears too easy pleased with the warm
breath of your attention. Wake. But waking
is not easy, how long your ears are
these days, fuzzy and soft, how long
your poems. The street curves up to meet the sun.
Again it is an island, one of your many
in this ancient archipelago your life.
When you were a very small boy horses still flew,
most things you ate tasted of fish, Africa
was close, clams tasted of the same
whole sea you years later would ask her
to bring you safe in her hand. It is almost noon
and your dream is a real drag, no wonder you don't
like dreaming, no wonder horses
always look so frightened, with their big eyes
rolling but their measureless will-power
keeps their scared skinny legs standing still.
A fearful thing this money is, burns,
fire in the pocket, kills birds, eats fish,
swims through the streets remembering numbers.

Money never forgets the house he lives in,
the man you still suppose yourself to want to become.
Or to want to have become already,
blue-visaged, ignorant as a mussel,
gaping, empty of alarm. Are you
even yet outside the dream,
are you even the one who dreamed? Trying
to find the footsteps of the morning
before you, just something to follow, you caress
the gorgeous infidelities that make you free.

[1992]

Gustaf Sobin

GIRANDOLE

1

towards dawn, the
taxis
        idle
before the glass doors . . .
. . . .
fuchsia,

where a blown hem flares
in the sudden
updraft,
then

settles
pearl, through
a broken
foam

of reflections.

~

an ankle
arches, as the
mouths open, and fill . . .
a world-

without.
what the instinct
would swell to: that

image, that
deep

ray-
headed mirror
in which the dark breath
un-

wrinkles.

. . . .

wrapt
shadows, swept
fates . . .

                    in the rush,
uptown, the
moon
slips, over and
over, off the polished
wings

of the streaked
fenders.

2

it's how the
scarf falls, and
the

soft
braided silver
of the shoes . . . their signs!
that sky! the
new

un-
declinated night!
whisper

chases whisper, edge
its edges,
as

an arm swims
toward the
cast
brass palmleaves
of the light.

~

break, but
where; shatter, a
wave, still
swelling, against what?...
....

... no
heaven, and
scarce-

ly an
earth, a-
wash in that last echo: a
mouth, as it

twists
to the fold of a shoulder.

IRISES
for Susanna

out of those wild, in-
visible circuits, a
hawkmoth flew in. was dawn (in
deep vases, the first
white lines of the iris).

---

way that they ruffle in
that rock windcell (that their buds un-
scroll and open: opened,

asking myself only for what I see . . . .).

---

like birds trapped in
those tall, still-
glistening frescoes: the errant etruscan's.

---

earth it-
self held
in

that silent
ven-
triloquy.

---

muscled in
washed golds or
waves of pale naples, these deep
androgynies: a

joust of buds and limp
relenting petals.

---

my lines, for an instant, become theirs (but
only
for the extravagation).

---

rise, loop-winged, in a volley
of light yellows, stalks caught
in slender rectangular jars . . . .

---

being invisible, we
sip at those open
emanations: tubers shot into tall
grottoes, emptied
wind- eaten tombs.

---

lovely, the irises in their deep
oblivion, wounds open on
what the poem would
close: catch in the purities of its fiction.

---

a surf of
frozen whites, for your eyelids; its
waves, that
pitched linen, for your sleep . . . .

(faïence de moustiers)

not the javelins stabbing
into their own azurous mass, but the bowl, the
cold, sun- broken round. . .

---

are corpses, too: the petals streaming
against the hard stalks, or
wizened, sack-
like, in the tissued shadows of their wings.

(Saint Vincent's)

those cold fires on
their piped stems don't flower, they
alight, perch there in pale,
insane violets…

(are prayers, are the smoke of prayers . . .).

---

are awe-

weights (for
weighing

a

grief
against . . .).

---

the dead go on drinking, speckle
the white table saffron
with their transparent inks . . . .

---

each iris: the shell
of an iris, the papery craters
of its spent
ebullience.

---

mass gutted for the sake of an inference.

---

are the lines of flight of
these floral chases (not the
blades, the buds, the skirts blown, buff-
white, over the draft of
their thighs),

but the lines   driven, quilled,
        into the drawn lips   of the invisible.

(viaticum)

the dried irises in the
    sleeves of the   oil lamps
are yours —for   your journey— for dimming
        those   gaudy winds with . . . .

from THE EARTH AS AIR: AN ARS POETICA

I

1

lapping of   light over
light,   dew podding the   tall
    ferns   nacreous, as
it
opens (that

~

even here, at
the   very edges it
    start up, this   teasing of
sound out
of

    substance: the
air
paired fibrous
with

syllables: *moss,*   *rock, air-*
it-
self-in-   syl-

lable, that
it

happen).

~

in twos, that
it ribbon forth, the
forked idiom's . . .

each thing
eithered to another, the *this*
whatevered to the
that, the
ark-

within-the-
lyre- propellant: *wind*
and *white roses*

wrapt in a taut, vibratory weave.

~

because poetry is passage. is an equipoise-in-motion, addressed *away.*

by juxtaposing syllable, word, word-cluster in a harmonious tension, the poem (both in its materials and its sonorities) channels that passage: determines its course.

(or atomically, by the poem's vibration; discursively, by its dialectic, its *tao*).

is the body's, first, its profound androgyny's.

fused, inarticulate: insufferable.

that the saying, in releasing, separates: investing each of its opposites, its multifarious twins, with a transparent identity.

that only as 'eviscerates' might they enter the relationship, the *passacaglia*, the poem.

as our breath's oscillating bodies. . . .

is *wind* that permits *white roses* (and inversely).

locked together in their lyric trajectories of attraction, contact, dispersal.

far, what the poem would gather, accord, scatter further.

the earth, in its longing, its shattered fragments—in twos—fluted through.

celebrants in the doom of their invisible transactions, the narrows of their weightless encounters.

that's neither the *enactment of* nor the *symbol for,* but the rites of process by which substance, through sound, is transmitted forth: towards. . . .

the lash-undulant of complements that's

2

neither the lily's
nor

the toad's, shem's nor shaun's, all
our adored decoys of
cognition . . .
(what language
had seized, set
echoing, reflexive,
through the chambered
spaces
of
our words.

the bounced clowns of history, one
the suspended
referent
to the other: ever, our
alien- commensurates).

but,
what rushes
be-

tween them:
slips
be-

tween
cabbage
and

spade, thumb
and
clay, in

a gust-
accelerant
of

ashes,
shadows,
of 'things

that are
not.'
neither

earth's
nor
air's, but

the
null
springing.

ebullient,
out
of

a fusion
of
either's. the

nei-
ther's, the
limp,

re-
lapsing
flora of

their
muscles
dulled in

the
wisp, the
wires, the

un-
elemented
rays

shot
from the
hinged

half-
shells: the
echoing

limbs
of these
lovers.

~

that
it happen!
that the

breath
leap, and
the dark

light
issue, be-
tween

our tongue
and
teeth!

[1984]

Susan Howe

THOROW

Author's note: During the winter and spring of 1987 I had a writer-in-residency grant to teach a poetry workshop once a week at the Lake George Arts Project, in the town of Lake George, New York. I rented a cabin off the road to Bolton Landing, at the edge of the lake. The town, or what is left of a town, is a travesty. Scores of two-star motels have been arbitrarily scrambled between gas stations and gift shops selling Indian trinkets, china jugs shaped like breasts with nipples for spouts, American flags in all shapes and sizes, and pornographic bumper-stickers. There are two Laundromats, the inevitable McDonald's, a Howard Johnson, assorted discount leather outlets, video arcades, a miniature golf course, two run-down amusement parks, a fake fort where a real one once stood, a Dairy-Mart, a Donut-land, and a four-star Ramada Inn built over an ancient Indian burial ground. Everything graft, everything grafted. And what is left when spirits have fled from holy places? In winter the Simulacrum is closed for the season.

I went there alone, and until I became friends with some of my students, I didn't know anyone. After I learned to keep out of town, and after the first panic of dislocation had subsided, I moved into the weather's fluctuation. Let myself drift in the rise and fall of light and snow, re-reading re-tracing once-upon

Narrative in Non-Narrative

I thought I stood on the shores of a history of the world where forms of wildness brought up by memory become desire and multiply.

Lake George was a blade of ice to write across not knowing what She.

Interior assembling of forces underneath earth's eye. Yes, she, the Strange, excluded from formalism. I heard poems inhabited by voices.

In the seventeenth century European adventurer-traders burst through the forest to discover this particular long clear body of fresh water. They brought our story to it. Pathfinding believers in God and grammar spelled the lake into *place*. They have renamed it several times since. In paternal colonial systems a positivist efficiency appropriates primal indeterminacy.

In March 1987, looking for what is looking, I went down to unknown regions of indifferentiation. The Adirondacks *occupied* me.

Gilles Deleuze and Felix Guattari have written in an essay called "May, 1914. One or Several Wolves?": "The proper name (*nom propre*) does not designate an individual: it is on the contrary when the individual opens up to the multiplicities pervading him or her, at the outcome of the most severe operation of depersonalization, that he or she acquires his or her true proper name. The proper name is the instantaneous apprehension of a multiplicity. The proper name is the subject of a pure infinitive comprehended as such in a field of intensity."

Thoreau once wrote to a friend: "am glad to see that you have studied out the ponds, got the Indian names straightened out—which means made more crooked—&c. &c."

Sir Humfrey Gilbert wrote in *A New Passage To Cataia:* "To proove that the Indians aforenamed came not by the Northeast, and that there is no thorow passage navigable that way."

Thoreau never visited the Adirondacks. His book about the wilderness and mountains in Maine is called *Ktaadn*.

Work penetrated by the edge of author, traverses multiplicities, light letters exploding apprehension suppose when individual hearing

Every name driven will be as another rivet in the machine of a universe flux

I

Go on the Scout they say
They will go near Swegachey

I have snow shoes and Indian shoes

Idea of my present
not my silence

Surprise is not so much
Hurried and tossed about
that I have not had time

From the Fort but the snow
falling very deep
remained a fortnight
Two to view the Fort & get a scalp
domain of transcendental subjectivity
Etymology the this

present in the past now
So many thread

———

Fence blown down in a winter storm

darkened by outstripped possession
Field stretching out of the world

this book is as old as the people

There are traces of blood in a fairy tale

———

The track of Desire
Must see and not see
Must not see nothing
Burrow and so burrow
Measuring mastering

When ice breaks up
at the farthest north
of Adirondack peaks
So empty and so empty
Go back for your body
Hindge

———

Dear Seem dear cast out
Sun shall go down and set

Distant monarchs of Europe
European grid on the Forest

so many gether togather
were invisible alway Love

———

at Fort Stanwix the Charrokey
paice

only from that Alarm
all those Guards

Constant parties of guards
up & down

Agreseror

Bearer law my fathers

Revealing traces
Regulating traces

———

The true Zeno
the immutable morality

Irruptives

thorow out all
the Five Nations

To cut our wete

of the Jentelmen

Fort the same
Nuteral

Revealing traces
Regulating traces

To Lake Superior to view

that time the Shannas & Dallaways

Home and I hope passage

Begun about the middle next

to Kittaning

Eating nothing but hominey

Scribbling the ineffable

See only the tracks of rabbit

A mouse-nest of grass

The German Flatts

Their women old men & children

Numerous than I imagined

Singing their War song

I am

Part of their encroachment

Speed & Bleave me &

a Good Globe to hang in a hall
with light

To be sent in slays
if we are not careful
To a slightly place
no shelter

Let us gether and bury
limbs and leves
Is a great Loast
Cant say for us now
Stillest the storm world
Thought

The snow
is still hear

Wood and feld
all covered with ise

seem world anew
Only step

as surveyor of the Wood
only Step

2

Walked on Mount Vision

New life after the Fall
So many true things

which are not truth itself
We are too finite

Barefooted and bareheaded
extended in space

sure of reaching support

Knowledge and foresight
Noah's landing at Ararat

Mind itself or life

quicker than thought

slipping back to primordial
We go through the word Forest

Trance of an encampment
not a foot of land cleared

The literature of savagism
under a spell of savagism

Nature isolates the Adirondacks

In the machinery of injustice
my whole being is Vision

The Source of Snow
the nearness of Poetry

The Captain of Indians
the cause of Liberty

Mortal particulars
whose shatter we are

A sort of border life
A single group of trees

Sun on our back

Unappropriated land
all the works and redoubts

Young pine in a stand of oak
young oak in a stand of pine

Expectation of Epiphany

Not to look off from it
but to look at it

Original of the Otherside
understory of anotherword

Thaw has washed away snow
covering the old ice

the Lake a dull crust

Force made desire wander
Jumping from one subject

to another
Besieged and besieged

in a chain of Cause
The eternal First Cause

I stretch out my arms
to the author

Oh the bare ground

My thick coat and my tent
and the black of clouds

Squadrons of clouds

No end of their numbers

Armageddon at Fort William Henry
Sunset at Independence Point

Author the real author
acting the part of a scout

The origin of property
that leads here Depth

Indian names lead here

Bars of a social system
Starting for Lost Pond

psychology of the lost
First precarious Eden

a scandal of materialism

My ancestors tore off
the first leaves

picked out the best stars
Cries accompany laughter

Winter of the great Snow
Life surrounded by snows

The usual loggers camp
the usual bark shelter

Fir floor and log benches

Pines seem giant phenomena

Child of the Adirondacks
taking notes like a spy

Most mysterious river

On the confined brink

Poor storm
all hallows

and palings around cabin

Spring-suggesting light

Bustle of embarkation
Guides bewildered

Hunt and not the capture

Underthought draws home
Archaism

Here is dammed water

First trails were blazed
lines

Little known place names

tossed away as little grave
pivot bravura

Long walk on Erebus

The hell latch Poetry

Ragged rock beside hemlock

Mist in deep gulfs

Maps give us some idea
Apprehension as representation

Stood on Shelving Rock

The cold Friday
as cold as that was

Flood of light on water
Day went out in storms

Well structure could fall
Preys troop free

I have imagined a center

Wilder than this region
The figment of a book

Scarce broken letters
Cold leaden sky

Laurentian system of Canada

Tuesday the instant May

Elegiac western Imagination

Mysterious confined enigma
a possible field of work

The expanse of unconcealment
so different from all maps

Spiritual typography of elegy

Nature in us as a Nature
the actual one the ideal Self

tent tree sere leaf spectre
Unconscious demarkations range

I pick my compass to pieces

Dark here in the driftings
in the spaces of drifting

Complicity battling redemption

3.

Cannot be
every
where I
entreat
snapt
R e s o lu t i o n

Picked up arrowhead
hieroglyph

Parted with the Otterware
at the three Rivers, & are
Gone to have a Treaty
with the French at Oswego
batteau
& singing their war song
islet
The French Hatchet
neck
Messages
drisk

At this end of the carry
sheen
Their Plenipo squall
disc
coin
splint
cedar
chip
grease
lily root
cusk
a very deep Rabbit
swamp
of which will not per[mit] of
wavelet
fitted to the paper, the Margins
shrub
mud
Frames should be exactly
Encampt Fires by night
wood
canoes
waterbug
c o v er y
Cove
Places to walk out to
Tranquillity of a garrison
Escalade
Traverse canon night siege Constant firing
Traverse canon night siege Constant firing

Gabion
Parapet

Gabion
Parapet

Traverse canon night siege Constant firing
Escalade

Tranquillity of a garrison

Places to walk out to
Cove

canoes

waterbug
The Frames should be exactly
Fires by night
wood
Encampt

mud
fitted to the paper, the Margins

shrub
of which will not per[mit] of

wavelet
swamp
a very deep Rabbit

cusk
lily root
cedar
grease
chip
coin

splint
disc
Their Plenipo

drisk
Messages
sheen

The French Hatchet
neck
At this end of the carry

& singing their war song
islet

batteau
The War Belt
hieroglyph

Messengers say
Picked up arrowhead

over the lakes

Of the far nations

You are of me & I of you, I cannot tell

Where you leave off and I begin

selving

forfending
Immeadeat Settlem
but wandering
Shenks Ferry people
unhoused
at or naer Mohaxt
elect
Sacandaga vläie
vision
Battoes are return
thereafter
They say
resurgent
"Where is the path"
laughter

ankledeep

answerable

last

PASSACAGLIA
Moon wading through cloud Strict counterpoint
reassemble
Union

Stress

distant day helter No mighty
nd
want lenght
Awake! top hill demon daunt defiant
brested Premis
a
on
ce
t
first

anthen   uplispth   enend

adamap   blue wov   thefthe

folled   floted   keen

Themis

thou sculling me
Thiefth

[1990]

Clark Coolidge

PERU EYE, THE HEART OF THE LAMP

There is a stone in the air
calls on me to quiet
all that moves and is not light

I sit on the solar spine
a stone so carved connects
to nothing but still
all the distance lights

•

And do you wander in a blue stone town,
plain liking own self to mountains, or
with others? Train signal of an anciency,
Jupiter and Saturn rise together. Bare round
powers. How did they lock the stones?

•

And I still stand cleaved between Incan walls,
stones hold. The harpman blind sings in the sand
that held his hand alert as cut corners.
The sun is out of line in the Indian past, settlings
of Mestizo stark wine. He whims and blends,
almost Appalachian latch, and the sun renders
a dolly racket on the Fanta fenders. Juice
neon green washes ash, and browning awning benders.
Still am in Peru, I doubt my start.

•

It was silent in the world with the voices
like soapstones. And in the yard the grass
we talked on they had sat on. Sun and
moon and on. Hats were trivets.
Stones that fit a leather sort of granite.
Since that homing on a ridge spine time
the humans have progressively retired. We had
to go there. We couldn't stop speaking so
we did.

•

She cried with grief that the boy would
    take her clasp as the walls tolled
There in overage Peru, under the
    powdered scrape of the Fanta sign
But we left the train, in a cloak of the soft
    ore bars returning to their stone
It was night, a night like a day that had
    not always returned

•

Where the light water flowed in spar streams
    not Greece, Peru, but the light was.
And the Indian girl ran down from the hill
    a lamb on her arm to be pictured for coin
But this taker was a mirror
    her spirit refused

•

We walked in single file along the shorn stones
the mists to recede and the mountains bump us
We could only imagine on   their compass intentions
the sun an only   part of their year

•

If you walk up this height
you will score the sky.

•

We sat there carefully and listened. It was a park. It was not. Sometimes you feel you are clinging up here. They have placed the stones as little apart as possible. Perhaps they had no concept of "on"? They had wanted to become part of the ground.

"All the separate stones hunger to be once again part of the great universal rock that they came from. We have been at some pains to oblige them."

We did not know where the sun was. Different portions of stone and plant lit up in pattern according to a mystery.

"The world is here. You have not come. You will not go."

•

Mystery is valuable and must be preserved
Heart of the lock the sky
Stones a bread of the woven time
And on trails the vines lock up into lamps
Mystery is valuable and must be preserved

And the soul so light a dense weight
And the soul so light a dense weight
The ticking of the trees, the box of stabs
Shaken

The critical is the penetrant, sidereal, the mystery
The mystery is valuable and must be preserved

Come back from love to crystal lace penetrable
The latches are a moss and arrangement of cliffs
Mystery is valuable and must be preserved
The man on the rock is not there, shock of hair
The combinant rhymes a struck match of lamps
The lamps are a tongue to the eye of the mass
And arrivals are mere, the mocks of a mist
The mystery is valuable and must be preserved

•

What does it mean to capture any thing in a picture?
The Incas worshipped the rainbow. It is said that
their priests threw kisses to the rising sun.
The reasons for things, for coming and leaving.
When I began walking in Machu Picchu I
felt the desire to climb higher in the
ruins. Each time I found myself in
a cul-de-sac from which I could exit only by
retracing my steps. It is said that when no
written language survives "nobody knows." The Incas
are gone but their stones. Sometimes
their sun and their stars.

•

In the stone still lives the Incan night.
You can see it in the line between the
ridge and light. More than lives, is
always nigh. The stir.

•

I have the feeling I'm only partly here
that I'm slipping down behind the images in my mind
and behind them the lamp
that projects what's left of me here.

•

The green snake on the blue rock
the blue snake on the black rock

There is no black snake

Bee Odor

thrumming turns of the trail
sun dropped gorge

There is water in the alley.
There is a tang to the tongue.
The rocks ripped from the leather
of an almost perfect forgettal.
Where voice has been there should be
stone.

Who *are* you?

(repeated blurred into pure vocal tones)

•

I saw man's universe at Machu Picchu and it was
not me. Nor the black millipede cut in two
by the staircase Ginsberg also noticed—there
is no repetition. Now I sit cold in a room
half under the ground in western Massachusetts and
imagine the density of the night, streets of Lima.
The impermeable black eyes, the darkness exhaled
from their noses, a palpable dark that stills things.
To enter on the endless walk that nobody owns.

•

The Dark Lamp of Peru

•

Then the Lamp of All the Colors. The blue
walls that are shirts of turquoise. The ore brown
of armed earth. The peaks lit but not warmed by the
sun. The lozenges of stone fit round
by Inca lips. Can't I forget, I can't
be all here.

•

And on the Andean Plain a railway lamp
winking at the high ice. One lone Indian
trudging to the terraced time star.

•

Machu Picchu is already an excavation in my life.

•

and became image-haunted afterwards.

[1982]

from *At Egypt*:

V

A new hunt
the morning bent
ferry from the crumble dock
a kid mass singing of its dust
all wanting our names and barely
the square barge floats its trucks of human
and skinning lessons all of one hour
to scout across the Nile, a morning world

Say I brought away a mouse
The heart of this town

Tombs, there are here kings
which tomb the key of tombs
which grotto the stairway one
and which underworld the painted touch?

Over there is an entrance to the underworld
and over there an other too many
standing in a world whirled white by blindmen
digging for the opening fret, the charting tone
for deep relief from figure, just a paper hanger

As if, given sufficient light, one could simply step
then again in the dream of the white Steinway
at the center of the earth he would approach
but only keep approaching, it was so heated
then I was close to the entrance of fully given figures
stalled in deep relief, they were so guarded
they were never fully entered, you see the crew's scrawl
trail off into the hollow of books

The Book of Caverns
The Book of Gates
The Book of the Total Slab

Where the snakes could be buried first by debris
and only then by our covered eyes
the snake that contained a ball
or the beetle that grasped the sunball
stood out straight in the underworld doors
and rigged humans blank with its wings
a hovering cobra turning to carbon
hollow as the mother of the angling gateway
curled out of hands of feathers and dooms
we dry in these rooms

The snake that covers the boat cabin, chair
the snake under the sex act signatory
the snake that pulls the boat, with the slaves
the snake that is ropes that are firehose coils
the snake that opens to anything, among the missing

We stand in rooms, deep in stone
beneath the dry light quarry, one room
space like a cartouche closed

That it is shut
He shuts
These words are shut
This wall

That one with the upside-down birdmen
await opal relief, or the dark hands sift
the hounds of their dots, a red not hairs
layered up the walls with stung paint, raised tongues
in shun mellow of cap off in the dry, the date
beyond you echo, the gone men slid
I'm amazed at my own slow straightening

But they appreciate
To go on over time
They walk and leave

Nights of blimps or lumps where there are no empty space
nights of a slight raising of the surface, every time
the wall is remarked, we see it being set up but
we do not see the spider lower and rise, writing this book
why does he dart to the ashes? approaching the machine of
any time for the words to appear, how do I notice
while being Am, reading the rocks, noting the surface
we did and always return to
my voice gets clipped and lost in all this

Haste of space
The god haste
The unspeakable leaving
Embossed it
Still says

I have been lost, that then I have loomed here
the men with penises straight out from navels
hands tied behind backs, heads cut off
big wastings going on in other sequences, try-outs
baboons that worship the globe, wasps on high lintels
layers of chert nodules in a very limestone sun
I have been backwards from this, I have not learned the tongue

And how does this say that was like his paintings?
how does that hollow for his pain, that snake
with the sphinx head on its back end turned backwards
as round and round cycled as a torque of Last Judgement
the art in its reversal teams not to express but magic
the remains, those hovers

Now whine, the electron tune in denatured avenues
muezzin rub its scale over the warping disco, in slab cell
hotel by the milding Nile and thought to grasp
such painted flatness, enter
now gain, the underground upside-down
the return backwards, scratched from the Beetle of Existence
and grinding off the grey chunks, word is weird

Now there's this world that I am not here, but brainless
in my case, batteries lacking, thought reels sinking slowing
the caked out land, turns on a tamp of hash and dry lamps
oxen husks and saddlery, the thought enough that
that the next world not under or above
but another dimension over

Red oxide on the empty drum
rubs a digit of it, as does rust
the tell of its former, the high grey rod
that later, a white fluorescent is left on
in place of, embraces the drain of
drip castle in a drier, climate and beachless
the armchair is on, an iron dock, flap

I see green over the hums of a January
the error children make fun of

As the back of his head disturbed the room
resting next to wasps of the doorsill
and the grey stamp vacancies nobody's bought
but brought anyway, the reducings of the inks
to dryings out and so on, so to stay
rapt and so *on*, so stain the light marks in
square empty time.

Break the dust
Remove your self
Sight
Of the back of his head
From what the shadow mouth
Says

That I stay rapt to see the ink dry
reversal emerge, solution in place, within
the market without, tendencies, snail cries
leaks of the internal sponge in the parlor funnel
bodiless eyes return here seeking the trail
napkin, smudge make it coffee if you will it
the sameside of the nail file in the mirror if it will

Look at it
Always from the wrong side
You do

He motions us to kneel into the crypt box and pick
out the pictures as lit by the angles of his mirror, sun led
from his entrance hand, stored remove
and I smile to see the stales, so bright of wheat
intimation, mile palaver and the carve, that the crease
hall of entry would then flatten into brightness pictured
back of the reach time longest, prong like jazz files
and the straws through which the gems are blown
the cemetery of the arches of his arm

Where the glass is a bucket
Where the wash is light

In the valley of the things
the standing girl in the door post
I almost missed with open palms
and unstable in line with those
who in one listening may too nobly infinitive
the once it was a shrimp upon her head

And does she return
Though I have seen
It does?

As is anyone we are
about as sure of the significance of any of
this signing as one could be of the relation
of Chattanooga Choochoo to the amethyst lamp panes of Venice
another stranded turn of made sense?
in the candied lights of shown fancies
you rate things but don't coin them or even
time them especially, they are here
and everywhere there again tomorrow, a sparrow
do we find our feet in
caught speculance, or even a single haunch?

No alabaster!
the call sign of this wander
at the window of this northeast sander
when it is cold then that means it will go well with you
standing out in the pre-dawn square, jeweled and hustled
we went there and saw the thing
I know because I have seen

A few decimal places in picture history past
a town you have homed on, but the dots
that come to approach and free from the snakes, those riots
and then the island of all you can eat of
the tiny sweet bananas, that glove left out
on the pharaoh's doorsill as he vanished into the square
empty time break the dust of your pencil columns
Hatshepsut has your numbers

Valley of the Things
Valley of a kinship
Among the Suffixes

But the bats of the dusk banks
why were they not depicted?
it was not an "underworld" where you would be going?
paraphernalia of a king starched by cubed time
into nothing but money, I drink aqua minerale
by her temple colonnade and watch all the stone heads snap back
the moon a wicket wire of beetalic hops
rolled off the impossible end
of its own table, Egypt

[1988]

Michael Palmer

from BAUDELAIRE SERIES

[. . .]

Here the image of a child on a hill
The grasses wave
Fire signals fire this is sleep
who meets you there

time bent to sight
in the radius of a phrase

Dear King Empty
Yesterday I tripped and fell
Today I will run in a race

I've had nothing to do with numbers

I do not remember personally torturing prisoners

though a name appears nonetheless
inside a pumpkin's lighted head—

this name or that—

a scattering of hours around some sound
Then *ego scriptor* gets blotted out

* * *

Barely anything to say, everything said. But you break, as a hooded traveller, scattering images across the plain, I among them and other I's. This prose, a

color sampler, is meant for you: *Voile bleu, Dame du Sud, Bleu Medicis,* fifty dead on the tarmac, creases of the hand. Is there still an outside, uncancelled as yet by other

codes appearing in service to what

revolutionary pleasures, what floods
of a matrix in slow dissolve

there on the screen, where everything is named difference, and is always the same for that reason, since you've watched it many times before and counted the limbs?

Glides and rests.

Let's say a particular music, in profile.

Let's say mythological figures, freeze dried, who—once immersed—emerge from their gelatin capsules: Syrinx, Polyeidos, the Dioskuroi; Earth Diver, Frog and Moon, Mephisto.

They refuse you their stories, pour soot on you
                                                                      and into you.

And that other music, sort of gasped out now by the synthetron, the instruments slightly more than real, if ontically problematic at best.

Or we might say just as you said, It's snowing in Paris, which does not exist.

(A painting of that.)

Or the problem we began with, that words have no letters.

And that each of those letters has a distinctive shape. Or shade. Impossible to remember.

* * *

Desire was a quotation from someone.

Someone says, This This. Someone says, Is.

The tribe confronts a landscape of ice.

He says, I will see you in the parallel life.

She says, A miser has died from the cold; he spoke all his sentences and meant no harm.

My voice is clipped, yours a pattern of dots.

Three unmailed have preceded this, a kind of illness.

Now I give you these lines without any marks, not even a breeze.

dumb words mangled by use

like reciting a lesson or the Lord's Prayer.

How lovely the unspeakable must be. You have only to say it and it tells a story.

A few dead and a few missing

and the tribe to show you its tongue. It has only one.

* * *

I killed a bee on the Street of Scissors
The bee was holding a picture of me

A woman walked past
There is a time, there

is a time before, she said
without turning her head

Then you carried no ink
Then you were not a photograph

* * *

I am an architect in Vienna
dead and a writer
in a blood red bed

I eat with a fork the meat, the violin

I've let go my practice of this violin

In Vienna there are no musicians

Is my violin broken again
I asked at age 9.10

So then I sat down and was going to get rid of this violin

I can't play it for beans anyway

I'm an architect in a town of architects

No buildings

All my brother architects are dead
or else asleep with their sisters in bed

Call me Eric
whose grandfather mended the violin

whose mother once taught him to hate the violin
and play dead

I've designed a circle and a bridge

My tears are for the person I miss, the down on her lip

* * *

We will call today
In Search of a Newt,

a language that is ordinary, the same
as language only smaller. The ship

did land, Michael, and the natives
did speak, so we killed them.

Souviens-toi? All things were as one
then, behind the electronic fence.

In tongues books were written, suns
rose wherever we placed them

and lawnchairs and trees too
were painted in. The Gasthaus

was Eros itself, with that ghost
of the dancer hovering about.

The more-than-grass
stretched toward the sea.

We floated
and it could be said that we floated.

* * *

Said the Speaker:
It is a great pleasure

to be not-dead
here again

and to be speaking to you
from this notebook or

journal or Book of the Dead
in the system of demicurves

and crests, veinous
gestures and radial splits

that is known to you
and was made by you

for this purpose
It is a great pleasure

to be cut

as a tongue or a knot

* * *

Said the Speaker:
Flat as tongues

the pages are spread out
before you to dry

Come and look
Come and see

the pages spread out
before you in the sun

curled like leaves
black as tongues

* * *

Nowness and nowness sings the crow
Whatness and whiteness sings the center
Then and then signs the hen

Hello to the break sings the left hand

Is there even a building here?
Even a body? Was it burning

        like a necklace burning?

Greener than loss or ice? Blind

as music and laughter? Final
        song in a sequence?

We are facing the nets
        says a sentence

We are alive we are covering our eyes
        tell the spires

SUN

Write this. We have burned all their villages

Write this. We have burned all the villages and the people in them

Write this. We have adopted their customs and their manner of dress

Write this. A word may be shaped like a bed, a basket of tears or an X

In the notebook it says, It is the time of mutations, laughter at jokes, secrets beyond the boundaries of speech

I now turn to my use of suffixes and punctuation, closing Mr. Circle with a single stroke, tearing the canvas from its wall, joined to her, experiencing the same thoughts at the same moment, inscribing them on a loquat leaf

Write this. We have begun to have bodies, a now here and a now gone, a past long ago and one still to come

Let go of me for I have died and am in a novel and was a lyric poet, certainly, who attracted crowds to mountaintops. For a nickel I will appear from this box. For a dollar I will have text with you and answer three questions

First question. We entered the forest, followed its winding paths, and emerged blind

Second question. My townhouse, of the Jugendstil, lies by Darmstadt

Third question. He knows he will wake from this dream, conducted in the mother-tongue

Third question. He knows his breathing organs are manipulated by God, so that he is compelled to scream

Third question. I will converse with no one on those days of the week which end in *y*

Write this. There is pleasure and pain and there are marks and signs.
A word may be shaped like a fig or a pig, an effigy or an egg
but

there is only time for fasting and desire, device and design, there is
only time to swerve without limbs, organs or face into a
scientific

silence, pinhole of light

Say this. I was born on an island among the dead. I learned language on this island but did not speak on this island. I am writing to you from this island. I am writing to the dancers from this island. The writers do not dance on this island

Say this. There is a sentence in my mouth, there is a chariot in my mouth. There is a ladder. There is a lamp whose light fills empty space and space which swallows light

A word is beside itself. Here the poem is called What Speaking Means to Say
though I have no memory of my name

Here the poem is called Theory of the Real, its name is Let's Call This, and its name is called A Wooden Stick. It goes yes-yes, no-no. It goes one and one

I have been writing a book, not in my native language, about violins and smoke, lines and dots, free to speak and become the things we speak, pages which sit up, look around and row resolutely toward the setting sun

Pages torn from their spines and added to the pyre, so that they will resemble thought

Pages which accept no ink

Pages we've never seen—first called Narrow Street, then Half a Fragment, Plain of Jars or Plain of Reeds, taking each syllable in her mouth, shifting position and passing it to him

Let me say this. Neak Luong is a blur. It is Tuesday in the hardwood forest. I am a visitor here, with a notebook

The notebook lists My New Words and Flag above White. It claims to have no inside

only characters like A-against-Herself, B, C, L and N, Sam, Hans Magnus, T. Sphere, all speaking in the dark with their hands

G for Gramsci or Goebbels, blue hills, cities, cities with hills, modern and at the edge of time

F for alphabet, Z for A, an H in an arbor, shadow, silent wreckage, W or M among stars

What last. Lapwing. Tesseract. X perhaps for X. The villages are known as These Letters—humid, sunless. The writing occurs on their walls

[1988]

RECURSUS

(to Porta)

The voice, because of its austerity, will often cause dust to rise.

The voice, because of its austerity, will sometimes attempt the representation of dust.

Someone will say, I can't breathe—as if choking on dust.

The voice ages with the body.

It will say, I was shaped by light escaping from a keyhole.

Or, I am the shape of that light.

It will say, For the body to breathe, a layer must be peeled away.

It will say, What follows is a picture of how things are for me now.

It will say, The rose is red, twice two is four—as if another were present.

The dust rises in spirals.

It will say, The distance from Cairo to anywhere is not great.

As if one had altered the adjustment of a microscope.

Or examined its working parts.

Possibly an instrument covered with dust and forgotten on a shelf.

Beside a hatbox and a pair of weathered boots.

The voice will expand to fill a given space.

As if to say, This space is not immeasurable.

This space is not immeasurable.

When held before your eyes.

And which voice is it says (or claims to say), Last night I dreamt of walls and courses of brick, last night I dreamt of limbs.

As you dream—always unwillingly—of a writing not visible and voices muffled by walls.

As if the question: lovers, prisoners, visitors.

The voice, as an act of discipline or play, will imitate other voices.

This is what I am doing now.

This is what I'm doing now.

The clock behind my back, its Fusée mechanism.

Voice one recognizes from years before.

Beneath water, hidden by a spark.

Here at the heart of winter, or let's say spring.

Voice with a history before its eyes.

With a blue dot before its eyes.

History of dust before its eyes.

It will say, as if remembering, the letter S stands for a slow match burning.

On the table before me.

No numbers on this watch.

And I live in a red house that once was brown.

A paper house, sort of falling down.

Such is the history of this house.

It looks like this.

Looks just like this.

We think to say in some language.

[1992]

AMERICAN POETRY SINCE 1950: A VERY BRIEF HISTORY

A READER'S BIBLIOGRAPHY

American Poetry Since 1950: A Very Brief History

There have been two great flowerings of American poetry in this century. The first, of course, occurred in the 1910's and 1920's, with Ezra Pound, William Carlos Williams, T.S. Eliot, H.D., Wallace Stevens, Mina Loy, Hart Crane, Langston Hughes, Marianne Moore, e.e. cummings and Gertrude Stein among its brightest lights, along with scores of lesser practitioners. In 1931, Louis Zukofsky attempted to launch a new generation of Modernists by gathering a group of largely disparate younger poets under the partially defined banner of "Objectivism": George Oppen, Charles Reznikoff, Lorine Niedecker (who was included later), the British poet Basil Bunting, Kenneth Rexroth, and Zukofsky himself, among others. The movement, however, and in a sense the entire generation, vanished soon after into personal obscurity, changing fashions in poetic taste, the Depression, and the Second World War. There would be nearly two decades until the next major developments.

Pound became largely concerned with economic matters and his support for Italian Fascism, wrote some of his dullest *Cantos*, and would not return to his earlier greatness until the *Pisan Cantos* of 1948. Williams' work became more conventional, and he turned to writing narrative fiction and an autobiography; he would return in the late 1940's and early 1950's with the long poem *Paterson* and his two late masterpieces, *The Desert Music* and *Journey to Love*. Eliot abandoned the avant-garde for England and the Church, produced the *Four Quartets* in the 1930's and 1940's, and then abandoned poetry altogether. Mina Loy stopped writing, and never wrote again in her long life. Crane committed suicide. By the 1940's most of Moore's and cummings' best poetry were behind them. H.D., an expatriate in England and Switzerland, was remembered only for her early Imagist poems; her greatest work, the wartime *Trilogy*, would not be published in the United States until thirty years later, ten years after her death. Hughes lived in the Soviet Union for some years, covered the Spanish Civil War as a journalist, and increasingly wrote prose; he would return to form, again in the 1950's, with *Montage of a Dream Deferred*—a work which, like all of Hughes' poetry, is inexplicably still primarily discussed in the context of African-American, and not American Modernist writing.

As for the young poets: George Oppen stopped writing for 25 years, devoting himself to the Communist Party in the 1930's, serving as an infantry man in the Second World War (the only important American poet since the Civil War to actually engage in combat), and living in exile from McCarthyism in Mexico in the 1950's. Louis Zukofsky worked as an English instructor at a technical school in Brooklyn, published a few pamphlets which went unnoticed, and wrote his life-work, *"A"*, which would not appear until the 1960's. Charles Reznikoff had to publish his own books until he was in his seventies. Lorine Niedecker spent nearly all her life in a small fishing village in Wisconsin where she scrubbed hospital floors to make a living; she too, would not be widely published until the 1960's. Muriel Rukeyser, who was not connected to the Objectivists, was visible quite early as a Yale Younger Poet in 1935 and throughout her life as a literary and political activist, but was nonetheless dismissed by the poetry establishment (most notably by Randall Jarrell) and never really formed alliances with the avant-garde—the source, perhaps, of her continuing neglect by nearly all poetic camps. Kenneth Rexroth finally published his first book in 1941 and, though he was entirely ignored at the time, became in retrospect the only poet of enduring interest to emerge in regularly published book form in that decade.

The age became dominated by the Anglican Eliot, and poets such as Allen Tate, John Crowe Ransom and Yvor Winters, who rejected the exuberance and excess of Modernism in favor of poems that were self-contained, ironic, and dense with elaborately constructed metaphors. Practitioners of the so-called New Criticism, they championed a return to traditional prosody and rhyme, and a reading of poetry that considered the "poem itself" as an entity separate from its author and its age (not that unlike contemporary deconstructionism). Its second generation, which emerged in the 1940's—Howard Nemerov, Randall Jarrell, Robert Lowell, Elizabeth Bishop, Delmore Schwartz, Richard Wilbur, Anthony Hecht, John Berryman, among many others—would fuse these techniques with postwar malaise, and an interest in psychoanalysis and existentialism, to produce works that often depended on a minor scandalousness, from the incorporation of impolite words like "pubic hair" in an otherwise traditional sonnet, to the "confession," in well-turned phrases, of one's neurotic and self-destructive life. Such self-indulgence—utterly timid compared to, say, the autobiographical spelunkings of Artaud or Vallejo or Celan—ultimately threatened no one, while reinforcing the American image of the poet as an overgrown disturbed child prodigy. Canonized early in their careers, these poets formed an Establishment for a new avant-garde, the century's second great flowering, to lay siege to—much as Pound and the others had seen as their task the demolition of *fin de siècle* English poetry.

The 1950's are remembered in the United States as a decade of conformity, placidity and prosperity—the short hair and long cars of Eisenhower America—yet it is astonishing how many subversive elements were loose in the land. In popular music, the mellow love songs sung by tuxedoed Italian-Americans were swiftly overwhelmed by the erotic carnival of rock & roll. At the movies, amidst the Doris Day-Rock Hudson comedies and the bright musicals, there was James Dean and *Vertigo* and the atomic mutants terrorizing small towns. And for all the proverbial "men in gray flannel suits" climbing the corporate ladder, there were also the Beats—who also, it has been forgotten, wore suits, but were less embarrassed to take them off. In fact nearly everything that was to happen in the unfettered 1960's was already in place in the 1950's: the youth culture was invented with rock & roll; the anti-Vietnam War movement had its roots and its organizing principles in the civil rights demonstrations in the South; the obsession with hallucinogens and other realities began with R. Gordon Wasson's highly publicized encounter with the Mazatec shaman María Sabina and her mushrooms in 1957; the Hippies were the spiritual children of the Beats; even 1960's slang was first coined by bebop and "cool" jazz musicians.

So too in American poetry: on the outskirts of the Official Verse Culture of middle-brow magazines, large publishers and literary prizes, armed bands of rebels were forming. Most visible, of course, were the Beats—including Allen Ginsberg, Gary Snyder and Leroi Jones (Amiri Baraka), with Kenneth Rexroth as reluctant father-figure—who, apart from their celebrated lifestyles, introduced iconoclastic humor, Eastern philosophy, anarchist politics, some taboo subjects and language, and brought orality back to American poetry through their populist readings at cafés and nightclubs and their collaborations with jazz musicians. In New York, poet-art critics like John Ashbery and Frank O'Hara, closely associated with the flourishing Abstract Expressionist scene, were importing certain aspects of French surrealism, including whimsical juxtaposition, free-floating fancy, random apprehensions of ordinary life, and, for O'Hara, the panorama of the street. O'Hara and Paul Blackburn perfected what became, for a while, the typical poem of New York, an endless flow of "now I am doing this" (a form whose ultimate source is Apollinaire's "Zone," perhaps the most influential poem, in any language, in the century). Blackburn in particular, following Williams and in this aspect surpassing him, caught the everyday speech of the streets, and his poems written on the subways were imitated by scores of young poets.

For a few years at Black Mountain, an experimental arts college in North Carolina, Charles Olson—along with other avant-gardists of the era, such as Willem DeKooning, John Cage, Merce Cunningham, Franz Kline and Robert Rauschenberg—was the centrifugal center of what was to become a major tendency in American poetry: the "Black Mountain school" (as they became known in the somewhat strained taxonomy of Donald Allen's immensely influential 1960 anthology, *The New American Poets*). The group included Olson (who compared himself to Mao in the Yennan caves), Robert Duncan, Robert Creeley, Denise Levertov, Paul Blackburn and others—some of whom had never visited the place. Though these poets were ultimately quite different, all subscribed to Olson's belief that a line of poetry, rather than depending on any inherited prosody, should correspond to a unit of breath; that, in Olson's words, "each perception should immediately lead to another perception" (without the Baroque ornamentation of the academics); and that musical composition—and even more, a new music for each poem—was paramount. (In Creeley's words: "Form is never more than an extension of content.") Olson, Duncan and Blackburn, inspired by the abstract painters, evolved a "field composition"—poems that were not dependent on the left-hand margin, but exploded over the page, with the spaces corresponding to calibrated moments of silence; and all emphasized, again like the contemporary painters, the process of creation, rather than its product. (Duncan: "A poem is an event; it is not the record of the event.") Both Duncan and Olson worked on open-ended long poems, much like the *Cantos*, capable of including anything, and intended to occupy one's entire writing life.

San Francisco saw its first important generation of poets: Kenneth Rexroth, William Everson (who for some years was a Dominican monk named Brother Antoninus), Jack Spicer, Robert Duncan and Gary Snyder, among others, who became known collectively as the "San Francisco Renaissance," though in fact it was more accurately the city's poetic nascence. Again, their cohesion is more a matter of personal temperament and geographical proximity than style. Rexroth, an unchained erudite and energy source, is one of the great figures in American poetry: his poems of the wilderness essentially invented the West in poetry, and opened the way for Snyder and many others; his furious political poems were a major influence on Ginsberg's "Howl"; he wrote the greatest heterosexual love poems in English in this century; and his perennial battles against the establishments (both political and literary), his heretical mysticism (which embraced both Zen Buddhism and the Christian mystics), and his belief in a brotherhood of artists amidst the cultural wasteland was an inspiration for countless poets. Duncan—along with Rexroth the most erudite American poet since Pound—proudly declared himself a "derivative" poet, one whose poems directly proceeded from earlier texts. The most musical of the poets, he, more than any of the academics, experimented with nearly all the traditional forms, finding a new music for them in the context of his "field" poetics, in a poetry that combined political rage, occultist beliefs, homoeroticism, and whole libraries into a dense elegy. Spicer, a professional linguist who died young, would be championed years later by the postmodernists as an early explorer of the abyss between signified and signifier—though unlike his descendants, he wrote with mordant and bitter humor. Everson, a Christian (and later erotic) ecstatic, working directly out of Robinson Jeffers, purified Jeffers' rhetorical excesses while retaining his long lines and vatic tone. Snyder would follow Rexroth to become the preeminent poet of the American wilderness in an exact and unsentimental landscape poetry learned from Pound and the Chinese poets, as well as an early populist champion of ecological causes.

To glide over some of the features of some of the poets and poems can only hint at the richness and eclecticism of the decade. There are no general characteristics of this poetry that can be applied to all, though the avant-garde tended to emphasize musicality, simultaneity (collage or "field") over the academic linearity, open-ended rather than closed forms, and the poem that "is" rather than the poem that is "about." In the end, what united these poets was, in opposition to the prevailing canon, Pound's exhortation to "Make it new"—whether it meant the small and perfect psychological meditations of Creeley or the bardic expansionism of Ginsberg, William Bronk's metaphysical speculations written with the smallest and simplest possible vocabulary or Ashbery's highly elaborated ironies, the clipped speech of Snyder in the Rockies or the streetwise slang of Blackburn in the subways.

Most important of all, for the first time in the century, American poetry was being written almost entirely in the United States. The age of the Modernist expatriates in Europe was over. Even Ezra Pound, though confined to a mental institution in Washington, D.C. for his wartime broadcasts, was back, writing some of his greatest *Cantos* and Greek and Chinese translations, receiving a stream of younger poets, and firing off thousands of letters on what to read and how to write.

And America became again—for the first time since Whitman—a subject for its own poetry. Williams, who had never expatriated, but had spent his life as a pediatrician in a dreary working-class suburb of New York, fighting for an American speech in poetry to counter the Anglophilia of Eliot, was immersed in the late 1940's and early 1950's in the composition of *Paterson*, a long poem that discovered the universe through the history and language of a nearby, previously undistinguished small city. Olson would similarly take his hometown, the fishing town of Gloucester, Massachusetts, as the locus for a personal mythology that stretched back to Mesopotamia. Rexroth, Everson and Snyder were opening the landscapes of the American West; Blackburn, O'Hara and Hughes were inseparable from downtown, midtown and uptown New York; Niedecker from her "life by water" in a village in Wisconsin.

But it was not a poetry of isolationism, nationalism or localism. Pound had taught that poetry should ideally include everything, and the lesson of Modernism itself was that anything could be an entry into the poem and the world—that, to take its most famous example, the way to an understanding of the "Waste Land" of modern life was through reference to the Holy Grail or the sermons of the Buddha. This meant, in the 1950's—and it would expand exponentially in the following decades—that the avant-garde was preoccupied with both American history and the news from abroad, with world mythology, with Jungian archetypes rather than Freudian family romances, various occultisms rather than existentialism, the new developments in painting and jazz, and world poetry in general. (Twenty-five of the thirty-five poets here also devoted themselves to translation, and the poetry of the period is inseparable from the simultaneous, and sometimes equally radical, work in translation.)

And though a few of the poets lived briefly in Europe—none permanently—more were looking west (to the East) and south. Japan was magnetic: Snyder and Rexroth (and later Eshleman) were to spend years there; Zen was the Beat obsession, and later the very serious practice of various poets; even the most influential poetry magazine of the decade, *Origin*, was edited in Kyoto by the poet Cid Corman. Rexroth and Snyder wrote magnificent translations of Chinese poetry; Cage based most of his literary and some of his musical compositions on the *I Ching*; Ginsberg, Snyder, Rexroth and Rukeyser traveled extensively in India, and later Ginsberg would consider himself a Tibetan Buddhist. And to the south: Oppen,

Rukeyser, Levertov and Olson lived in Mexico; Blackburn, Ginsberg, Bronk and many others wrote there; Ginsberg and Bronk (and later Tarn and Eshleman) were also in Peru. (The academic poets, meanwhile, tended to take their Guggenheims in Florence.) One of the central poetics texts of the era is Olson's letters to Creeley from the Yucatán, where he discovered in the Mayan hieroglyphs—much as Pound had found in Chinese—the image of an ideal language for poetry, a language where each word had weight and was inexpendable, and in the contemporary Mayas themselves, a people still in touch, he believed, with primeval forces.

This interest in Latin America would explode in the 1960's with Rukeyser, Levertov, Blackburn, Eshleman, Rothenberg, Tarn and Ginsberg translating Paz, Neruda, Vallejo, Parra, Huidobro, Cuban poets, Nahuatl and other indigenous works. William Bronk wrote a magnificent prose meditation on the Mayan and Incan ruins, *The New World*; and one of the most important magazines of the era was the bilingual *El Corno Emplumado*, edited by Sergio Mondragón and Margaret Randall from Mexico City. [Even the preferred mode in the Establishment—typified by such poets as Robert Bly, Mark Strand and W.S. Merwin—became an amalgam of diluted Latin American surrealism, particularly Neruda, and the postwar existential surrealism of the Eastern Europeans.]

Indeed, the 1960's was a moment when previously conspicuous absences suddenly were present everywhere. Robert Duncan hoisted the flag in a famous statement calling for a "symposium of the whole": "The drama of our time is the coming of all men into one fate, 'the dream of everyone, everywhere.' [...] all the old excluded orders must be included. The female, the proletariat, the foreign; the animal and vegetative; the unconscious and the unknown; the criminal and failure—all that has been outcast and vagabond must return to be admitted in the creation of what we consider we are."

It was the decade of black nationalist poetry—concurrent with the militancy that marked the second stage of the civil rights movement—and its huge and genuinely populist audience. The movement effectively admitted African-American speech into poetry (something the Harlem Renaissance, with the notable exception of Hughes, had refused to do), had a close and exciting working relationship with jazz and some rock musicians (the now-forgotten grandparents of rap and hip-hop), offered scathing commentaries on whites and white "verse," and brought in a great deal of African and African-American history, mythology and religion previously absent in American poetry. [That this poetry was considered politically threatening became obvious during the trial of Amiri Baraka, following the 1967 Newark riots: though the charges, later dismissed, were assault and possession of a deadly weapon, his own poems were used as evidence against him.]

It was the decade of poetry written and read against the Vietnam War, an extraordinary time when American poets buried their aesthetic differences in the name of a democratic vision of a republic of letters. It was the first collective political poetry in the country since the 1930's, and perhaps the only moment when American poets were recognized as the intellectual consciences of the country, when poetry itself was seen as a legitimate and effective form of political protest. Although many of the poems can be read now only as period pieces, some of the work—particularly by Levertov and Duncan—still retains tremendous force.

It was the decade whose most vital movement or tendency, invented by Jerome Rothenberg and made manifest in his magazine *Alcheringa* and anthologies including *Technicians of the Sacred* and *America a Prophecy*, was "ethnopoetics." Essentially an American revision and expansion of Surrealism—itself a response to a war and a prophecy of the next war—ethnopoetics attempted to forge a chain from the tribal to the European heterodoxies to the early vanguardist Modernists to the contemporary avant-garde. A poetry not of the People, but of peoples, it not only introduced a huge amount of American Indian and other indigenous works, but also presented a re-reading of American literature, discovered all sorts of strange and forgotten poets, emphasized oral performance and poetry rituals and talismans, offered new theories and practices of translation, and, perhaps most of all, proposed an image of the poet, based on the archaic, as a vital, necessary member of the community.

The decade also marked the return from silence or obscurity of the poets of the 1930's: Louis Zukofsky, whose masterpiece *"A"* is a long poem in twenty-four sections, written over forty years; an intensely musical, sometimes impossibly dense exploration of American speech that is filled with secret codes and strengths (in one section, for example, the letters "n" and "r" are placed according to the formula for a conic section; in another—*"A"*-15, included here—English words recreate the Hebrew sounds of the opening of the Book of Job, much as his famous homophonic translation of Catullus attempts to "breathe" the Latin into English). George Oppen, survivor from the Party and the War, whose powerful restrained lyrics were an extended meditation on how the individual perceives and lives in the crush of history and humanity. Lorine Niedecker, writing crystalline observations of the life around her, and poems of historical biography (on Darwin, Jefferson and others) reduced to its telling details, all written in a Debussy-like music of precise syllables. Muriel Rukeyser—who essentially stopped writing for almost twenty years—alternating blunt speech and lush rhetoric, an early feminist in her revisionings of classical mythology and in her incorporation of the female body into the poem. And Charles Reznikoff, the quintessential invisible walker in the city, capturing like a photographer the "decisive moments" of urban life, and whose later poetry was devoted to a seemingly artless and utterly terrifying condensation of criminal court cases from turn-of-the-century America and the Nuremberg trials.

It was as though Pound's dream of the vortex had been realized: the whole world was rushing into American poetry. Consider the career of one of the poets to emerge in that decade, Nathaniel Tarn: born Anglo-French, he published books, articles and monographs (under various names) as a French Surrealist poet, a student of Gnosticism, an anthropologist working in the Atitlán region of Guatemala, a British poet, a Mayanist, and as an authority on the monastic system of Burma, before becoming an American poet in the late 1960's. Or consider the contents of a single issue of the most important poetry magazine of the period—amidst a proliferation of small magazines and poetry presses—Clayton Eshleman's *Caterpillar*: Ryunosuke Akutagawa's last writings before his suicide; articles comparing translations of Catullus and Rilke; Gary Snyder's journals as a forest ranger including Buddhist sutras and American Indian songs; poems by Robert Kelly incorporating imagery from the Kabbalah, the Maya and the history of astronomy; a poem on a shipwreck in the Great Lakes that ends up with the Cro-Magnons; photographs of child napalm victims, Jerome Rothenberg's invocations of the prewar Poland of his parents; a long poem by Eshleman written entirely under the influence of LSD; an essay on phonetics that ranges from Sanskrit to Middle English to current slang; a translation of the Martiniquean surrealist Aimé Césaire; writings on nutrition by the Japanese founder of Macrobiotics; an essay on the comic strip *Little Orphan Annie*; paintings by Leon Golub; and Lorine Niedecker's detailed evocation of her local flora, among other contributions. [In contrast, the establishment magazines of the time, like nearly all magazines today, tended to be 90% lyric poetry with a few reviews of poetry books in the back.]

To be an American avant-gardist poet at that moment, one had to know a lot about something, and a little about everything. Of the poets who emerged in the 1960's, Eshleman would become the primary translator of Vallejo, Artaud and Césaire, and spend years studying the Paleolithic caves in Europe; Tarn would carry his interest in nearly everything into a systematic exploration of the American continent; the immensely prolific

Kelly would assimilate the world's religious heterodoxies into an endless lyric; David Antin, an art theorist, would abandon his seemingly "found" but highly manipulated deadpan poems to devote himself to "talking," the transcription of spontaneous performance monologues; Rothenberg, as the prime force of ethnopoetics, would become the repository for countless oral traditions and early avant-gardist practices, and his exploration of his Polish roots would continue into *Khurbn*, a shattering medium-length poem on the Holocaust; Cage and Jackson Mac Low would subject given texts or their own words to highly complex chance operations and rules of play; and Ronald Johnson, following Zukofsky, would roam through the dictionaries and science books to create the elaborate musical structures of the multi-volume, still mainly unpublished *ARK*, which includes, among many other things, a partial erasing of Milton's *Paradise Lost*. In many ways their work continues to maintain the spirit of a moment in American poetry that—much like the events in the daily papers then, or the films of Godard, or the metamorphoses of the Beatles—created a state of continual surprise.

In the 1970's, the life of the poet in American society radically changed. In response to the students' demand for "relevancy" in what they were studying, universities, for the first time, began teaching contemporary poetry and offering courses and advanced degrees in something called "creative writing." [In 1914, the Dadaist poet and boxer Arthur Cravan, fulminating against the current vogue for art schools, had written: "I am astonished that some crook has not had the idea of opening a writing school."] Hundreds of universities and community arts centers supplemented their writing courses with regular series of poets reading their own works, institutionalizing what had begun as the spontaneous Beat café scene. And despite (or because of) the growing militancy of the poets against the Vietnam War and the black nationalists, Lyndon Johnson founded and Richard Nixon implemented the creation of the National Endowment for the Arts, while arts councils were formed in each state—all of them giving money not only directly to writers, small magazines and presses, but also to the mushrooming arts "service" organizations and their attendant bureaucrats, which were also handing out money and sponsoring readings, workshops, prizes, and fellowships.

Poetry, almost overnight, became a respectable middle-class career. One could now graduate with a degree in creative writing, take a job teaching creative writing, and augment one's income with readings and grants. The eco-system had become unbalanced by the elimination of the poets' main predator: money. In the past, the exigencies of earning a living had discouraged all but the most committed (or more exactly, obsessed) and those who held on were nevertheless forced out into the world as workers, journalists, capitalists, bohemians—all of which, in turn, had nourished the poetry. Now anyone could remain forever on campus in the springtime of adolescent poetry-writing. The result was, and continues to be, not only a demographic explosion of poets: an endless array of things to read as bewildering as the selection of laundry soaps in an American supermarket. It has meant that poets, once largely centered in, or in communication with, the urban metropolises, are now scattered through the diaspora of colleges and universities—a loss of what little community they had. It has meant that poets, especially bad poets, tend to distinguish themselves from the mob not by aesthetic beliefs and practices, but according to extra-literary categories such as ethnic background and sexual preference. It has meant that, with so many poets on one form or another of the government dole, there has been virtually no political poetry, even during the racial and economic injustices and warmongering of the Reagan and Bush administrations. And above all it has meant that a sameness of lives is producing a sameness of poetry.

Worst of all, it has become increasingly difficult for an individual poet to be heard in the collective racket. Where the leading anthologies of the previous decades, both on the aesthetic left and right, had primarily featured poets under thirty-five, it now became normal—even for collections of the "latest"—to concentrate on poets over forty. It is difficult to think of a single poet born after 1945 who has had the impact or the recognition achieved by dozens of poets under forty, from all the poetry camps, in the 1950's and 60's. It may well be a long time until we sort out what has happened in the last twenty years. For the moment, what has dominated the era has been the increasingly interesting work of those who were younger poets in the period between World War II and the Vietnam War.

Since 1970, the most visible kind of poetry—that being written by the teachers and students of the writing workshops—has been autobiographical, anecdotal, and written in prose syntax with apparently arbitrary line-breaks. The reigning dogma has been that the function of poetry is to transform our perception of everyday matters. [Curiously, the establishment hero is now Williams, who was reviled by the establishment for most of his life as a crackpot or a naïf. But it is the Williams of "The Red Wheelbarrow," not the exuberant, collaged, sometimes "automatic" writings that still remain little known: the poems of his 1923 book *Spring and All*, say, and not the prose poems of that same book.] And though the academy and its publications and reading series now pride themselves on "diversity," it is one based on ethnicity, not poetry: it is sometimes astonishing how such varied backgrounds can lead to the same poems.

There have been two collectivized responses to this dominant mode: On the ultra-right, reacting to the undisciplined free expression of the workshops, a group of young poets declared themselves to be the New Formalists and, in the pages of neoconservative political magazines, they championed a return to traditional prosody and rhyme, taking as their spiritual fathers New Critics like Ransom and Tate. Meanwhile, on the poetic left, as in the universities, European theory (the other New Formalism) took hold, setting adrift signifier and signified, dismantling the "authorities" and "hierarchies" of syntax, voice, meaning, content. Not only were reams of critical prose written by poets: both avant-gardists and academics were writing in the identical technocratic jargon. And the poetry (the so-called praxis) that these theories produced—reacting to the unexamined free expression of the workshops—ranged from strictly non-referential arrays of words to unending prose poems and lyrics that, like a ghazal on amphetamines, kept changing the subject with every line: the poem as MTV, under the guise of a preoccupation with "surface texture" and pure "language." It was a sign of the times that the avant-garde presented its most militant polemics not in a Beat café or in an underground magazine, but at the annual meetings of the Modern Language Association.

The one evidently positive new force in American poetry in the period—and it continues to be so—was feminism. The first generation of feminists were responsible for resurrecting and bringing back into print such neglected poets such as H.D., Niedecker, Mina Loy and Gertrude Stein; they wrote devastating attacks on the patriarchal assumptions of Modernism, and began an exploration into new forms, new speech, and new responses to the traditions of history and mythology, among other topics: a women's writing to set against the men who had dominated the first half of the century. Their second generation—women now in their twenties and thirties—may well be the most vibrant and promising tendency in American poetry today.

Central to the new writing by women has been the work of Susan Howe, who is ironically the true heir of a poet who didn't recognize women poets, Charles Olson. Like Olson, she has evolved a "field" poetics: her words sometimes cover the page like the shrapnel of an exploded etymological dictionary. And both share a preoccupation with New England history: her *My Emily Dickinson* and the essays collected in *The Birth-Mark* stand alongside Olson's study of Melville, *Call Me Ishmael*, not only as remarkable readings of American classics, but as extraordinary books of poet's prose. Her poems are not so much meditations on the ruins of history, as ruins themselves, full of passionate stories that at times are impossible to reconstruct.

Of the poets born before 1945 who have emerged in the last twenty years, three have been included here: Gustaf Sobin, who has lived in a small village in France most of his adult life—perhaps the only important expatriate American poet in the second half of the century—and who condenses local observation and metaphysical speculation into ecstatic syllables; Clark Coolidge, an inexhaustible writer capable of taking a subject, any subject, and improvising endless bebop glissandos around it; and Michael Palmer, who combines Surrealist imagery, the concentrated and self-critical lyricism of Oppen or Celan, and postmodernist skepticism of the meaning of meaning into flat sentences of remarkable resonance. His 1988 poem "Sun" (not to be confused with the shorter "Sun" included here), deliberately the exact same length as "The Waste Land," is one of the major works of a still-unnamed new poetry, and has already had many imitators. Palmer, the last poet born before Hiroshima, and the first of the poets to come of age in that new world, stands on the cusp between this volume and another.

I take American poetry to be, with French and Spanish (as written in both the Old and New Worlds), one of the great poetries of the century. This is not a matter of national pride: American poetry has always been written in spite of, not because of, the culture it inhabits. With rare exceptions, it has remained an underground activity. Few poets have been considered as actively contributing to the intellectual life of the country; few, in their lifetimes, are well known, even among people who read books. Unlike the poets in the rest of the world, few have ever been interviewed by, or published anything other than an occasional book review in a newspaper. The idea of an American poet-ambassador, a Claudel or Neruda, Seferis or Paz, is unimaginable: they are never official symbols of national cultural achievement. "There is no place for a poet in American society," wrote Kenneth Rexroth. "No place at all for any kind of poet at all." And yet it is precisely isolation and neglect, particularly in the anti-establishment, that has helped to create the extraordinary diversity of 20th century American poetry. In a literature that has been so little codified or canonized, each poet—like a new immigrant to a land of immigrants—must invent his or her self, and continue to work largely unmodified by outside opinion.

Unlike any other poetry, the range of referents that inform it is limitless. This has been seen by some as a sign of an absence of a culture of its own, but it is more exactly a reflection of its identity as a composite of countless cultures. Thanks to the vastness and precision of the English language, with by far the largest vocabulary in the world, American poetry has been much less abstract and rhetorical than the poetries written in the European languages. Thanks to the Modernist interest in Chinese poetry and the inheritance from Whitman, it has been preoccupied with the detailed observation of the world around: an epic of particulars. And thanks to Pound it has believed that everything is suitable subject matter. The extraordinary range of possible sounds in the English language, particularly the hard consonants it received from Anglo-Saxon, has led its poets to experiment, more than elsewhere, with an enormous variety of musical compositions. And plain-speaking American English, unlike many of the world's languages, does not easily assume mellifluous or sonorous tones: its elegies tend to be composed in fragments.

These qualities are difficult to translate, and most of these poets remain little known abroad. A great deal, perhaps too much, of American poetry is concerned with the intricacies of American speech. But it is precisely these poems that are babbles of accented voices, simultaneities of perceptions and collages of imagery and ideas, histories and natural histories, that—far more than American prose—recreate and enlarge the culture in which they were written.

—Eliot Weinberger

A Reader's Bibliography

The following bibliography of the poets included in the anthology is not a complete listing of their published works. Rather it is intended as a guide for readers seeking most of the poet's work in the latest available editions. Thus individual volumes which are reprinted in later editions, such as a *Collected Poems*, are not included. Most fugitive pamphlets, issued by small presses and now difficult to obtain, are omitted. The books are listed in the chronological order of their original publication, but only their most recent editions are cited. [Original date of composition or publication is given in square brackets, when this represent a significant lapse of time.] Secondary material, such as critical studies and biographies, has not been included.

DAVID ANTIN (b. 1932)

SELECTED EDITION:

Selected Poems: 1963–1973. Sun & Moon, 1991.

OTHER POETRY:

Talking at the Boundaries. New Directions, 1976.
Tuning. New Directions, 1984.
What It Means To Be Avant-Garde. New Directions, 1993.

JOHN ASHBERY (b. 1927)

SELECTED EDITIONS:

Selected Poems. Penguin, 1985.
Reported Sightings: Art Chronicles 1957–1987. Harvard, 1991.

OTHER POETRY:

Some Trees [1956]. Ecco, 1978.
The Tennis Court Oath. Wesleyan, 1962.
Rivers and Mountains [1966]. Ecco, 1977.
The Double Dream of Spring [1970]. Ecco, 1976.
Three Poems. Viking, 1972.
The Vermont Notebook. Black Sparrow, 1975.
Self-Portrait in a Convex Mirror. Viking, 1975.
Houseboat Days. Viking, 1977.
As We Know. Viking, 1979.
Shadow Train. Viking, 1981.
A Wave. Viking, 1984.
April Galleons. Viking, 1987.
Flow Chart. Knopf, 1991.
Hotel Lautréamont. Knopf, 1992.

OTHER WORKS:

A Nest of Ninnies (novel), with James Schuyler. Z Press, 1975.
Three Plays. Z Press, 1978.

AMIRI BARAKA (Leroi Jones) (b. 1934)

SELECTED AND COLLECTED EDITIONS:

Three Books: The Dead Lecturer [poems, 1964], *System of Dante's Hell* [novel, 1965], *Tales* [1967]. Grove, 1975.
Selected Poems. Morrow, 1979.
Selected Plays and Prose. Morrow, 1979.
The Leroi Jones-Amiri Baraka Reader, ed. William J. Harris. Thunder's Mouth, 1991.

OTHER POETRY:

Black Magic: Poetry 1961–1967. Bobbs-Merrill, 1969.
Reggae or Not! Contact II, 1982.

PLAYS:

Dutchman and The Slave. Morrow, 1964.
The Baptism and The Toilet. Grove, 1967.
Four Black Revolutionary Plays. Calder and Boyars, 1971.
The Motion of History and Other Plays. Morrow, 1978.
The Sidney Poet Heroical. Reed & Cannon, 1979.

OTHER PROSE:

Blues People: Negro Music in White America. Morrow, 1963.
Home: Social Essays. Morrow, 1966.
Black Music. Morrow, 1967.
In Our Terribleness: Some Elements and Meaning in Black Style. Bobbs-Merrill, 1970.
Raise Race Rays Raze: Essays Since 1965. Random House, 1971.
Daggers and Javelins: Essays 1974–1979. Morrow, 1984.
The Music: Reflections on Jazz and Blues. Morrow, 1987.

AUTOBIOGRAPHY:

The Autobiography of Leroi Jones/Amiri Baraka. Freundlich, 1984.

ANTHOLOGIES:

The Moderns: New Writing in America. Corinth, 1964.
Black Fire: An Anthology of Afro-American Writing. Morrow, 1968.
Confirmation: An Anthology of African-American Women. Morrow, 1983.

PAUL BLACKBURN (1926–1971)

SELECTED AND COLLECTED EDITIONS:

The Collected Poems, ed. Edie Jarolim. Persea, 1985.
The Parallel Voyages, ed. Clayton Eshleman & Edie Jarolim. Sun-Gemini, 1987.
Selected Poems, ed. Edie Jarolim. Persea, 1989.

TRANSLATIONS:

The Cid. American R.D.M., 1966.
Proensa: An Anthology of Troubadour Poetry [1953–1968]. Paragon, 1986.
Lorca / Blackburn: Poems of Federico García Lorca. Momo's Press, 1979.
Julio Cortázar, *End of the Game and Other Stories.* Pantheon, 1967.
Julio Cortázar, *Cronopios and Famas.* Pantheon, 1969.

WILLIAM BRONK (b. 1918)

COLLECTED EDITIONS:

Life Supports: New and Collected Poems. North Point, 1981.
Vectors and Smoothable Curves: Collected Essays. North Point, 1983.

OTHER POETRY:

Manifest and Furthermore. North Point, 1987.
Death is the Place. North Point, 1989.
Living Instead. North Point, 1991.
Some Words. Moyer-Bell, 1993.

JOHN CAGE (1912–1992)

WRITINGS:

Silence [1961]. M.I.T., 1966.
A Year from Monday. Wesleyan, 1967.
M: Writings '67–'72. Wesleyan, 1973.
Empty Words: Writings '73–'78. Wesleyan, 1979.
X: Writings '79–'82. Wesleyan, 1983.
Themes and Variations. Station Hill, 1988.
First: Sixth. Harvard, 1990.
I–IV. Harvard, 1990.

CLARK COOLIDGE (b. 1939)

SELECTED EDITIONS:

Solution Passage: Poems 1978–1981. Sun & Moon, 1986.
Sound As Thought: Poems 1982–1984. Sun & Moon, 1989.

OTHER POETRY:

Space. Harper & Row, 1970.
The Maintains. This, 1974.
Polaroid. Adventures in Poetry and Big Sky, 1975.
Smithsonian Depositions / Subject to a Film. Vehicle, 1980.
A Geology. Potes & Poets, 1981.
American Ones. Tombouctou, 1981.
Research. Tuumba, 1982.
Mine: The One That Enters The Stories. The Figures, 1982.
The Crystal Text. The Figures, 1986.
Melencolia. The Figures, 1987.
Mesh. In Camera, 1988.
At Egypt. The Figures, 1988.
Baffling Means (with Phillip Guston). O-blek, 1991.
Odes of Roba. The Figures, 1991.
The Book of During. The Figures, 1991.

ROBERT CREELEY (b. 1926)

SELECTED AND COLLECTED EDITIONS:

Collected Poems 1945–1975. University of California, 1982.
Collected Prose (fiction). University of California, 1988.
Collected Essays. University of California, 1989.
Selected Poems. University of California, 1991.

OTHER POETRY:

Hello: A Journal. New Directions, 1978.
Later. New Directions, 1979.
Mirrors. New Directions, 1983.
Memory Gardens. New Directions, 1986.
Windows. New Directions, 1990.

LETTERS:

Charles Olson & Robert Creeley: The Complete Correspondence, ed. George Butterick. (9 vols.) Black Sparrow, 1980–1990.

H.D. (Hilda Doolittle) (1886–1961)

SELECTED AND COLLECTED EDITIONS:

Collected Poems 1912–1944, ed. Louis L. Martz. New Directions, 1983.
Selected Poems, ed. Louis L. Martz. New Directions, 1988.

OTHER POETRY:

Trilogy [1942–1944]. New Directions, 1973.
By Avon River [1949]. Black Swan, 1989.
Helen in Egypt [1956]. New Directions, 1974.
Vale Ave [1957]. Black Swan, 1991.
Hermetic Definition [1957–1961]. New Directions, 1972.

PROSE:

Notes on Thought and Vision [1919]. City Lights, 1982.
Tribute to Freud [1948]. New Directions, 1984.
End to Torment: A Memoir of Ezra Pound [1958]. New Directions, 1979.

FICTION:

Paint It Today [1921]. New York University, 1992.
The Hedgehog [1924]. New Directions, 1988.
Hedylus [1926]. Black Swan, 1980.

Palimpsest [1926]. Southern Illinois, 1968.
HERmione [1927]. New Directions, 1981.
Nights [1935]. New Directions, 1986.
The Gift [1943]. New Directions, 1982.
Bid Me to Live [1949]. Black Swan, 1983.

TRANSLATIONS:

Euripides, *Hippolytus Temporizes* [1927]. Black Swan, 1985.
Euripides, *Ion* [1937]. Black Swan, 1985.

LETTERS:

A Great Admiration: H.D./Robert Duncan: Correspondence 1950–1961, ed. Robert Bertholf. Lapis, 1992.

ROBERT DUNCAN (1919–1987)

SELECTED EDITIONS:

The Years as Catches: First Poems (1939–1946). Oyez, 1977.
The First Decade: Selected Poems 1940–1950. Fulcrum (England), 1968.
Derivations: Selected Poems 1950–1956. Fulcrum (England), 1968.
Fictive Certainties (selected essays). New Directions, 1985.
Selected Poems, ed. Robert Bertholf. New Directions, 1993.

OTHER POETRY:

The Opening of the Field [1960]. New Directions, 1973.
Roots and Branches [1964]. New Directions, 1969.
Bending the Bow. New Directions, 1968.
Ground Work: Before the War. New Directions, 1984.
Ground Work II: In the Dark. New Directions, 1987.

LETTERS:

A Great Admiration: H.D./Robert Duncan: Correspondence 1950–1961, ed. Robert Bertholf. Lapis, 1992.

CLAYTON ESHLEMAN (b. 1935)

SELECTED EDITIONS:

The Name Encanyoned River: Selected Poems 1960–1985. Black Sparrow, 1986.
Antiphonal Swing: Selected Prose 1962–1987. MacPherson, 1988.
Conductors of the Pit: Major Works by Rimbaud, Vallejo, Césaire, Artaud and Holan. Paragon, 1988.

OTHER POETRY:

Indiana. Black Sparrow, 1969.
Altars. Black Sparrow, 1971.
Coils. Black Sparrow, 1973.
The Gull Wall. Black Sparrow, 1975.
What She Means. Black Sparrow, 1978.
Hades in Manganese. Black Sparrow, 1981.
Fracture. Black Sparrow, 1983.
Hotel Cro-Magnon. Black Sparrow, 1989.

OTHER PROSE:

Novices: A Study of Poetic Apprenticeship. Mercer & Aitchison, 1988.

TRANSLATIONS:

César Vallejo, *The Complete Posthumous Poetry.* University of California, 1978.
Antonin Artaud, *Four Texts.* Panjandrum, 1982.
Aimé Césaire, *The Collected Poetry.* University of California, 1983.
Michel Deguy, *Given Giving: Selected Poems.* University of California, 1984.
Bernard Bador, *Sea-Urchin Harakiri.* Panjandrum, 1986.
Aimé Césaire, *The Lyric and Dramatic Poetry.* University of Virginia, 1989.
César Vallejo, *Trilce.* Marsilio, 1992.

WILLIAM EVERSON (Brother Antoninus) (b. 1912)

SELECTED AND COLLECTED EDITIONS:

The Residual Years: Poems 1934–1946. New Directions, 1968.
The Veritable Years: Poems 1949–1966. Black Sparrow, 1978.
Earth Poetry: Selected Essays and Interviews, ed. Lee Bartlett. Oyez, 1980.
Naked Heart: Selected Interviews, ed. Lee Bartlett. University of New Mexico, 1992.

OTHER POETRY:

Man-Fate: The Swan Song of Brother Antoninus. New Directions, 1974.
River Root: A Syzygy for the Bicentennial of These States [1976]. Broken Moon, 1990.
The Masks of Drought. Black Sparrow, 1979.
The Engendering Flood. Black Sparrow, 1990.

OTHER PROSE:

Archetype West: The Pacific Coast as a Literary Region. Oyez, 1976.
Birth of a Poet, ed. Lee Bartlett. Black Sparrow, 1982.
The Excesses of God: Robinson Jeffers as a Religious Figure. Stanford, 1988.

ALLEN GINSBERG (b. 1926)

COLLECTED EDITION:

Collected Poems 1947–1980. Harper & Row, 1984.

OTHER POETRY:

White Shroud. Harper & Row, 1986.
Howl: Original Draft Facsimile, Fully Annotated. Harper & Row, 1986.

OTHER PROSE:

Indian Journals. City Lights, 1970.
Allen Verbatim: Lectures on Poetry, Politics, Consciousness, ed. Gordon Ball. McGraw-Hill, 1974.
Journals Early Fifties Early Sixties, ed. Gordon Ball. Grove, 1977.
Composed on the Tongue. Grey Fox, 1980.

LETTERS:

The Yage Letters (with William Burroughs). City Lights, 1963.
As Ever: Collected Correspondence of Allen Ginsberg & Neal Cassady. Creative Arts, 1977.
Straight Hearts Delight: Love Poems and Selected Letters 1947–1980 with Peter Orlovsky. Gay Sunshine, 1980.

SUSAN HOWE (b. 1937)

COLLECTED EDITION:

The Europe of Trusts. Sun & Moon, 1990.

OTHER POETRY:

Hinge Picture. Telephone, 1974.
The Western Borders. Tuumba, 1976.
Secret History of the Dividing Line. Telephone, 1978.
Cabbage Gardens. Fathom, 1979.
Articulation of Sound Forms in Time. Awede, 1987.

The Bibliography of the King's Book; or, Eikon Basilike. Paradigm, 1989.
Singularities. Wesleyan, 1990.
The Nonconformist's Memorial. New Directions, 1993.

PROSE:

My Emily Dickinson. North Atlantic, 1985.
The Birth-Mark: Unsettling the Wilderness in American History. Wesleyan, 1993.

LANGSTON HUGHES (1902–1967)

SELECTED EDITIONS:

The Langston Hughes Reader. Braziller, 1958.
Selected Poems [1959]. Random House, 1990.
The Best of Simple [1961]. Farrar, Straus & Giroux, 1990.
Five Plays. Indiana University, 1963.
Good Morning Revolution, ed. Faith Berry. Lawrence Hill, 1973.

OTHER POETRY:

The Weary Blues. Knopf, 1926.
Fine Clothes to the Jew. Knopf, 1927.
Shakespeare in Harlem. Knopf, 1942.
Fields of Wonder. Knopf, 1947.
One-Way Ticket. Knopf, 1949.
Montage of a Dream Deferred. Henry Holt, 1951.
Ask Your Mama. Knopf, 1961.
The Panther and the Lash [1967]. Random House, 1992.

FICTION:

Not Without Laughter. Knopf, 1930.
The Ways of White Folks [1934]. Random House, 1990.
Simple Speaks His Mind. Simon & Schuster, 1950.
Laughing to Keep from Crying. Henry Holt, 1952.
Simple Takes a Wife. Simon & Schuster, 1953.
Simple Stakes a Claim. Rinehart, 1957.
Something in Common and Other Stories. Hill & Wang, 1963.
Simple's Uncle Sam. Hill & Wang, 1967.

AUTOBIOGRAPHY:

The Big Sea [1940]. Thunder's Mouth, 1986.
I Wonder as I Wander [1956]. Thunder's Mouth, 1986.

PLAYS:

Mule Bone (with Zora Neale Hurston) [1930]. HarperCollins, 1991.
Tambourines to Glory. John Day, 1959.

TRANSLATIONS:

Jacques Roumain, *Masters of the Dew.* Reynal & Hitchcock, 1947.
Nicolás Guillén, *Cuba Libre.* Ward Ritchie, 1948.
Federico García Lorca, *Gypsy Ballads.* Beloit Poetry Journal, 1951.
Gabriela Mistral, *Selected Poems.* Indiana University, 1957.

ANTHOLOGIES:

The Poetry of the Negro 1746–1949. Doubleday, 1949.
The Book of Negro Folklore. Dodd, Mead, 1958.
An African Treasury. Crown, 1960.
Poems from Black Africa. Indiana University, 1963.
New Negro Poets: U.S.A. Indiana University, 1964.
The Book of Negro Humor. Dodd, Mead, 1966.
The Best Short Stories by Negro Writers. Little, Brown, 1967.

RONALD JOHNSON (b. 1937)

POETRY:

A Line of Poetry, A Row of Trees. Jargon, 1965.
The Book of the Green Man. Norton, 1967.
Valley of the Many-Colored Grasses. Norton, 1969.
Eyes & Objects. Jargon, 1976.
RADIOS. Sand Dollar, 1977.
ARK: The Foundations. North Point, 1980.
ARK 50: Spires 34–50. Dutton, 1984.

ROBERT KELLY (b. 1935)

POETRY:

Finding the Measure. Black Sparrow, 1968.
Songs I–XXX. Pym-Randall, 1968.
The Common Shore, Books I–V: A Long Poem About America in Time. Black Sparrow, 1969.
Kali Yuga. Goliard Grossman, 1971.
Flesh: Dream: Book. Black Sparrow, 1971.

The Mill of Particulars. Black Sparrow, 1973.
The Loom. Black Sparrow, 1975.
The Convections. Black Sparrow, 1978.
The Cruise of the Pnyx. Station Hill, 1979.
Kill the Messenger Who Brings Bad News. Black Sparrow, 1979.
Spiritual Exercises. Black Sparrow, 1981.
The Alchemist to Mercury, ed. Jed Rasula. North Atlantic, 1981.
Under Words. Black Sparrow, 1983.
Not This Island Music. Black Sparrow, 1987.
The Flowers of Unceasing Coincidence. Black Sparrow, 1988.
A Strange Market. Black Sparrow, 1992.

FICTION:
The Scorpions [1967]. Station Hill, 1985.
A Transparent Tree. McPherson, 1985.
Doctor of Silence. McPherson, 1988.
Cat Scratch Fever. McPherson, 1991.

ANTHOLOGY:
A Controversy of Poets. Doubleday, 1965.

DENISE LEVERTOV (b. 1923)

SELECTED AND COLLECTED EDITIONS:
Collected Earlier Poems 1940–1960. New Directions, 1979.
Poems 1960–1967. New Directions, 1983.
Poems 1968–1972. New Directions, 1987.
New and Selected Essays. New Directions, 1992.

OTHER POETRY:
The Freeing of the Dust. New Directions, 1976.
Life in the Forest. New Directions, 1978.
Candles in Babylon. New Directions, 1982.
Oblique Prayers. New Directions, 1984.
Breathing the Water. New Directions, 1987.
A Door in the Hive. New Directions, 1989.
Evening Train. New Directions, 1992.

PROSE:
The Poet in the World. New Directions, 1973.
Light Up the Cave. New Directions, 1981.

TRANSLATIONS:

Guillevic, *Selected Poems.* New Directions, 1961.

In Praise of Krishna: Songs from the Bengali. University of Chicago, 1981.

Jean Joubert, *Black Iris.* Copper Canyon, 1988.

JACKSON MAC LOW (b. 1922)

SELECTED EDITION:

Representative Works: 1938–1985. Roof, 1986.

OTHER POETRY:

The Pronouns—A Collection of 40 Dances—For the Dancers [1964]. Station Hill, 1979.

22 Light Poems. Black Sparrow, 1968.

Stanzas for Iris Lezak. Something Else, 1972.

4 trains. Burning Deck, 1974.

Asymmetries 1–260. Printed Editions, 1980.

"Is That Wool My Hat?" Membrane, 1982.

From Pearl Harbor Day to FDR's Birthday. Sun & Moon, 1982.

Bloomsday. Station Hill, 1984.

French Sonnets [1984]. Membrane, 1989.

The Virginia Woolf Poems. Burning Deck, 1985.

Words nd Ends from Ez. Avenue B, 1989.

Twenties: 100 Poems: 24 February 1989–3 June 1990. Roof, 1991.

Pieces o' Six: Thirty-three Poems in Prose. Sun & Moon, 1993.

42 Merzgedichte in Memoriam *Kurt Schwitters.* Station Hill, 1993.

PLAYS:

The Twin Plays: Port-au-Prince & Adams County Illinois. Something Else, 1966.

Verdurous Sanguinaria. Southern University, 1967.

LORINE NIEDECKER (1903–1970)

SELECTED AND COLLECTED EDITIONS:

My Life by Water: Collected Poems 1936–1968. Fulcrum (England), 1970.

From This Condensery: The Complete Writing, ed. Robert Bertholf. Jargon, 1985.

The Granite Pail: Selected Poems, ed. Cid Corman. North Point, 1985.

OTHER POETRY:

Harpsichord & Salt Fish [1969], ed. Jenny Penberthy. Pig Press (England), 1991.

LETTERS:

Between Your House and Mine: Letters to Cid Corman, ed. Lisa Pater Faranda. Duke, 1986.

FRANK O'HARA (1926–1966)

SELECTED AND COLLECTED EDITIONS:

The Collected Poems, ed. Donald Allen. Knopf, 1971.

The Selected Poems, ed. Donald Allen. Knopf, 1974.

Early Writing, ed. Donald Allen. Grey Fox, 1977.

Poems Retrieved, ed. Donald Allen. Grey Fox, 1977.

Selected Plays. Full Court, 1978.

Standing Still & Walking in New York, ed. Donald Allen. Grey Fox, 1983.

Art Chronicles 1954–1966. Braziller, 1990.

CHARLES OLSON (1910–1970)

COLLECTED AND SELECTED POETRY:

The Maximus Poems, ed. George Butterick. University of California, 1983.

The Collected Poems, ed. George Butterick. University of California, 1987.

A Nation of Nothing But Poetry: Supplementary Poems, ed. George Butterick. Black Sparrow, 1989.

Selected Poems, ed. Robert Creeley. University of California, 1993.

OTHER SELECTED AND COLLECTED EDITIONS:

Selected Writings, ed. Robert Creeley. New Directions, 1966.

Additional Prose, ed. George Butterick. Four Seasons, 1974.

The Fiery Hunt & Other Plays, ed. George Butterick. Four Seasons, 1977.

Muthologos: The Collected Lectures and Interviews, ed. George Butterick. (2 vols.) Four Seasons, 1978 & 1979.

OTHER PROSE:

Call Me Ishmael: A Study of Melville [1947]. City Lights, 1967.

Human Universe and Other Essays. Grove, 1967.

Charles Olson & Ezra Pound: An Encounter at St. Elizabeths, ed. Catherine Seelye [1975]. Paragon, 1990.

LETTERS:

Charles Olson & Robert Creeley: The Complete Correspondence, ed. George Butterick. (9 vols.) Black Sparrow, 1980–1990.

Charles Olson & Cid Corman: Complete Correspondence, ed. George Evans. (2 vols.) National Poetry Foundation, 1987 & 1991.

In Love, In Sorrow: The Complete Correspondence of Charles Olson and Edward Dahlberg, ed. Paul Christensen. Paragon, 1990.

GEORGE OPPEN (1908–1984)

COLLECTED EDITION:

Collected Poems. New Directions, 1975.

OTHER POETRY:

Primitive. Black Sparrow, 1978.

LETTERS:

Selected Letters, ed. Rachel Blau DuPlessis. Duke, 1990.

MICHAEL PALMER (b. 1943)

POETRY:

Blake's Newton. Black Sparrow, 1972.

The Circular Gates. Black Sparrow, 1974.

Without Music. Black Sparrow, 1977.

Notes for Echo Lake. North Point, 1981.

First Figure. North Point, 1984.

Sun. North Point, 1988.

ANTHOLOGY:

Code of Signals: Recent Writings in Poetics. North Atlantic, 1983.

EZRA POUND (1885–1972)

SELECTED AND COLLECTED POETRY:

Selected Poems. New Directions, 1957.

Translations. New Directions, 1963.

The Cantos. New Directions, 1970.

Selected Cantos. New Directions, 1970.

Collected Early Poems, ed. Michael King. New Directions, 1976.

Personae: Collected Shorter Poems, ed. Lea Baechler & A. Walton Litz. New Directions, 1990.

OTHER SELECTED AND COLLECTED EDITIONS:

Literary Essays, ed. T.S. Eliot. New Directions, 1968.

Selected Prose 1909–1965, ed. William Cookson. New Directions, 1973.

Ezra Pound and Music, ed. R. Murray Schafer. New Directions, 1977.

Ezra Pound and the Visual Arts, ed. Harriet Zinnes. New Directions, 1980.

Ezra Pound and Japan: Letters and Essays, ed. Sanehide Kodama. Black Swan, 1986.

OTHER PROSE:

The Spirit of Romance [1910]. New Directions, 1968.

A Walking Tour in Southern France [1912], ed. Richard Sieburth. New Directions, 1992.

Gaudier-Brezska: A Memoir [1916]. New Directions, 1970.

ABC of Reading [1934]. New Directions, 1960.

Guide to Kulchur [1938]. New Directions, 1968.

"Ezra Pound Speaking": Radio Speeches of World War II, ed. Leonard Doob. Greenwood, 1978.

Pavannes and Divagations [1958]. New Directions, 1975.

OTHER TRANSLATIONS:

The Classic Noh Theatre of Japan [1916]. New Directions, 1959.

Confucius, *The Great Digest, The Unwobbling Pivot, The Analects* [1928, 1947]. New Directions, 1969.

Sophocles, *Elektra* [1949]. New Directions, 1990.

Shih-Ching: The Classic Anthology Defined by Confucius. Harvard, 1954.

Sophocles, *Women of Trachis* [1956]. New Directions, 1969.

ANTHOLOGY:

Confucius to Cummings. New Directions, 1964.

LETTERS:

Pound/Joyce, ed. Forrest Read. New Directions, 1968.

Selected Letters 1907–1941, ed. D.D. Paige. New Directions, 1971.

Pound/Ford: the Story of a Literary Friendship, ed. Brita Lindberg-Seyersted. New Directions, 1982.

Pound/Lewis, ed. Timothy Materer. New Directions, 1985.

Ezra Pound and Dorothy Shakespear: Their Letters 1909–1914, ed. Omar Pound & A. Walton Litz. New Directions, 1985.

Pound/Zukofsky, ed. Barry Ahearn. New Directions, 1987.

Pound/The Little Review, ed. T.L. Scott, M.J. Friedman & J.R. Bryer. New Directions, 1988.

KENNETH REXROTH (1905–1982)

SELECTED AND COLLECTED EDITIONS:

The Collected Shorter Poems. New Directions, 1966.

The Collected Longer Poems. New Directions, 1968.

Selected Poems, ed. Bradford Morrow. New Directions, 1984.

World Outside the Window: Selected Essays, ed. Bradford Morrow. New Directions, 1989.

Flower Wreath Hill: Later Poems. New Directions, 1991.

OTHER PROSE:

Bird in the Bush: Obvious Essays. New Directions, 1959.

Assays. New Directions, 1961.

The Alternative Society. Herder & Herder, 1970.

With Eye and Ear. Herder & Herder, 1970.

American Poetry in the Twentieth Century. Seabury, 1973.

The Elastic Retort: Essays in Literature and Ideas. Seabury, 1973.

Communalism: Its Origins to the Twentieth Century. Seabury, 1974.

Classics Revisited. New Directions, 1986.

More Classics Revisited. New Directions, 1989.

PLAYS:

Beyond the Mountains. New Directions, 1951.

AUTOBIOGRAPHY:

An Autobiographical Novel. New Directions, 1991.

TRANSLATIONS:

O.V. de L. Milosz, *Fourteen Poems* [1952]. Copper Canyon, 1982.
100 Poems from the French [1955]. Pym-Randall, 1972.
100 Poems from the Japanese. New Directions, 1955.
100 Poems from the Chinese. New Directions, 1956.
30 Spanish Poems of Love and Exile. City Lights, 1956.
Poems from the Greek Anthology. University of Michigan, 1962.
Pierre Reverdy, *Selected Poems.* New Directions, 1969.
Love in the Turning Year: 100 More Poems from the Chinese. New Directions, 1970.
Women Poets of China [1972]. New Directions, 1982.
100 More Poems from the Japanese. New Directions, 1974.
Women Poets of Japan [1977]. New Directions, 1982.
Kazuko Shiraishi: *Seasons of Sacred Lust.* New Directions, 1978.
Li Ch'ing Chao: *Complete Poems.* New Directions, 1979.

CHARLES REZNIKOFF (1894–1976)

COLLECTED EDITION:

Poems 1918–1975: The Complete Poems, ed. Seamus Cooney. Black Sparrow, 1989.

OTHER POETRY:

Holocaust. Black Sparrow, 1975.
Testimony: The United States (1885–1915): Recitative [1965–1975]. (2 vols.) Black Sparrow, 1978 & 1979.

PROSE:

Testimony. Objectivist Press, 1934.
Family Chronicle [1936, 1963]. Wiener, 1986.

FICTION:

By the Waters of Manhattan [1930]. Wiener, 1986.
The Lionhearted. Jewish Publication Society, 1944.
The Manner "Music" [1950's]. Black Sparrow, 1977.

JEROME ROTHENBERG (b. 1931)

SELECTED EDITIONS:

Poems for the Game of Silence 1960–1970. New Directions, 1975.
New Selected Poems 1971–1985. New Directions, 1986.

OTHER POETRY:

Poland / 1931. New Directions, 1974.
A Seneca Journal. New Directions, 1978.
Vienna Blood. New Directions, 1980.
That Dada Strain. New Directions, 1983.
Khurbn and Other Poems. New Directions, 1989.
The Lorca Variations. New Directions, 1993.

PROSE:

Pre-Faces & Other Writings. New Directions, 1981.

ANTHOLOGIES:

Technicians of the Sacred: A Range of Poetries from Africa, Ameica, Asia & Oceania [1968]. University of California, 1985.
Shaking the Pumpkin: Traditional Poetry of the Indian North Americas [1972]. University of New Mexico, 1991.
America a Prophecy: A New Reading of American Poetry from Pre-Columbian Times to the Present. Random House, 1973.
Revolution of the Word: A New Gathering of American Avant-Garde Poetry 1914–1945. Seabury, 1974.
Exiled in the Word: Poems & Other Visions of the Jews from Tribal Times to the Present [1978]. Copper Canyon, 1989.
Symposium of the Whole: A Range of Discourse Toward an Ethnopoetics. University of California, 1983.

MURIEL RUKEYSER (1913–1980)

COLLECTED AND SELECTED EDITIONS:

The Collected Poems. Norton, 1978.
Out of Silence: Selected Poems, ed. Kate Daniels. Triquarterly, 1992.

PROSE:

Willard Gibbs [1942]. Ox Bow, 1988.
The Life of Poetry [1948]. Wyn, 1968.
The Orgy. Coward-McCann, 1965.
The Traces of Thomas Hariot. Random House, 1970.

TRANSLATIONS:

Octavio Paz, *Sun Stone* [1962], now in *Selected Poems.* New Directions, 1984.
Octavio Paz, *Early Poems* [1963]. New Directions, 1973.

Gunnar Ekelöf, *Selected Poems.* Twayne, 1967.
Gunnar Ekelöf, *A Mölna Elegy.* Cambridge University, 1979.

GARY SNYDER (b. 1930)

SELECTED AND COLLECTED EDITIONS:

A Range of Poems. Fulcrum (England), 1966.
No Nature: New and Selected Poems. Pantheon, 1992.

OTHER POETRY:

Riprap & Cold Mountain Poems [1959, 1965] North Point, 1990.
Six Sections from Mountains and Rivers Without End. Four Seasons, 1970.
The Back Country. New Directions, 1968.
Regarding Wave. New Directions, 1970.
Turtle Island. New Directions, 1974.
Axe Handles. North Point, 1983.
Left Out in the Rain: New Poems 1947–1985. North Point, 1986.

PROSE:

Earth House Hold: Technical Notes & Queries to Follow Dharma Revolutionaries. New Directions, 1969.
The Old Ways: Six Essays. City Lights, 1977.
The Real Work: Interviews & Talks 1964–1979. New Directions, 1980.
Passage Through India. Grey Fox, 1984.
The Practice of the Wild. North Point, 1990.

GUSTAF SOBIN (b. 1935)

POETRY:

Wind Chrysalid's Rattle. Montemora, 1980.
Celebration of the Sound Through. Montemora, 1982.
The Earth As Air. New Directions, 1984.
Voyaging Portraits. New Directions, 1988.

FICTION:

Venus Blue. Little, Brown, 1992.
Dark Mirrors. Bloomsbury (England), 1992.

TRANSLATIONS:

Henri Michaux, *Ideograms of China.* New Directions, 1984.

JACK SPICER (1925–1965)

COLLECTED EDITIONS:

The Collected Books, ed. Robin Blaser. Black Sparrow, 1975.
One Night Stand & Other Poems, ed. Donald Allen. Grey Fox, 1980.

NATHANIEL TARN (b. 1928)

SELECTED EDITIONS:

Atitlan / Alashka: Selected Poems and Prose. Brillig Works, 1979.
Palenque: Selected Poems 1972–1984. Oasis/Shearsman (England), 1986.
Views from the Weaving Mountain: Selected Essays in Poetics & Anthropology. University of New Mexico, 1991.

OTHER POETRY:

Old Savage / Young City. Random House, 1965.
Where Babylon Ends. Cape Goliard, 1968.
The Beautiful Contradictions. Cape Goliard, 1969.
October. Trigram (England), 1969.
A Nowhere for Vallejo. Random House, 1971.
Lyrics for the Bride of God. New Directions, 1975.
The House of Leaves. Black Sparrow, 1976.
At the Western Gates. Tooth of Time, 1985.
Seeing America First. Coffee House, 1990.

TRANSLATIONS:

Pablo Neruda, *The Heights of Macchu Picchu.* Farrar, Straus & Giroux, 1966.
Con Cuba: An Anthology of Cuban Poetry of the Last 60 Years. (editor & co-translator). Cape Goliard, 1969.
Victor Segalen, *Stelae.* Unicorn, 1969.
Pablo Neruda, *Selected Poems.* (editor & co-translator). Delacorte, 1970.

WILLIAM CARLOS WILLIAMS (1883–1963)

SELECTED AND COLLECTED POETRY:

Selected Poems, ed. Charles Tomlinson. New Directions, 1985.

Collected Poems: 1909–1939, ed. A. Walton Litz & Christopher MacGowan. New Directions, 1986.

Collected Poems: 1939–1962, ed. Christopher MacGowan. New Directions, 1988.

Paterson, ed. Christopher MacGowan. New Directions, 1992.

OTHER SELECTED AND COLLECTED EDITIONS:

The Farmers' Daughters: Collected Short Stories. New Directions, 1961.

Many Loves and Other Plays: The Collected Plays. New Directions, 1961.

Selected Essays. New Directions, 1969.

Imaginations: Collected Early Prose. New Directions, 1970.

The Embodiment of Knowledge: Early Essays, ed. Ron Loewinsohn. New Directions, 1974.

A Recognizable Image: William Carlos Williams on Art and Artists, ed. Bram Dijkstra. New Directions, 1978.

The Doctor Stories, ed. Robert Coles. New Directions, 1984.

Something to Say: William Carlos Williams on Younger Poets, ed. James E.B. Breslin. New Directions, 1985.

OTHER PROSE:

In the American Grain [1925]. New Directions, 1956.

Yes, Mrs. Williams [1959]. New Directions, 1982.

FICTION:

A Voyage to Pagany [1928]. New Directions, 1970.

White Mule [1937]. New Directions, 1967.

In the Money [1940]. New Directions, 1967.

The Build-Up [1952]. New Directions, 1968.

AUTOBIOGRAPHY:

The Autobiography of William Carlos Williams [1951]. New Directions, 1967.

I Wanted to Write a Poem: The Autobiography of the Works of a Poet [1958], ed. Edith Heal. New Directions, 1978.

TRANSLATION:

Philippe Soupault, *Last Nights of Paris* [1929]. Full Court, 1982.

LETTERS:

Selected Letters, ed. John Thirwall. New Directions, 1985.

LOUIS ZUKOFSKY (1904–1978)

COLLECTED EDITIONS:

"A". University of California, 1978.

Prepositions: Collected Critical Essays. University of California, 1981.

Collected Fiction. Dalkey Archive, 1990.

Complete Short Poetry. Johns Hopkins, 1991.

OTHER PROSE:

Bottom: On Shakespeare [1963]. University of California, 1986.

ANTHOLOGY:

A Test of Poetry [1948]. Norton, 1981.

LETTERS:

Pound/Zukofsky, ed. Barry Ahearn. New Directions, 1987.

DAVID ANTIN: "a list of the delusions of the insane," and "defintions for mendy" from *Selected Poems 1963-1973*. Copyright © 1991 by David Antin. Reprinted by permission of Sun & Moon Press.

JOHN ASHBERY: "Into the Dusk-Charged Air," "Syringa" and selections from "The Skaters" from *Selected Poems*. Copyright © 1985 by John Ashbery. Reprinted by permission of Georges Borchardt, Inc.

AMIRI BARAKA: "Return of the Native," "For Maulana Karenga & Pharoah Sanders," "The Minute of Consciousness," "Study Peace," "Poem for Deep Thinkers," "When We'll Worship Jesus," and "Dope" from *Selected Poetry*. Copyright © 1979 by Amiri Baraka. Reprinted by permission of Sterling Lord Literistic, Inc.

PAUL BLACKBURN: "At the Well" and selections from "The Selection of Heaven" from *The Collected Poems*. Copyright © 1985 by Joan Blackburn. Reprinted by permission of Persea Books. "Two poems by Bernart de Ventadorn" from *Proensa*. Copyright © 1978 by Joan Blackburn. Reprinted by permission of the University of California Press.

WILLIAM BRONK: "At Tikal," "Metonymy as an Approach to a Real World," "The Mayan Glyphs Unread," "Corals and Shells," "The Plainest Narrative," "I Thought It Was Harry," "Where It Ends," "The World," "Life Supports" and "The Strong Room of the House" from *Life Supports*. Copyright © 1981 by William Bronk. Reprinted by permission of Moyer Bell.

JOHN CAGE: Selections from "Diary: How to Improve the World (You Will Only Make Matters Worse)" from *A Year from Monday*. Copyright © 1967 by John Cage, Wesleyan University Press. Reprinted by permission of the University Press of New England.

CLARK COOLIDGE: "Peru Eye, The Heart of the Lamp" copyright © 1983 by Clark Coolidge. Selections from *At Egypt*. Copyright © 1988 by Clark Coolidge. Reprinted by permission of the author.

ROBERT CREELEY: "Mazatlán: Sea" from *The Collected Poems*. Copyright © 1983 by The Regents of the University of California. Reprinted by permission of the University of California Press.

H.D.: "Red Rose and a Beggar" from *Hermetic Definition*. Copyright © 1972 by Norman Holmes Pearson. Reprinted by permission of New Directions Publishing Corporation and the Estate of Hilda Doolittle.

ROBERT DUNCAN: "Passages 1," "Passages 5," "Passages 13," "Passages 25," and "Passages 27" from *Bending the Bow*. Copyright © 1968 by Robert Duncan. "Passages 34" from *Ground Work*. Copyright © 1984 by Robert Duncan. Reprinted by permission of New Directions Publishing Corporation and the Estate of Robert Duncan.

CLAYTON ESHLEMAN: "Hades in Manganese" from *Hades in Manganese*. Copyright © 1981 by Clayton Eshleman. "Deeds Done and Suffered by Light" from *The Name Encanyoned River*. Copyright © 1986 by Clayton Eshleman. Reprinted by permission of Black Sparrow Press.

WILLIAM EVERSON: "A Canticle to the Waterbirds" from *The Veritable Years*. Copyright © 1978 by William Everson. Reprinted by permission of Black Sparrow Press.

ALLEN GINSBERG: "The Change: *Kyoto-Tokyo Express*" and "Wales Visitation" from *Collected Poems 1947-1980*. Copyright © 1984 by Allen Ginsberg. Reprinted by permission of HarperCollins, Inc.

SUSAN HOWE: "Thorow" from *Singularities*. Copyright © 1990 by Susan Howe, Wesleyan University Press. Reprinted by permission of University Press of New England.

LANGSTON HUGHES: Selections from "Montage of a Dream Deferred" from *Selected Poems.* Copyright © 1951 by Langston Hughes; copyright © renewed 1979 by George Houston Bass. Reprinted by permission of Harold Ober Associates Incorporated.

RONALD JOHNSON: "Beam 4," "Beam 7," and "Beam 25" from *ARK: The Foundations.* Copyright © 1980 by Ronald Johnson. "ARK 37" from *ARK 50.* Copyright © 1984 by Ronald Johnson. Reprinted by permission of the author.

ROBERT KELLY: "Those Who Are Beautiful" from *Under Words.* Copyright © 1983 by Robert Kelly. "Studying Horses" from *A Strange Market.* Copyright © 1992 by Robert Kelly. Reprinted by permission of Black Sparrow Press.

DENISE LEVERTOV: "The Jacob's Ladder" from *The Jacob's Ladder.* Copyright © 1961 by Denise Levertov Goodman. "To the Muse" from *O Taste and See.* Copyright © 1964 by Denise Levertov Goodman. "The Wings" from *The Sorrow Dance.* Copyright © 1966 by Denise Levertov. "Advent 1966" and "A Tree Telling of Orpheus" from *Relearning the Alphabet.* Copyright © 1970 by Denise Levertov Goodman. Reprinted by permission of New Directions Publishing Corporation.

JACKSON MAC LOW: Selections from "The Presidents of the United States of America" from *Representative Works 1938-1985.* Copyright © 1986 by Jackson Mac Low. Reprinted by permission of the author.

LORINE NIEDECKER: "Who was Mary Shelley?" from *From This Condensery.* Copyright © 1985 by the Estate of Lorine Niedecker. "Paean to Place" from *The Granite Pail.* Copyright © 1985 by the Estate of Lorine Niedecker. "Darwin" from *Harpsichord & Salt Fish.* Copyright © 1991 by the Estate of Lorine Niedecker. Reprinted by permission of Cid Corman, literary executor for the Estate of Lorine Niedecker.

FRANK O'HARA: "In Memory of My Feelings" from *The Selected Poems.* Copyright © 1958 by Maureen Granville-Smith, Administratrix of the Estate of Frank O'Hara. Reprinted by permission of Alfred A. Knopf, Inc.

CHARLES OLSON: "The Kingfishers" and "The chain of memory is resurrection" from *The Collected Poems.* Copyright © 1987 by the Estate of Charles Olson [previously published poetry] and copyright © 1987 by the University of Connecticut [previously unpublished poetry]. "Poem 143. The Festival Aspect" from *The Maximus Poems: Volume Three.* Copyright © 1975 by the Estate of Charles Olson and the University of Connecticut. Reprinted by permission of the University of California Press.

GEORGE OPPEN: "Route" from *Of Being Numerous.* Copyright © 1968 by George Oppen. Selections from "Some San Francisco Poems" from *Collected Poems.* Copyright © 1974 by George Oppen. Reprinted by permission of New Directions Publishing Corporation and the Estate of George Oppen.

MICHAEL PALMER: "Sun" and selections from "Baudelaire Series" from *Sun.* Copyright © 1988 by Michael Palmer. "Recursus" copyright © 1991 by Michael Palmer. Reprinted by permission of the author.

EZRA POUND: "Canto XC," "*from* Canto CXV," and "Canto CXVI" from *The Cantos.* Copyright © 1965, 1970 by Ezra Pound. Copyright © 1972 by the Estate of Ezra Pound. Reprinted by permission of New Directions Publishing Corporation and the Trustees of the Ezra Pound Literary Trust. Selections from *The Confucian Odes*: Copyright © 1954 by the President and Fellows of Harvard College, copyright © renewed 1982 by Mary de Rachewiltz and Omar Pound. Reprinted by permission of Harvard University Press.

KENNETH REXROTH: "The Signature of All Things," "Lyell's Hypothesis Again," and "Andree Rexroth" from *The Collected Shorter Poems.* Copyright © 1966 by Kenneth Rexroth. Selections from "The Love Poems of Marichiko" from *The Morning Star.* Copyright © 1979 by Kenneth Rexroth. Reprinted by permission of New Directions Publishing Corporation and the Kenneth Rexroth Trust.

CHARLES REZNIKOFF: "Massacres" from *Holocaust.* Copyright © 1975 by Charles Reznikoff. Reprinted by permission of Black Sparrow Press.

JEROME ROTHENBERG: "Seneca Journal 1: A Poem of Beavers," "Hunger," and "Visions of Jesus" from *New Selected Poems.* Copyright © 1986 by Jerome Rothenberg. Reprinted by permission of New Directions Publishing Corporation. "The 12th Horse Song of Frank Mitchell (Blue)" from *Shaking the Pumpkin.* Copyright © 1972 by Jerome Rothenberg. Reprinted by permission of the author.

MURIEL RUKEYSER: "Iris," and "In the Underworld" from *The Collected Poems.* Copyright © 1978 by Muriel Rukeyser. "The Speed of Darkness" from *Out of Silence.* Copyright © 1992 by William L. Rukeyser. Reprinted by permission of William L. Rukeyser.

GARY SNYDER: "What You Should Know to Be a Poet" and "Burning Island" from *Regarding Wave.* Copyright © 1970 by Gary Snyder. "What Happened Here Before" from *Turtle Island.* Copyright © 1974 by Gary Snyder. Reprinted by permission of New Directions Publishing Corporation. "The Hump-Backed Flute Player" copyright © 1973 by Gary Snyder. "Earrings Dangling and Miles of Desert" copyright © 1992 by Gary Snyder. Reprinted by permission of the author.

GUSTAF SOBIN: "Girandole," "Irises" and selections from "The Earth As Air" from *The Earth as Air.* Copyright © 1984 by Gustaf Sobin. Reprinted by permission of New Directions Publishing Corporation.

JACK SPICER: "Thing Language" and "*A Book of Music*" from *The Collected Books.* Copyright © 1975 by the Estate of Jack Spicer. Reprinted by permission of Black Sparrow Press.

NATHANIEL TARN: "Section: America (2): Seen as a Bird" from *Lyrics for the Bride of God.* Copyright © 1975 by Nathaniel Tarn. Reprinted by permission of New Directions Publishing Corporation. "Journal of the Laguna de San Ignacio" from *At the Western Gates.* Copyright © 1985 by Nathaniel Tarn. Reprinted by permission of the author.

WILLIAM CARLOS WILLIAMS: "The Desert Music" from *The Collected Poems Vol. II: 1939-1962.* Copyright © 1954, 1966 by William Carlos Williams. Copyright © 1988 by William Eric Williams & Paul H. Williams. Reprinted by permission of New Directions Publishing Corporation and the Estate of William Carlos Williams.

LOUIS ZUKOFSKY: "A-11," and selections from "A-15" and "A-18" from *"A".* Copyright © 1979 by Celia Zukofsky and Louis Zukofsky. Reprinted by permission of the University of California Press. Selections from "Catullus LXIV" from *Complete Short Poems.* Copyright © 1969 by Celia and Louis Zukofsky. Reprinted by permission of Johns Hopkins University Press.

ELIOT WEINBERGER'S essays are collected in *Works on Paper* and *Outside Stories*, both published by New Directions. With Octavio Paz he is the co-author of a study of the translation of Chinese poetry, *19 Ways of Looking at Wang Wei*. He is the editor and translator of over a dozen books by Octavio Paz, including *The Collected Poems 1957–1987*. Among his other translations are *Seven Nights* by Jorge Luis Borges, *Altazor* by Vicente Huidobro and *Nostalgia for Death* by Xavier Villaurrutia. He was the founder and editor of the literary magazine *Montemora* (1975–1982), and is currently a contributing editor of *Sulfur* and the New York correspondent for *Vuelta* in Mexico. A Spanish translation of a shorter version of this anthology has recently been published in Mexico and Spain and other editions are forthcoming in Italy and Brazil.